IMAGES
*of America*

# BRIDGEWATER

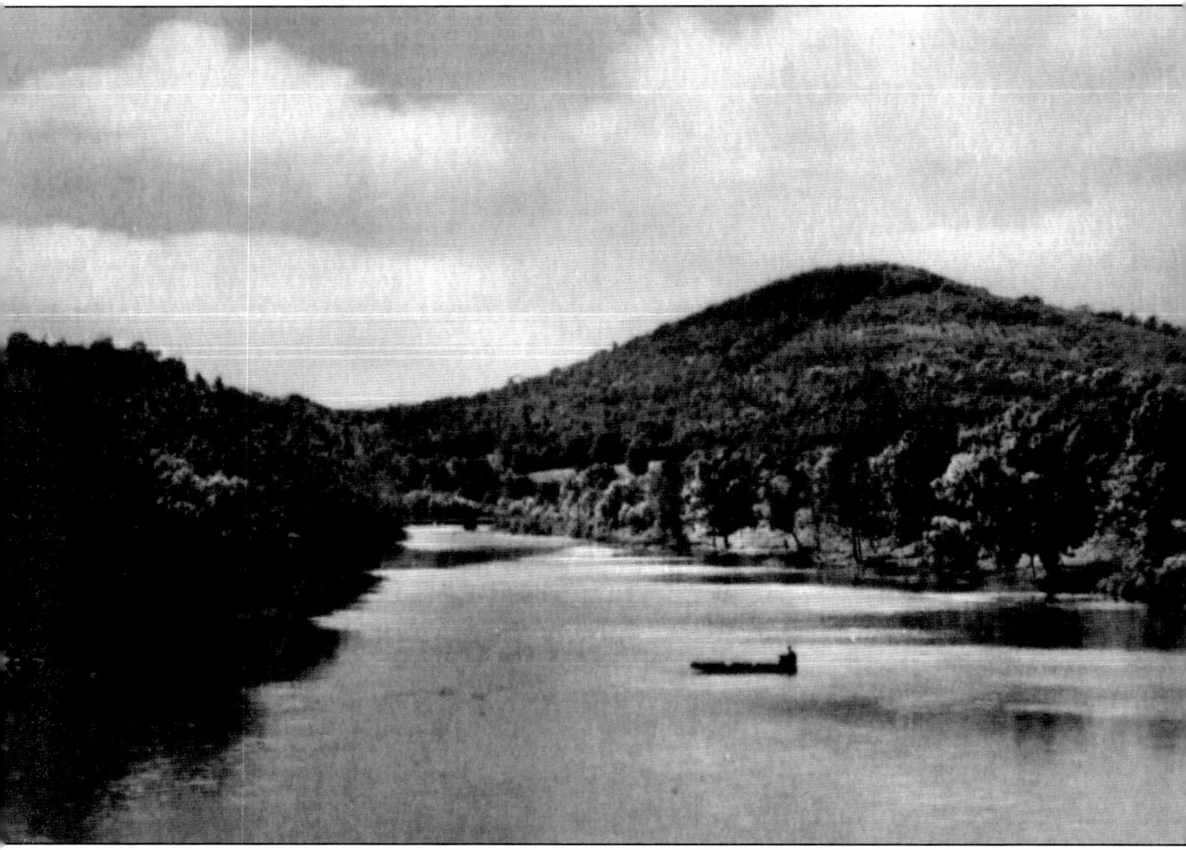

Without the North River, there would be no Bridgewater. It was this river that attracted the first Scotch-Irish immigrants who turned the wilderness into settlements that set the stage for those who would follow. The river was ready-made transportation for flat boats carrying pig iron and lumber to the north and bringing necessary supplies on the return trip. As the community grew, the river's energy was harnessed to provide power for at least five mills in the Bridgewater area. While most of what the river brought was good, there were times when its floodwaters would destroy homes, crops, and lives. Over the years, Bridgewater has learned to live with what the North River offers, both good and bad.

**ON THE COVER:** Seven bridges have crossed North River connecting Bridgewater to the outside world. When it was time to replace a bridge, ferries became the typical means of transportation and could move supplies, livestock, buggies, and automobiles across the water. On the cover is one such ferry and a youngster enjoying this novel experience.

IMAGES
*of America*

# BRIDGEWATER

Bob F. Holton and Carleen Loveless

ARCADIA
PUBLISHING

ISBN 978-0-7385-8650-2

Published by Arcadia Publishing
Charleston, South Carolina

Printed in the United States of America

Library of Congress Control Number: 2010925441

For all general information contact Arcadia Publishing at:
Telephone 843-853-2070
Fax 843-853-0044
E-mail sales@arcadiapublishing.com
For customer service and orders:
Toll-Free 1-888-313-2665

Visit us on the Internet at www.arcadiapublishing.com

*To Bridgewater's former town attorney Donald D. Litten,*
*whose wisdom, strength of character, and perseverance*
*guided Bridgewater through five decades.*

# Contents

# ACKNOWLEDGMENTS

Unless named otherwise, all pictures included in this book have come from the town's historical archives and were donated over the years by citizens and friends of the town of Bridgewater. Our profound thanks go to Wade Bodkin, Howard Shull, Judy Galang, and others who have freely shared their memories and their photographs. In addition, we would like to thank the following individuals for granting us permission to reprint photographs from their collections: the Harrisonburg-Rockingham Historical Society (HRHS), Bridgewater College Alexander Mack Memorial Library (BCAMML), Bridgewater Rescue Squad (BRS), various news articles from the *Bridgewater Herald* or *Daily News Record*, and Glenn Felix who provided sketches of photographs we did not have or that were too damaged to reproduce.

# SELECTED BIBLIOGRAPHY

Heatwole, John L. *The Burning: Sheridan in the Shenandoah Valley*. Charlottesville, VA: Rockbridge Publishing, an imprint of Howell Press, Inc.

Hinkle, Ken, and Galen Dellinger. *Bridgewater United Methodist Church—1841–2004*. Harrisonburg, VA: Campbell Copy Center, 2004.

May, C. E. *Life Under Four Flags in North River Basin of Virginia*. Verona, VA: McClure Press, 1976.

Wayland, John W. A. *History of Rockingham County, Virginia*. Dayton, VA: Ruebush-Elkins Company, 1912.

# INTRODUCTION

The story of Bridgewater is one of survival. Since its founding in 1835, Bridgewater has endured six major floods, economic crises, and a war that took place on its own soil. Despite the adversity it faced, the town not only prevailed but developed into one of the strongest and most progressive towns in Virginia.

Prior to the nation's founding, Bridgewater was known as Magills' Ford due to a shallow place in the North River where travelers could cross from one side to the other. The early settlers were Scotch-Irish pioneers who generally landed in New Castle, Delaware, or Philadelphia, Pennsylvania, and made their way south where land was available in greater quantities and at lower prices.

Over time, the majority of the original settlers migrated west as did many others in the nation. However, the village of Magills' Ford continued to grow as the nation developed, and more settlers of English, Dutch, and Welsh descent arrived in the Shenandoah Valley. The new name of Bridgeport was eventually adopted due to the proximity of the North River and its development as a port for lumber, iron, and other goods.

After the Revolutionary War, German settlers arrived in the valley and became the largest ethnic group in the Bridgeport area. In 1833, the first road, known as the Harrisonburg-Warm Springs Turnpike, was chartered by the general assembly and connected Bridgeport to the outside world. This prompted further development in the community and created an interest among the citizens in establishing an independent town. Their petition to the general assembly in 1835 was approved, and the community's name was changed to Bridgewater.

The following years were ones of growth for the nation, but that did not occur without conflict. The increasing debate over slavery affected all communities, large and small. Around 1840, Jacob Dinkle leased a lot and frame building on Main Street for the sole purpose of establishing a Methodist church in his community. He stipulated that the land would become the property of the Town of Bridgewater if it ceased to be used by the Methodist Episcopal Church of North America. Because of disagreement over slavery, the Methodist Church divided into north and south branches prior to the Civil War, thus causing the Bridgewater branch of the church to lose all rights to the church property. They were allowed to continue holding services at this site for several more years but eventually moved to a new sanctuary located farther north on Main Street.

By 1860, secession was the main topic of discussion, but Bridgewater was against it. In choosing delegates to a state convention charged with the responsibility of deciding whether Virginia should secede from the Union, two were selected who opposed secession and one who favored it. Nevertheless, by the following year, opinions had changed due to the fall of Fort Sumter and Lincoln's call for volunteers to force seceding states back into the Union. Bridgewater citizens voted unanimously in favor of leaving the Union. During the Civil War, Bridgewater was alternately occupied by troops of both sides and suffered the consequences of war such as the loss of buildings, crops, and lives.

In the years after the war, most American towns got caught up in "railroad fever," and Bridgewater was no exception. At least three attempts to establish a major rail line through Bridgewater are known. In the end, the Chesapeake and Western (C&W) did come to the area, and a local line connected the towns of Bridgewater, Harrisonburg, and Elkton. From Harrisonburg, a train could be taken south to Staunton and then go on to any part of the nation that had rail service. As a result, commercial expansion boomed, bringing prosperity to Bridgewater previously not seen. This growth continued until the popularity of the automobile increased until it became a commonplace means of traveling to larger communities. It then prompted the demise of the railroad and many local businesses as a result.

The turn of the 20th century was a major event for Bridgewater. By this time, electric service had arrived. At the same time, outbreaks of typhoid and other waterborne diseases had prompted town officials to develop the first public water system. However, first does not necessarily mean best. In today's world, it is hard to imagine a network of water pipes made up of wooden slats and metal bands, but that is what the town council selected. That decision was regretted from the moment the pumps were turned on at the springhouse. Frequent and dramatic leaks occurred throughout the system. The following seven years were devoted to fruitless attempts at minimizing the leaks, but by 1920, the decision had been made to scrap the whole system and start anew.

Despite these economic factors and the harsh realities of the Great Depression, Bridgewater survived and grew, only to face a devastating flood in 1949. It happened in the middle of a summer night. Floodwaters breached the banks of the North and Dry Rivers causing $1 million of damage and ending the lives of three women whose homes stood in the flood's path. Two years later, the U.S. Army Corps of Engineers invested a substantial amount of money to construct a flood-control levee between Bridgewater and the path of future floods. Their effort proved successful, as the flood-control levy withstood major floods in 1985 and 1996, minimizing damage that would have otherwise occurred.

The effect of the 1949 flood was devastating and only added to Bridgewater's economic woes. Nationwide, the post-war years were noted for prosperity, but Bridgewater did not share in this growth. Perhaps the dire straits this community faced were best expressed by Mayor Nelson T. Huffman on Christmas Day 1949, when he announced to the citizenry that funds were not even available for Christmas decorations and that someone should string lights around a tree at town hall to show that the spirit of Christmas was still alive.

It was not until the 1960s that a combination of factors prompted the revival of Bridgewater. Since that time, Bridgewater has taken off and achieved levels never before imagined. The town is home to Bridgewater College, a 1,500-student liberal arts school that has produced graduates who have become leaders in medicine, law, and politics. Bridgewater Retirement Community (formerly the Bridgewater Home) provides all levels of care, from independent living to state-of-the-art Alzheimer care, for more than 600 citizens. Add to this industries like Perdue Farms, Marshalls, and Good Printers, and one can see that Bridgewater has matured into a thriving community.

One of earliest written descriptions of Bridgewater came from the diary of a Confederate soldier in 1862 as he passed through town during Jackson's Valley Campaign. He wrote, "We reached Bridgewater about 4 p.m. It was a place of which I had never heard, and a beautiful village it proved to be, buried in trees and flowers." To this day, Bridgewater continues to be the village this young man admired so many years ago.

# *One*

# Continuity in the Midst of Change

All communities change over time. That is a basic fact of life. Bridgewater has gone through many of the same struggles as other localities, and it is obvious that on the surface, at least, this community has changed.

However, one feature of Bridgewater that has contributed to its survival and success is continuity. Those who grow up in this town or move here at some point in their lives tend to stay. The men and women selected to lead our town are usually in office long enough to make a difference.

On the governmental level, Bridgewater has had only two mayors over the last 35 years. Roland Z. Arey, a lifelong resident of Bridgewater, served a total of 40 years, first as councilman and later as mayor. His successor, Hallie D. Dinkel, who is a direct descendent of the founders of the town, has been a councilman and later mayor for more than 20 years. Former town attorney Donald D. Litten represented the town for a remarkable 50-year period only to be followed in office by his son Jay Litten who continues as town attorney today.

The theme of continuity is obvious among the churches of Bridgewater. Whether Lutheran, Brethren, United Methodist, Presbyterian, or Baptist, each can trace their lineage in Bridgewater back more than 100 years. In the case of the United Methodist church, it was established with the aid of the founders of Bridgewater and continues to this day not two blocks away from their original site.

Bridgewater College and Bridgewater Retirement Community, both off-shoots of the Brethren church, add to the continuity of our town. D. C. Flory started the college in the 1880s with only three students. Today it has grown into a private liberal arts school that can boast of prominent leaders in many fields who point to Bridgewater College as their alma mater. The retirement community began its operations in the 1960s with just a nursing home. Today it includes comprehensive independent-living and assisted-care housing up to and including a special wing for Alzheimer patients. Many of their residents were either born in Bridgewater, moved here as college students, or made this their home as their career ended.

On the following pages, some of the people and places that have tied the past to the present and built a sense of continuity in a changing world are pictured.

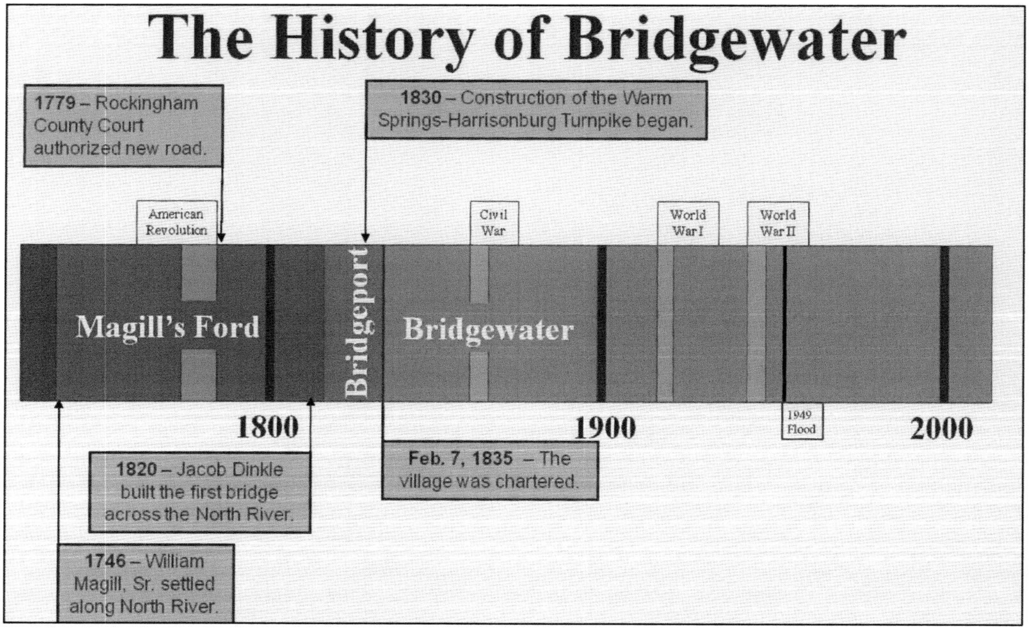


The Scotch-Irish, led by William Magill Sr., arrived in this area 30 years before the American Revolution. The Magills came from Northern Ireland as did most of their neighbors in this new land. These Scotch-Irish pioneers started life in the new world in Pennsylvania but moved on to the Shenandoah Valley where land was available in greater quantities and at lower prices. They were followed by English, Dutch, Welsh, and German immigrants, many of whom made Bridgewater their permanent home.

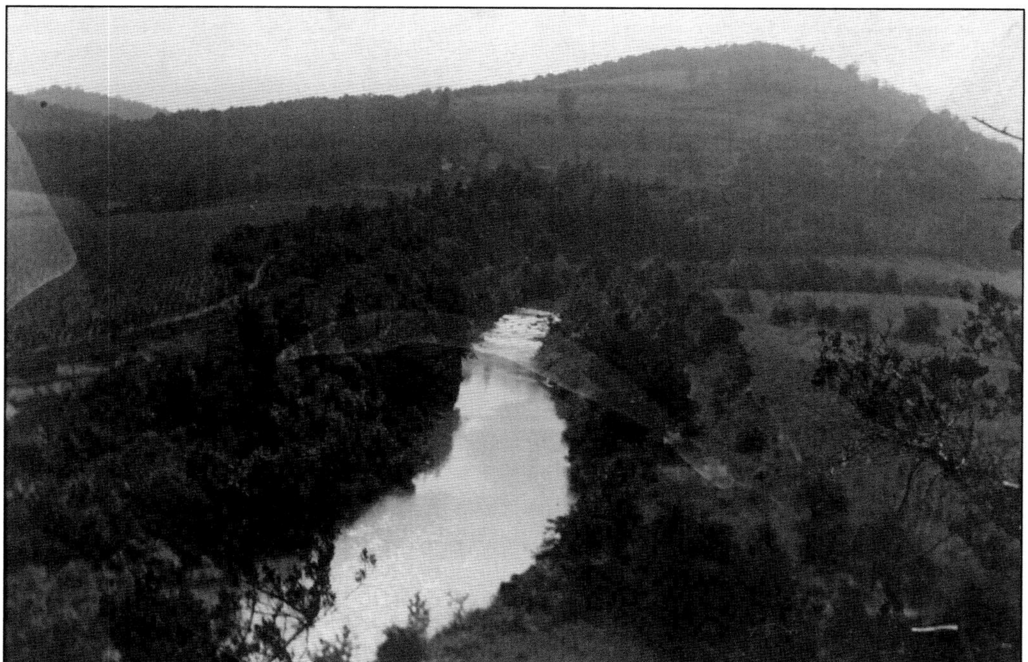

While the North River is the most defining feature of Bridgewater, the prominence of Round Hill situated just across the western banks of the river has also been an identifying feature.

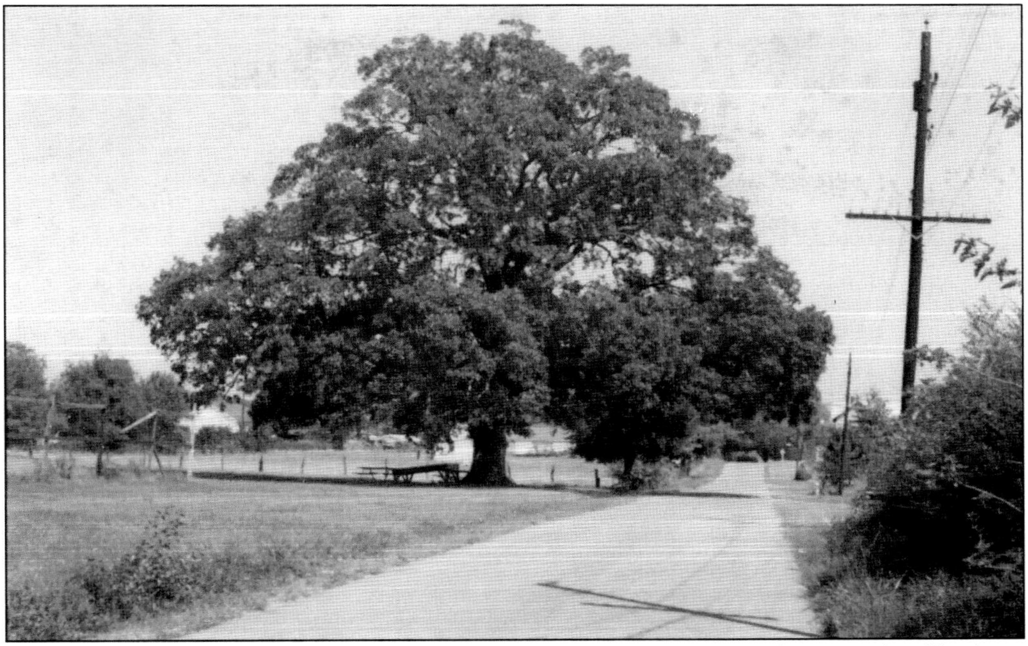
The large White Oak on First Street was a full-grown tree before the first settlers arrived and has been a landmark fixture in this community for more than 300 years. Along with North River and Round Hill, it remains one of the more distinctive geographical features of the Bridgewater community.

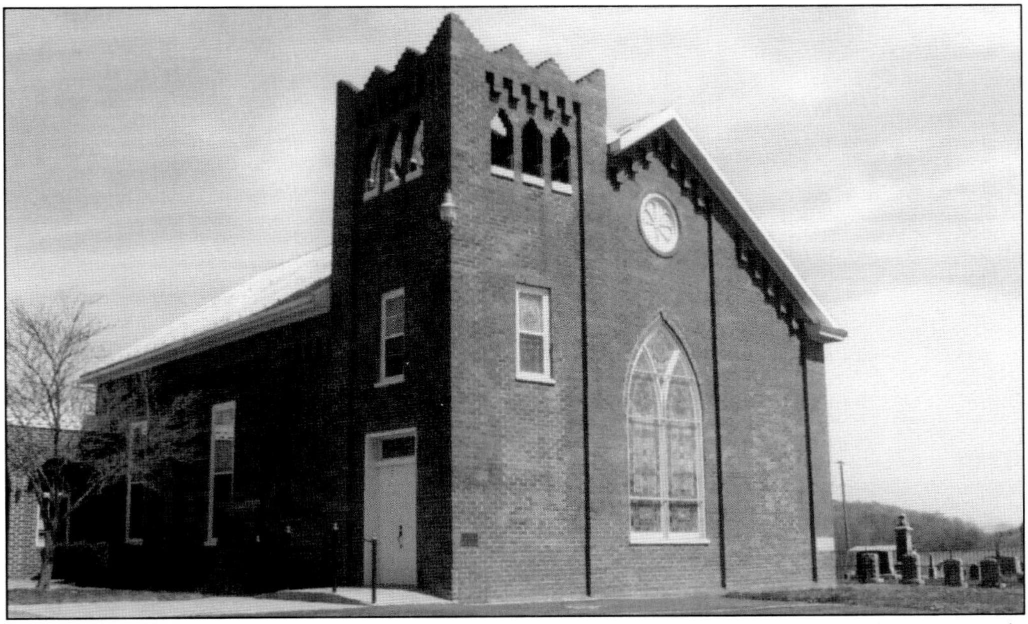
With the arrival of German immigrants in the 1780s, many of the Scotch-Irish families were ready to move to the new frontier and eagerly sold their farms to the newcomers. These new arrivals organized a German-speaking congregation and built several churches. The first of these was constructed shortly after the American Revolution and used by both Lutheran and Reformed congregations. Located a short distance outside the town boundary, it is still in use and known as St. Michael's United Church of Christ. It is interesting to note that their first pastor, the Reverend Benjamin Henkel, was buried under the pulpit after his death in 1794.

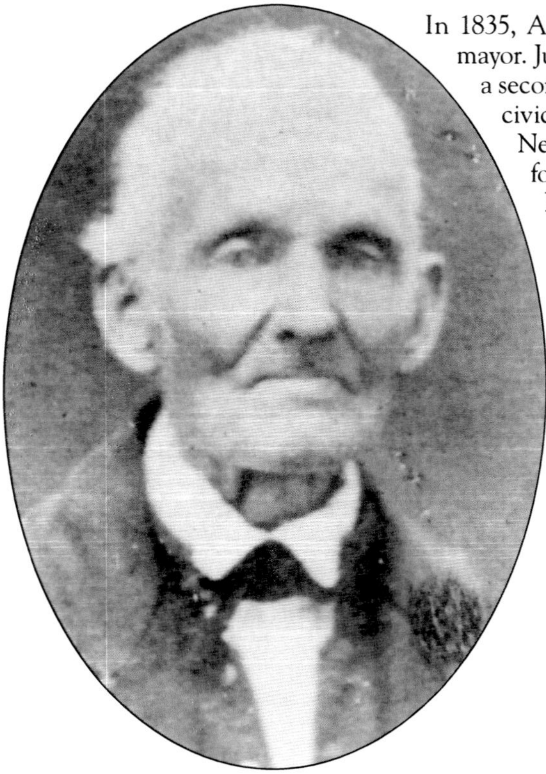

In 1835, Adam Radar was elected Bridgewater's first mayor. Just prior to the Civil War, he was reelected to a second term and remained active in Bridgewater's civic and business affairs throughout his long life. News accounts reported one of his last duties as follows, "On June 18, 1873, ground was broken at Bridgewater for the construction of the North River railroad. The first shovel full of dirt was thrown by Adam Radar, the oldest resident of the town." Mayor Radar died in 1881, just one month before his 90th birthday.

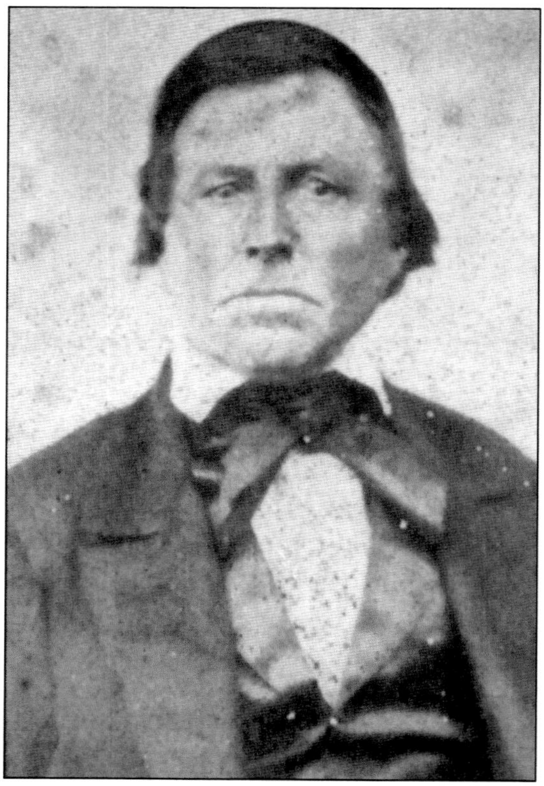

As soldiers returned from the Civil War, the focus of daily life changed from the battlefield to the rebuilding of communities. John Altaffer was elected mayor in 1866, serving two terms before he left office; he returned in 1880 for one more term. Like many of his compatriots, he was a member of the Masonic Lodge.

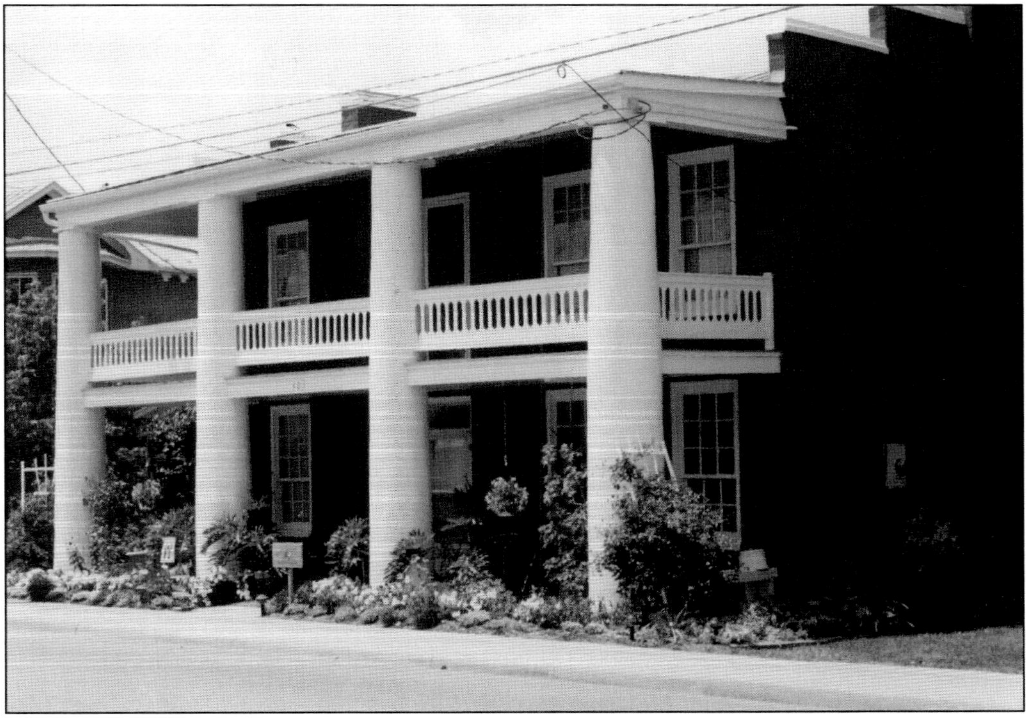

The Barbee House is one of the oldest homes on the north end of Main Street. It illustrates a style of architecture popular during the 1840s in the Shenandoah Valley. It was enlarged several times by the late 19th century when Col. Gabriel Barbee ran an inn called the Barbee Hotel. He also used the house as his personal residence, and for a while, his daughter operated a private school within its walls.

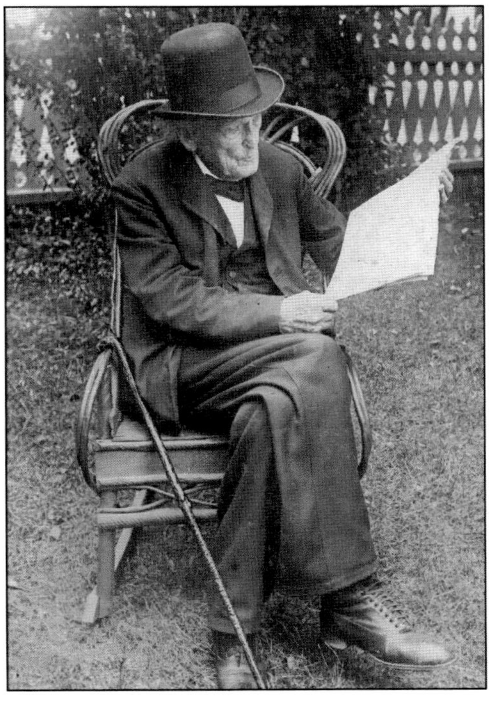

Colonel Barbee was a prominent Bridgewater citizen. He served as a Virginia state senator, acted as president of the Virginia Farmers Alliance, was a member of the board of visitors at the University of Virginia, and, most importantly to his hometown, he served two terms as mayor in the 1870s.

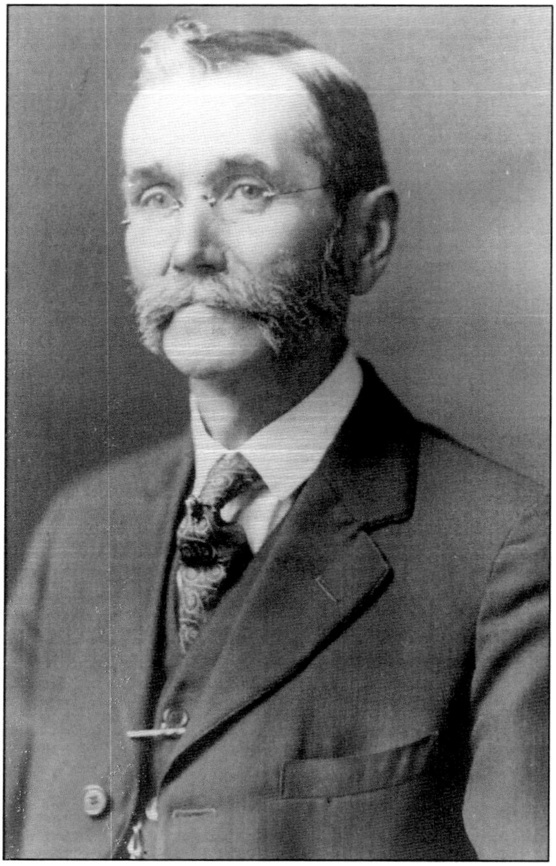

J. A. Riddel served as both councilman and mayor of Bridgewater from 1910 until 1924. As mayor, Riddel had to make the tough decision to increase taxes 400 percent in order to replace the deficient water system plaguing Bridgewater. He was accustomed to making pivotal business choices and was considered to be one of the more successful entrepreneurs at the turn of the 20th century. It was said that his investments grossed more than $10,000 annually. While that might not sound like much today, in 1910 it was quite a fortune.

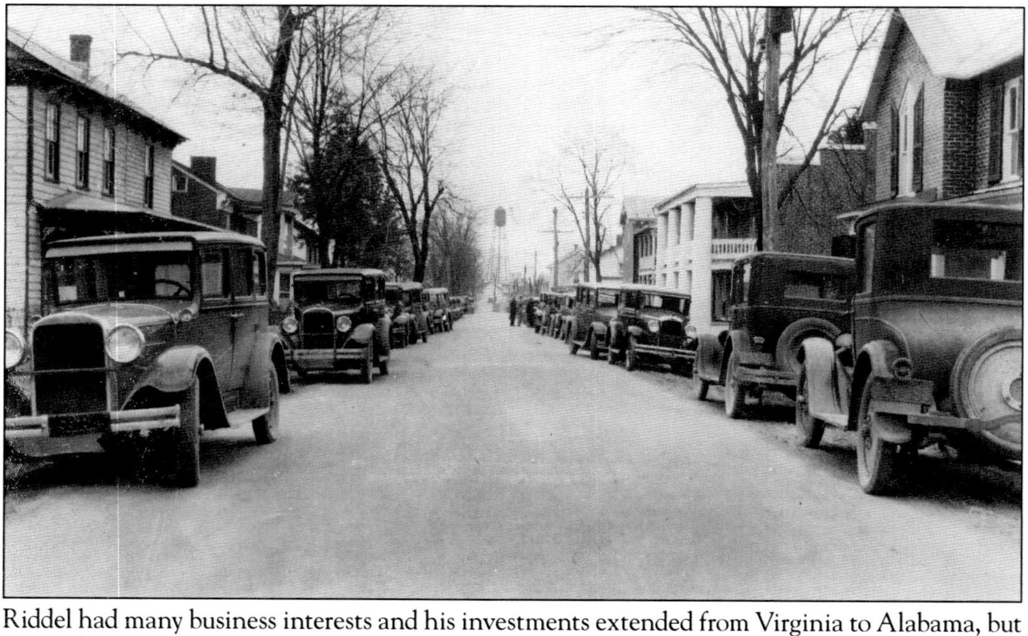

Riddel had many business interests and his investments extended from Virginia to Alabama, but most of Bridgewater associated him with the lumberyard bearing his name. When he passed away on January 8, 1929, it seemed the whole town turned out for his funeral.

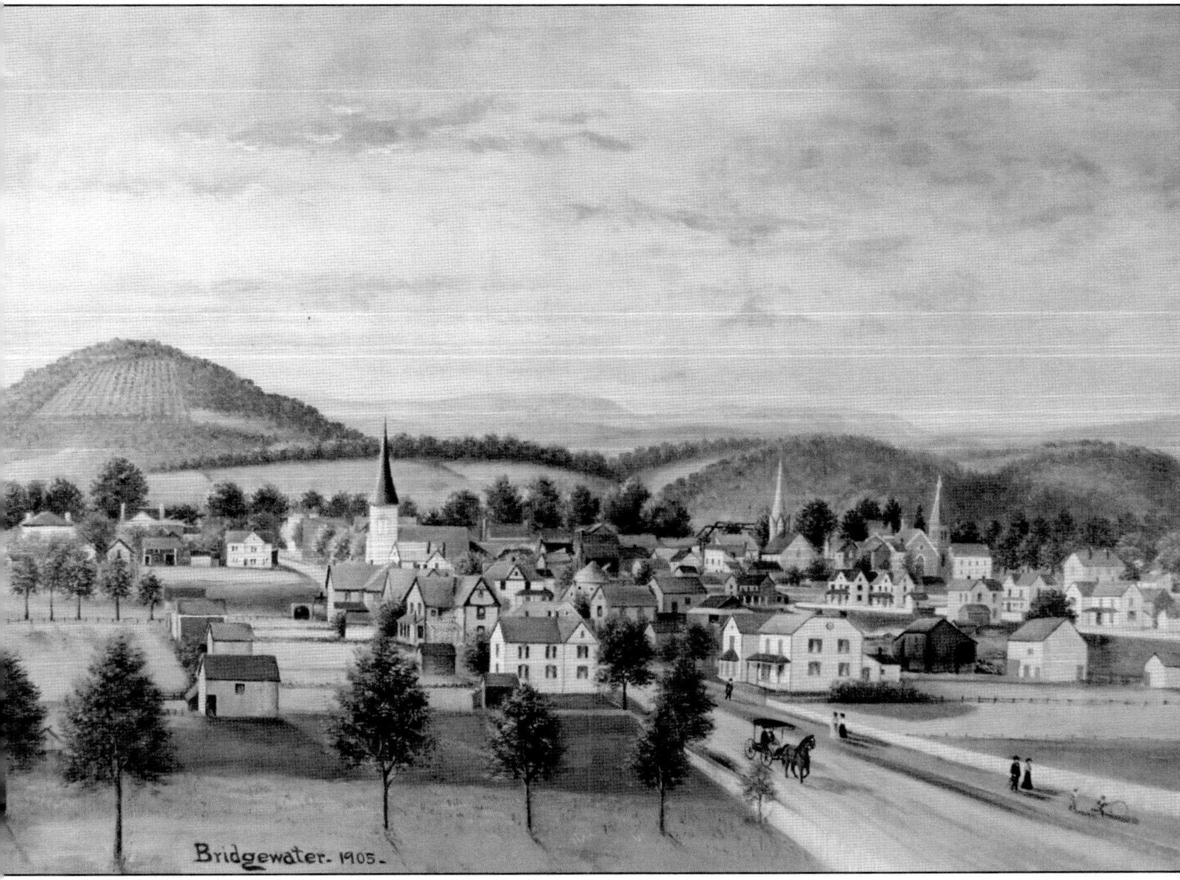


Rebecca Bowman was born in Rockingham County on June 14, 1871, and had 11 brothers and sisters. As each married, she painted a wedding portrait for the newlyweds. She also taught art at Bridgewater College from 1894 until 1913. Her most famous work is this painting of the town of Bridgewater in 1905 that now hangs in the treasurer's office at Bridgewater College.

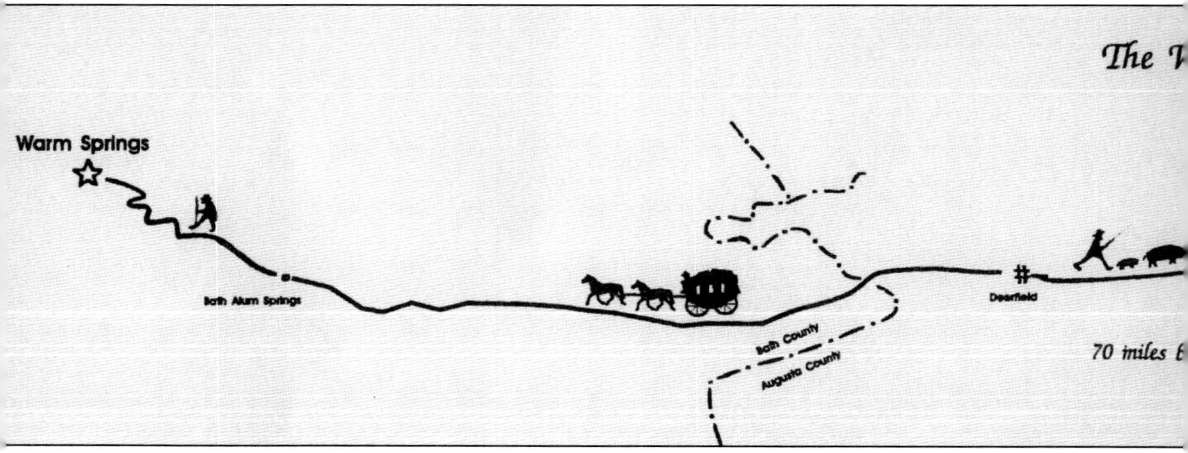


In the 1829–1830 session of the Virginia General Assembly, an act was passed incorporating the Warm Springs and Harrisonburg Turnpike Company. An improved roadbed was to be constructed to follow an old country road that had existed in portions of the route since the colonial era. The Warm Springs Turnpike Act preceded the Valley Turnpike (present-day U.S. Route 11) legislation by several years, indicating the particular importance of this highway. The construction of the road did away with the custom of residents who lived along the road being required to break rocks with knapping hammers for several days a year to fill in ruts with crushed stone. Investors in the new turnpike company would initiate repairs that would be paid for with road-use tolls. Along the roadway at each town, village, or stream crossing, a tollgate was established to collect money for road

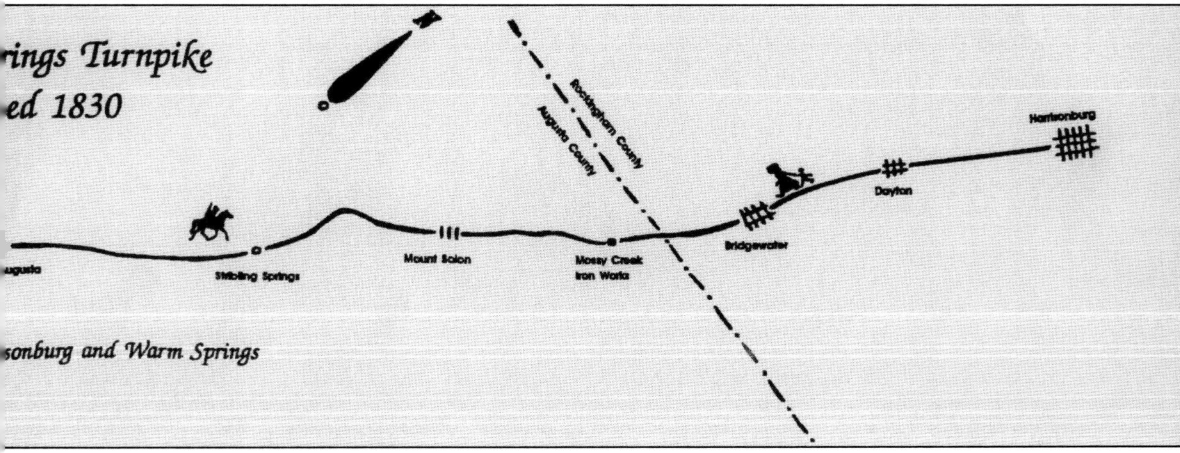


use, road repairs, and hopefully to generate a profit for investors. Tolls were set by the legislature. There was one toll for foot travelers, another for those on horseback, and separate tolls for two-wheeled carts and four-wheeled wagons. Stagecoaches paid tolls based on the number of horses needed to pull the vehicle. Herds of cattle, horses, sheep, hogs, and even ducks, turkey, and geese had different tolls per head in the drove. In 1867, a toll was initiated to cross the bridge over the North River at Bridgewater; it was 3¢ per person. Main Street in Bridgewater follows the bed of the old turnpike, as does U.S. Route 42, to a point about a mile south of the Augusta County line. The last tollgates along the turnpike were closed in 1912, when Rockingham County took over the maintenance of the thoroughfare within its borders.

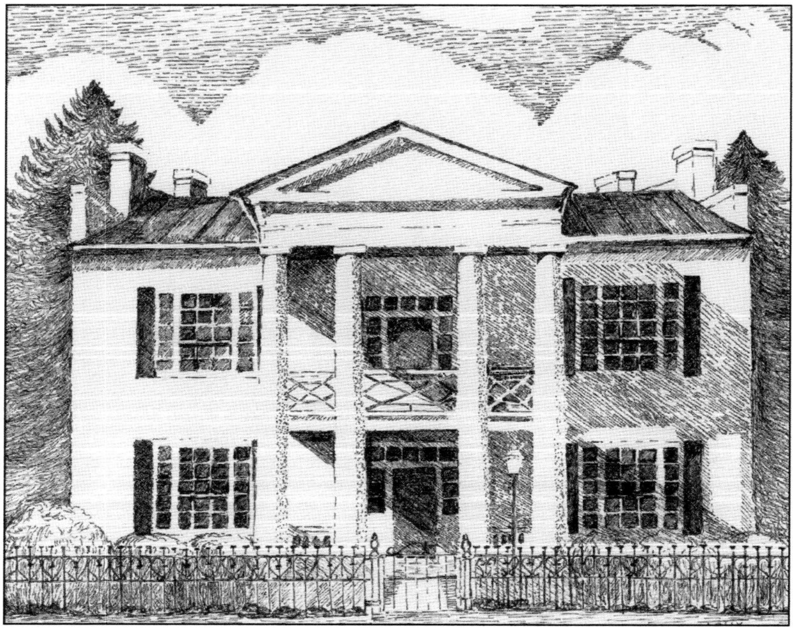

Dr. J. G. Brown's house on South Main Street was built in 1849 and remains one of the more impressive homes in Bridgewater. Dr. Brown was a physician, planter, money lender, and politician. He was a member of the Rockingham County Court from 1848 to 1857 and a member of the Virginia House of Delegates in 1847 and again in 1857.

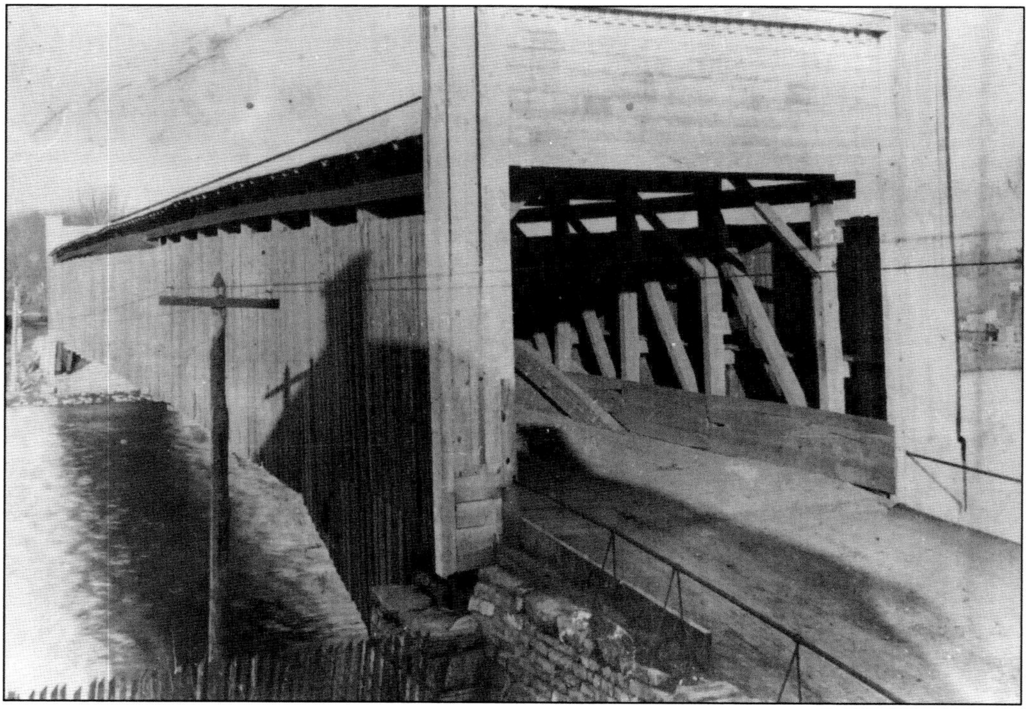

Seven bridges have crossed the North River since Bridgewater's founding in 1835. Some of these were merely low-water structures that were washed away by floods, while others have stood the test of time. The most famous of these is the wooden-covered bridge that served Bridgewater from 1877 to 1916.

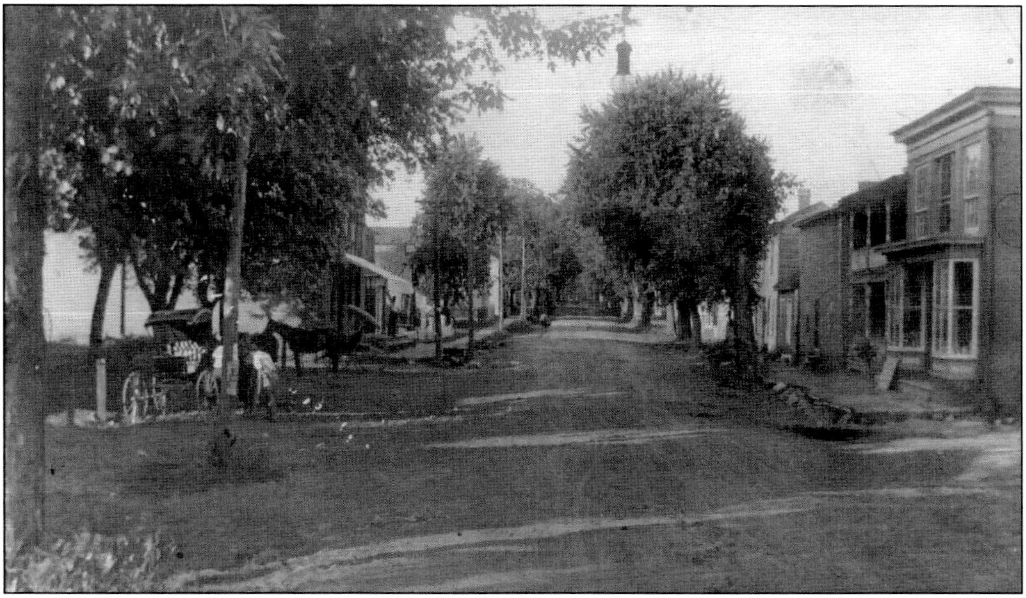

This is how South Main Street looked at the dawn of the 20th century. Notice the streetlight at the top center of the picture. Town records indicate that electricity came to Bridgewater as early as 1900, and that the council approved using electricity for streetlights in 1904. Telephones came several years later.

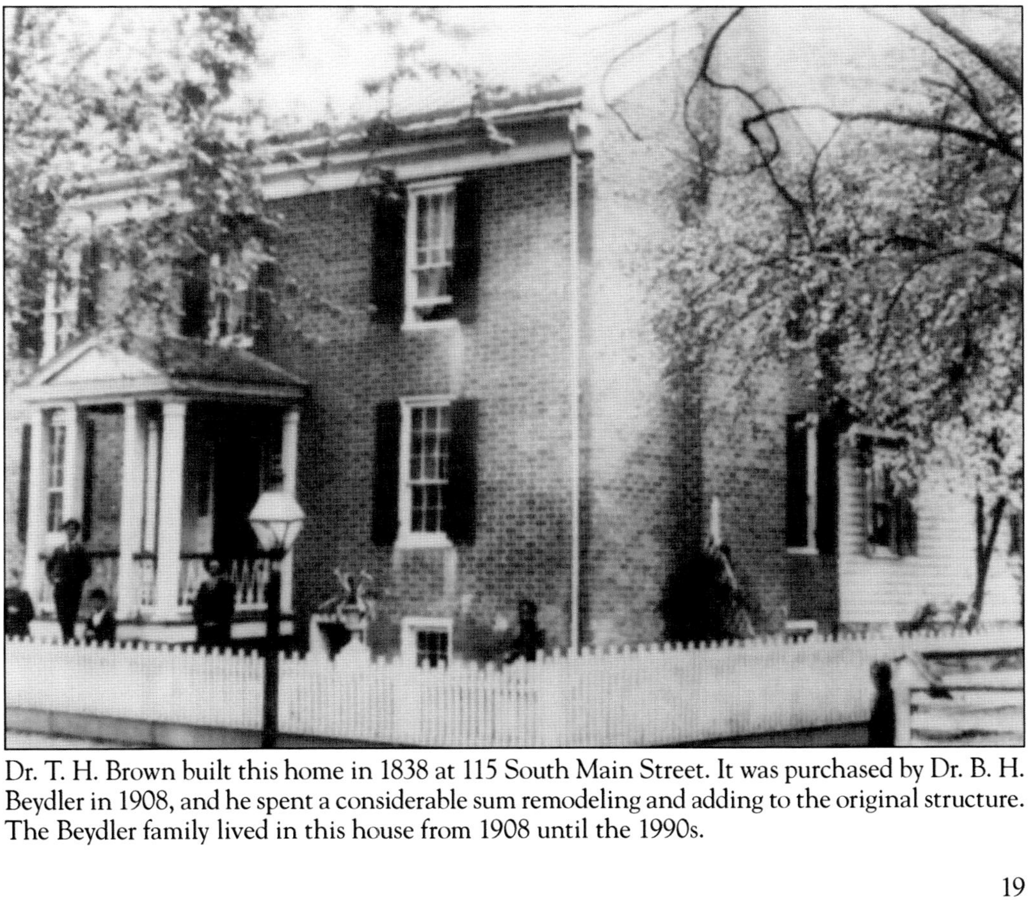

Dr. T. H. Brown built this home in 1838 at 115 South Main Street. It was purchased by Dr. B. H. Beydler in 1908, and he spent a considerable sum remodeling and adding to the original structure. The Beydler family lived in this house from 1908 until the 1990s.

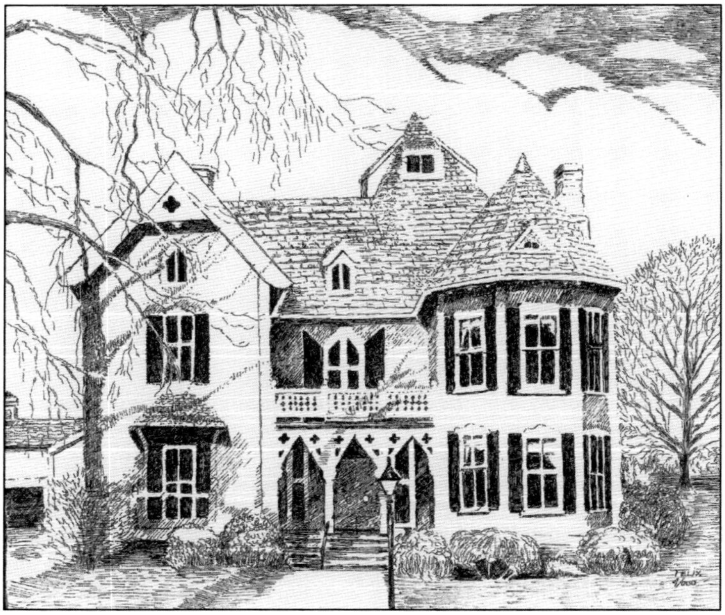

This stately home on West College Street is a derivative of Victorian style called Carpenter's Gothic. It was built in 1877 for Rev. J. S. Loose. Reverend Loose had dual careers that rarely go together. In addition to his ministry, he served as an officer and employee of Farmers Bank. It was said of him, "He is endowed with rare financial capacity for one of the clergy. He is a gentlemen of polish, yet plain and easy to address, and as a consequence is universally popular."

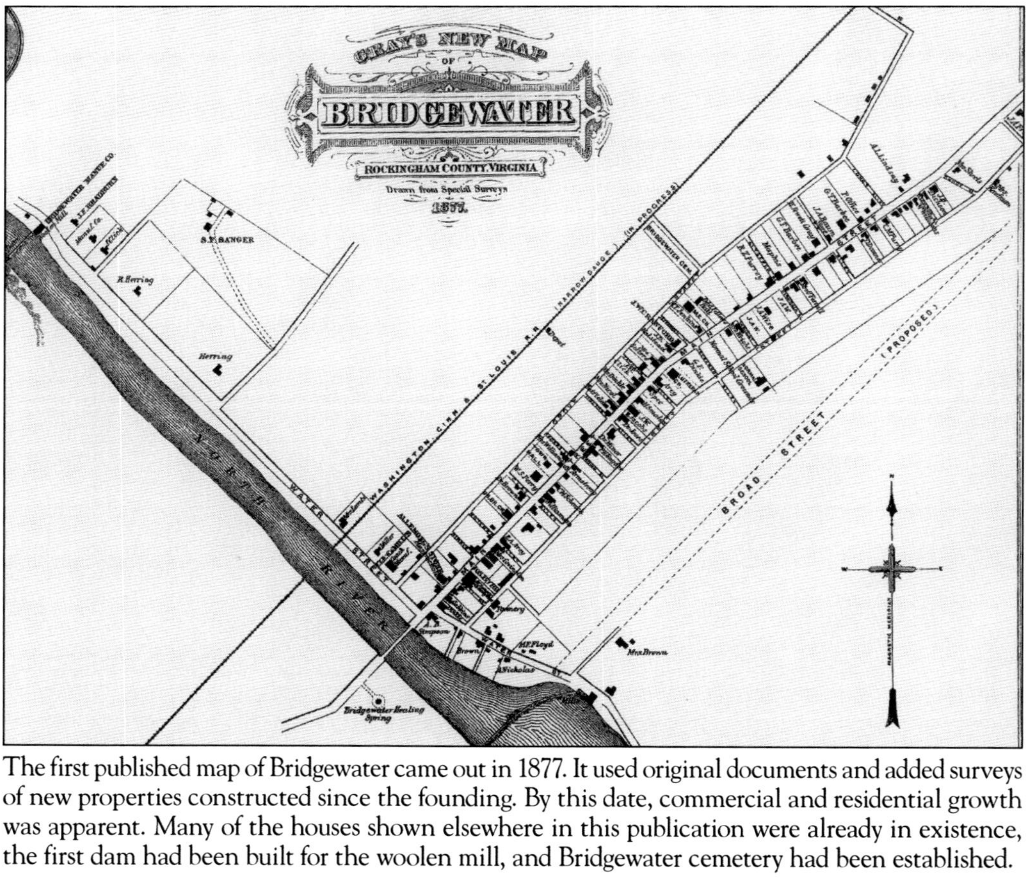


The first published map of Bridgewater came out in 1877. It used original documents and added surveys of new properties constructed since the founding. By this date, commercial and residential growth was apparent. Many of the houses shown elsewhere in this publication were already in existence, the first dam had been built for the woolen mill, and Bridgewater cemetery had been established.

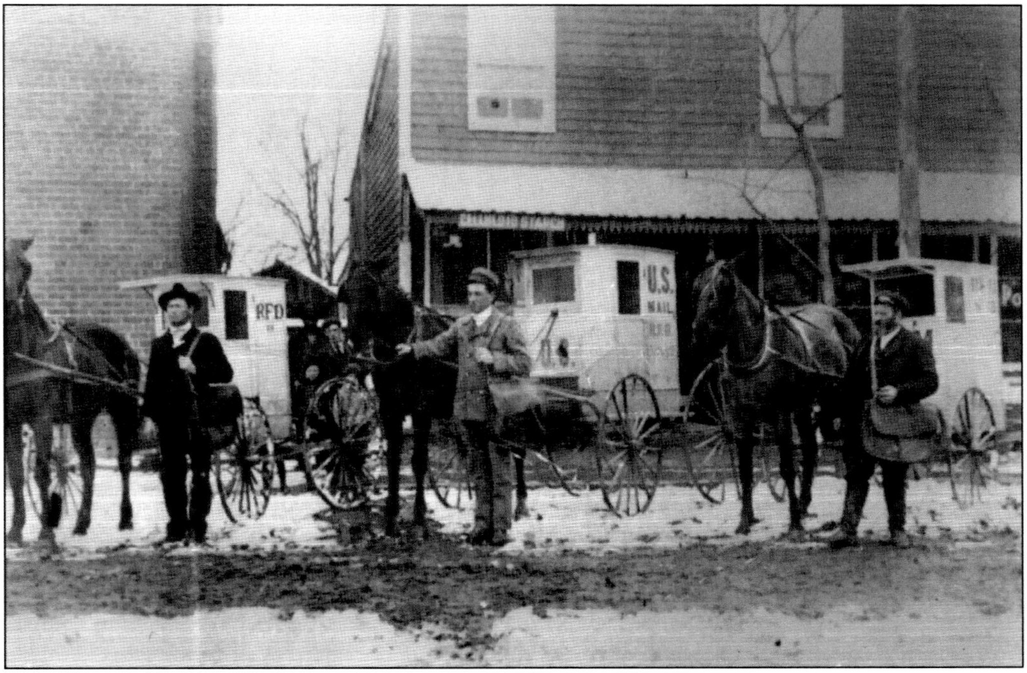


"RFD" stood for Rural Free Delivery and linked the smallest town in rural America to any city or village across the nation. For only a penny, a letter or card could be sent anywhere in the country, and letter writing became a popular pastime throughout America. The area around Bridgewater was served by three rural mail carriers. From left to right they were John Dovel, John Click, and Gabe Miller.

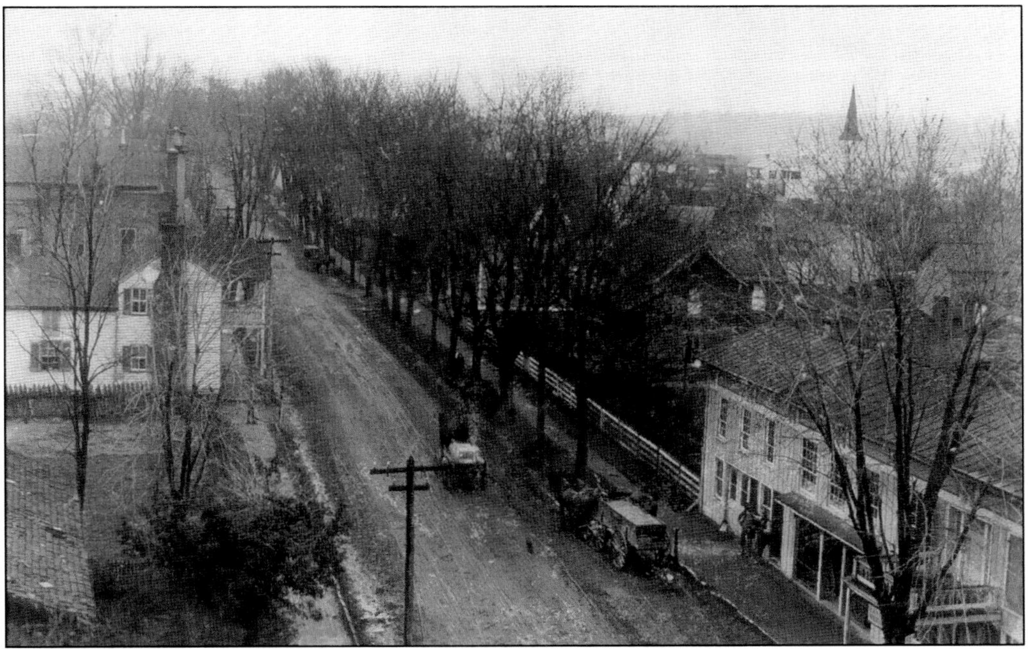

A horse-drawn hearse pulls away from Rosenberger Funeral Home to begin its journey to the cemetery only a few blocks away. It is believed that this picture was taken more than a century ago from the Masonic Lodge located on the third floor of Robson and Robson store.

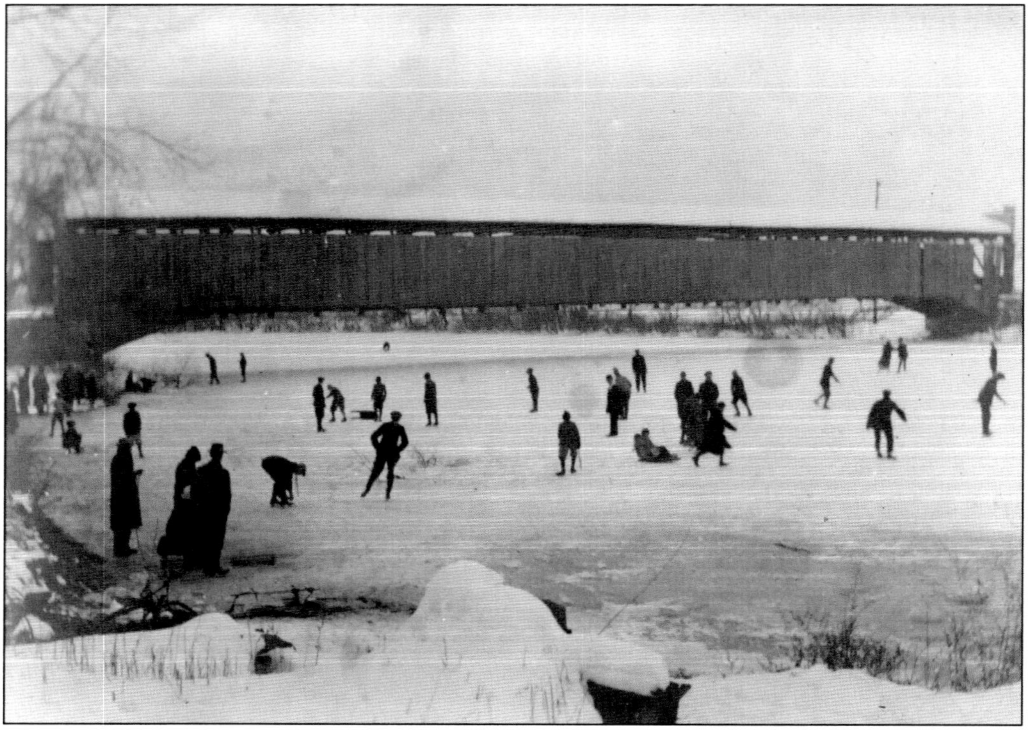

This is not a Courier and Ives painting. Instead, it is a typical scene from the early 1900s in Bridgewater. While the North River did not freeze every winter, it became a popular meeting place when it did. Of course, ice skating was the number one event, but this occasion was also used to cut blocks of ice out of the river, place them in an ice house, and cover them with sawdust to be saved and used during warm weather months.

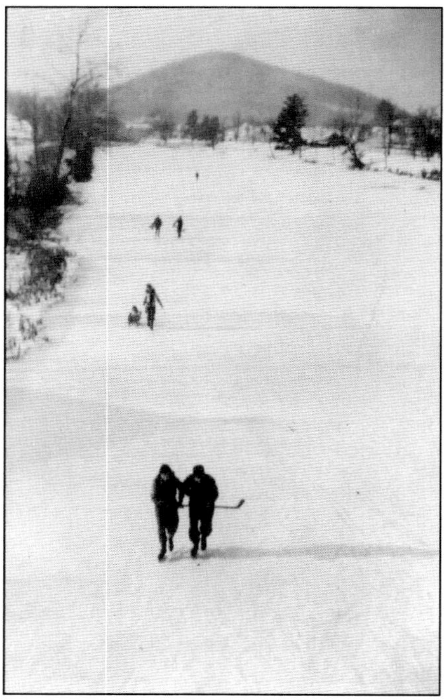

This picture, taken from the bridge over North River, shows skaters both in the foreground and at a distance. The North River borders Bridgewater for almost 3 miles. On days that it is frozen, it becomes one of the largest winter playgrounds one will ever see.

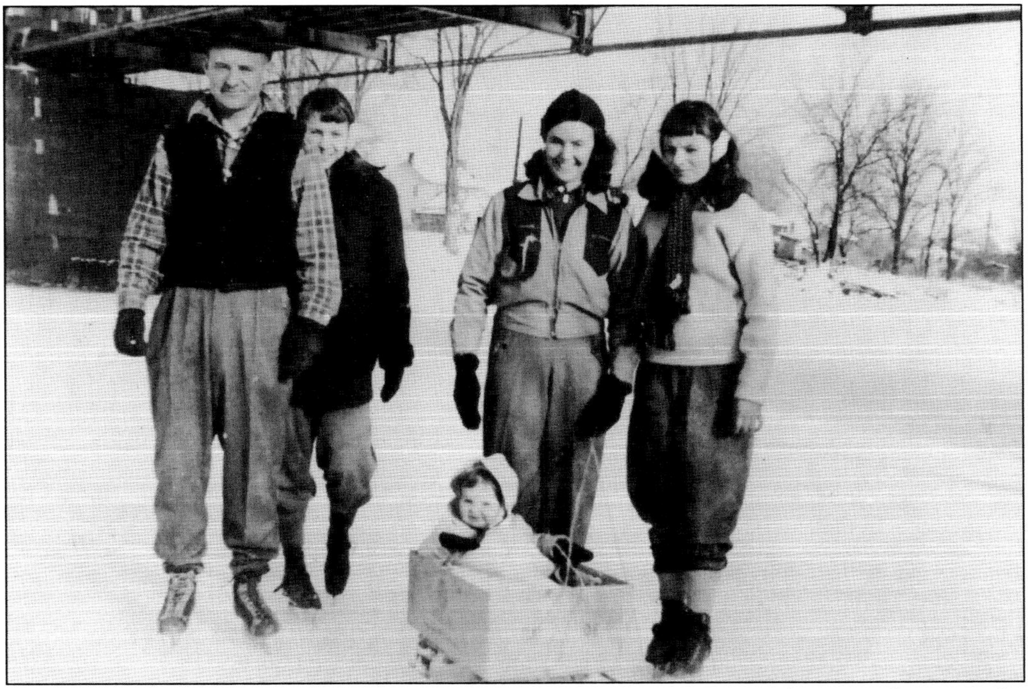

The winter of 1947 brought out more than ice hockey enthusiasts. Families were drawn to the river through all four seasons, but especially during those rare times when it would freeze from bank to bank. Here Dick Elliott and his family enjoy an afternoon out of the house on a cold winter day.

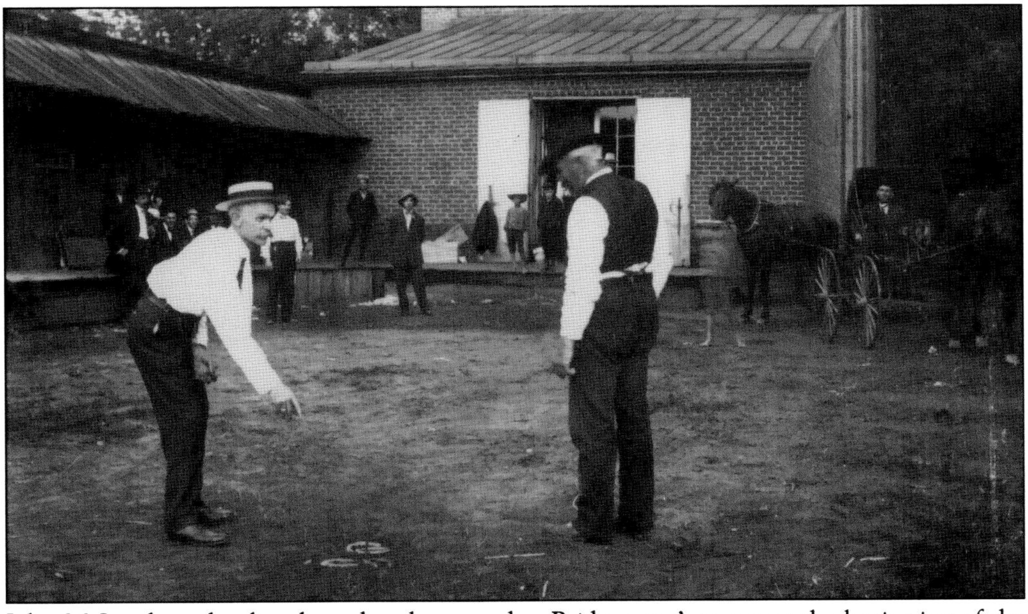

John McLeod, a schoolteacher who also served as Bridgewater's mayor at the beginning of the 20th century, plays horseshoes with his friend J. H. Lindsey in back of Robson's store. In the days before radio, television, and electronic media, social interaction was very important. Men especially would find time to hang around local stores to discuss politics, play games, and catch up on the latest gossip.

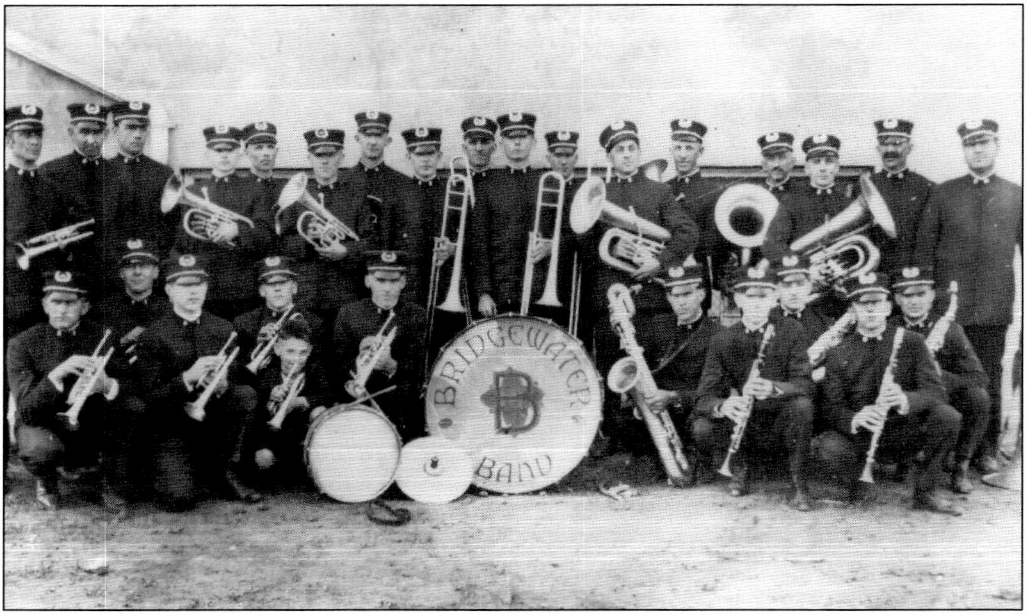


Most small towns had a community band, and Bridgewater was no exception. Weekend concerts were common during the summer months, and the band was in every parade whether it be Fourth of July, Labor Day, or Memorial Day. The Bridgewater band was widely reputed to be one of the best and often was asked to perform in other localities.

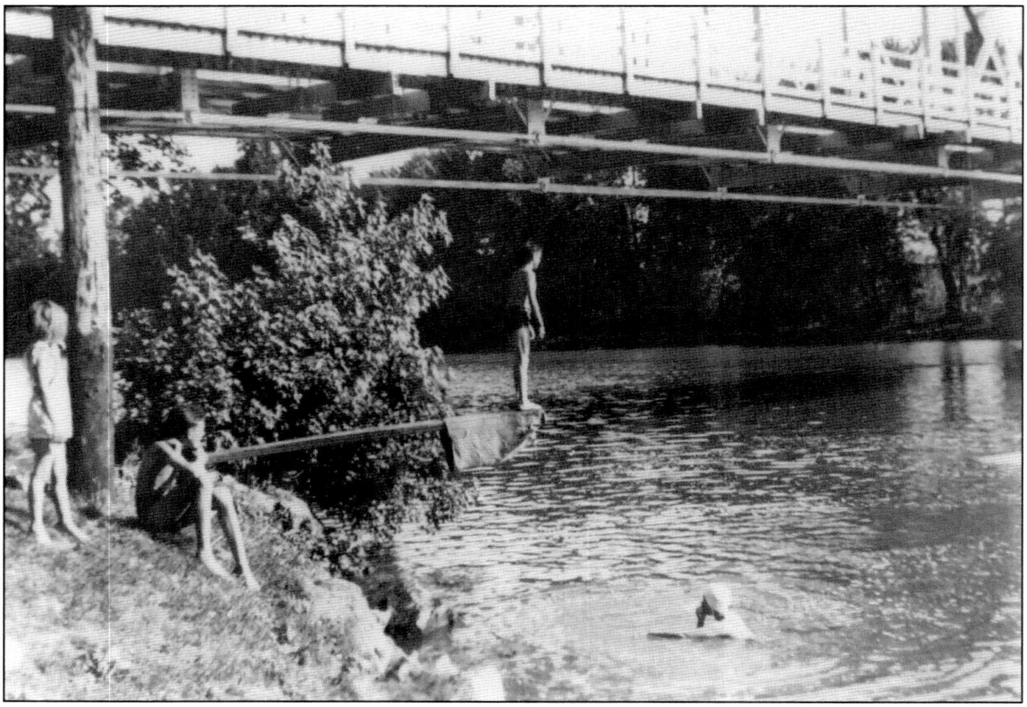

In the summer, the river was a favorite spot for young boys. Here they spent a lot of time catching frogs and swimming. It is said that every kid in Bridgewater used to jump off the bridge. Until about 10 years old, boys jumped from the main part and after that, from the top.

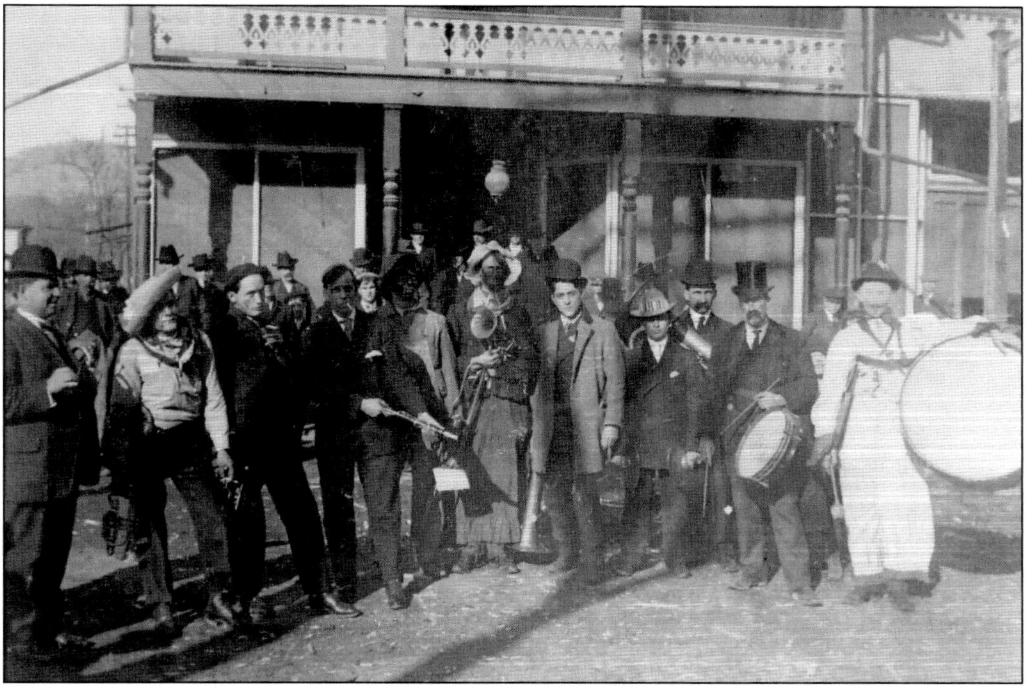

It is hard to imagine a world without television, the Internet, or a local movie theater. Entertainment seems to be a basic human need, and those living in the 1800s found ways to fill the week with local and traveling entertainment. Most families had a piano, and many evenings were spent singing hymns or popular tunes. Special events, such as the circus or other traveling shows such as seen above, were always welcomed in town.

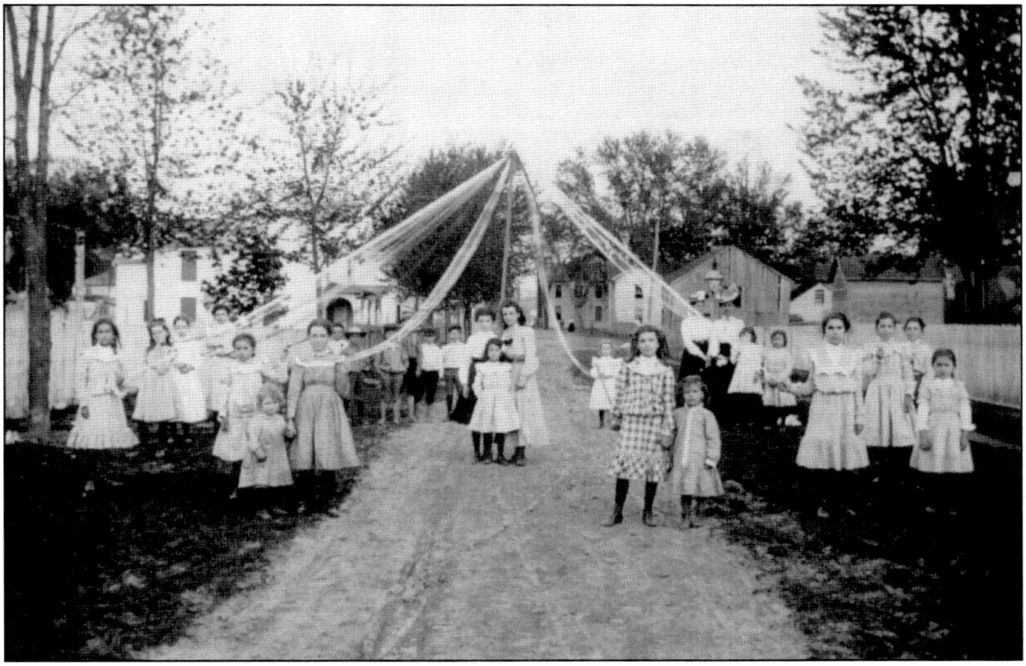

May Day celebrations were once a big event in towns such as Bridgewater. Young Bridgewater students from a century ago are shown celebrating this long-forgotten holiday.

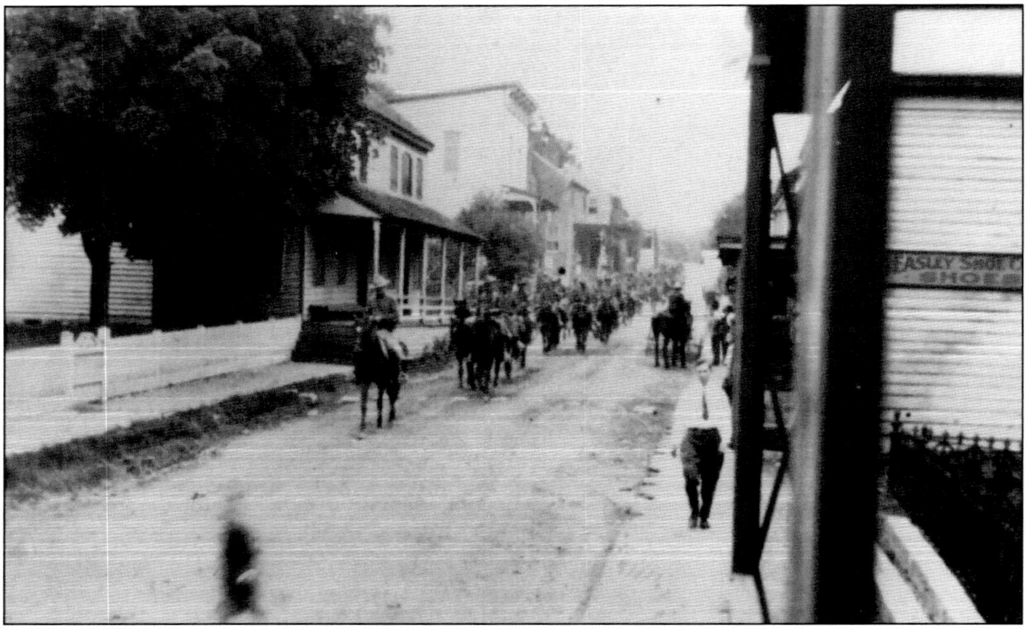

Small-town life in the 1800s was far different than it is today. One of the highlights was the arrival of the circus, minstrel, or Wild West show to the community. In this picture is the cast of a Wild West show parading down Main Street in Bridgewater. Spontaneous parades of this nature often occurred to promote the show that would be coming later that night.

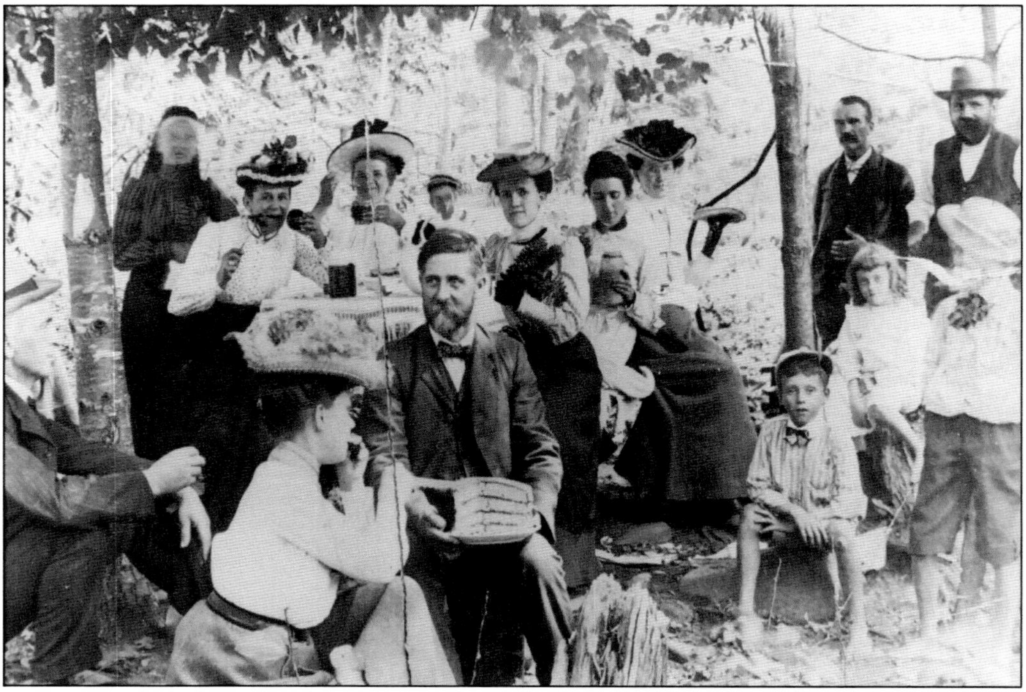

Churches held oyster suppers, ice cream socials, and strawberry festivals. Sunday school picnics and revivals were major events. Social events years ago were much more formal than they are today. Even a picnic such as this prompted men to wear their Sunday best, while women were adorned in their favorite hats even during the hottest afternoon.

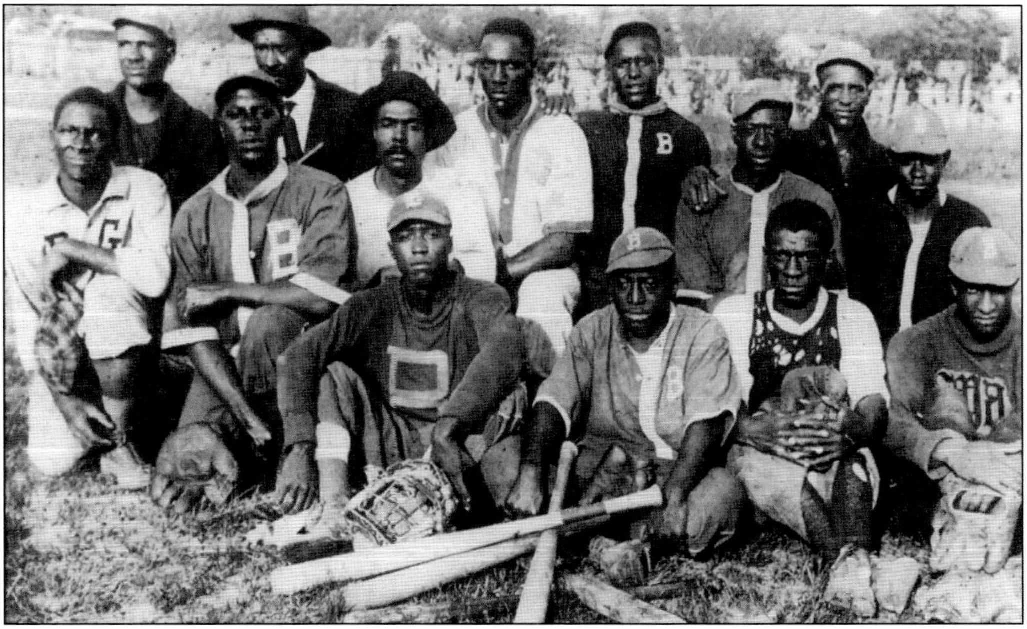

Before integration, all aspects of life were segregated, including sports. In Bridgewater, Roscoe Burgess (third row with "B" on shirt) led a team that traveled up and down the Shenandoah Valley to play baseball. It is believed that some of the players on this team had the potential to play professionally. Unfortunately they were never given the chance. Today Roscoe Burgess serves as a member of the Bridgewater Town Council.

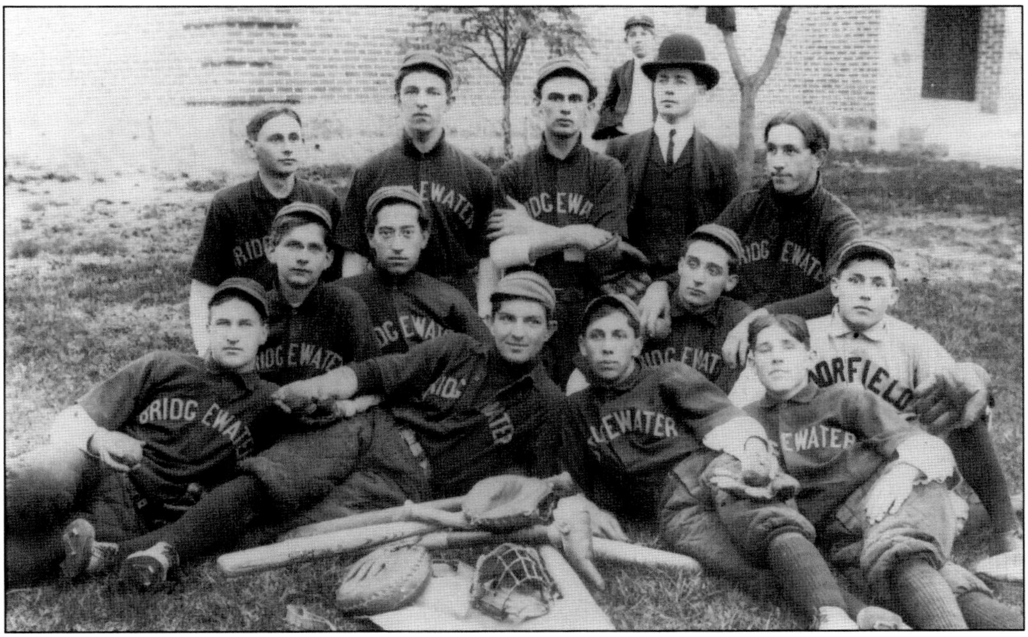

One cannot imagine how popular baseball was in small-town America in the late 1800s and early 1900s. Most towns had a team, and the rivalry was intense. For a while, baseball was not considered a family activity, because fights often broke out between fans and players in addition to the unending stream of insults directed towards umpires. On occasion, a police officer would have to escort the umpires out of town for their own protection.

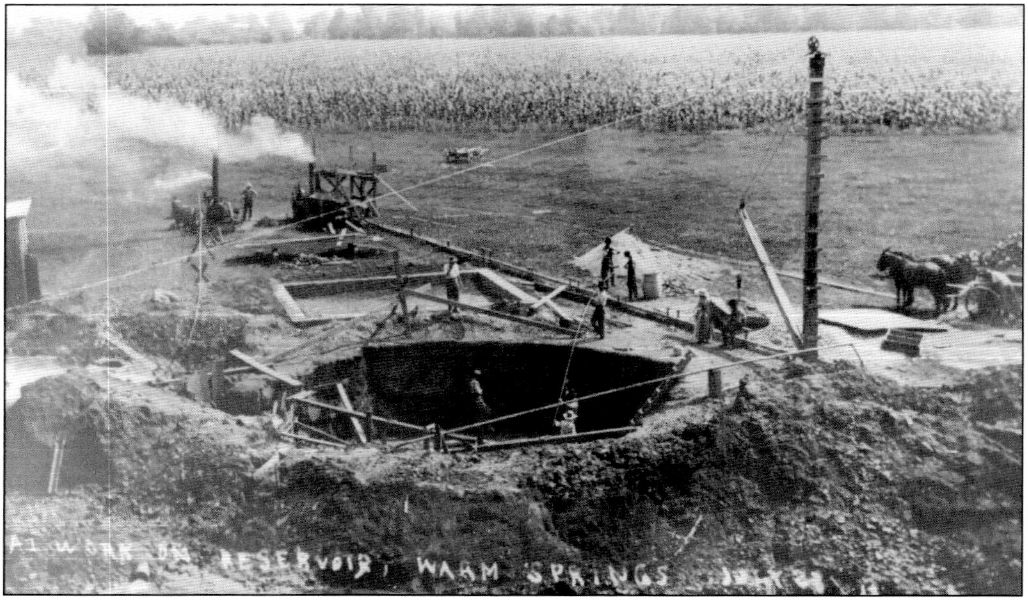


Outbreaks of typhoid and other waterborne diseases prompted Bridgewater to construct its first water-treatment system in 1913. In most modern countries, waterborne diseases are not a part of everyday life, but prior to public water systems, they were a major health problem.

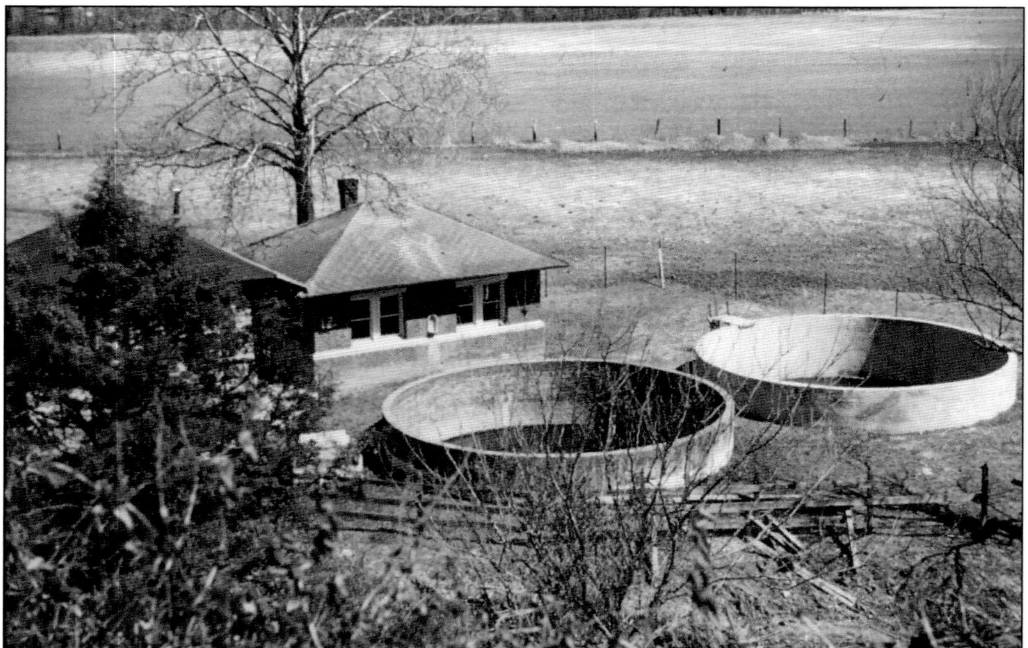

This is how the first water-treatment plant looked when completed in 1913. By modern standards, it was not much to look at, merely a spring and facilities to chlorinate and soften the mineral-laden springwater.

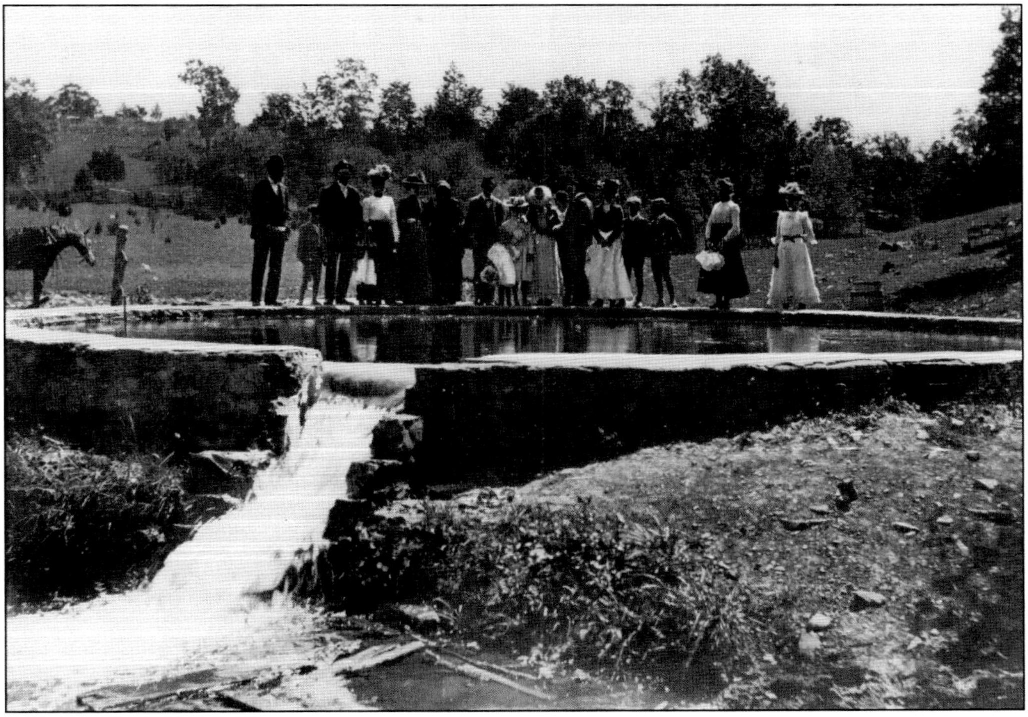

The grand opening of a spring is hardly cause for celebration, but that is exactly what happened in 1913. The first public water supply meant the end to cholera and other waterborne diseases.

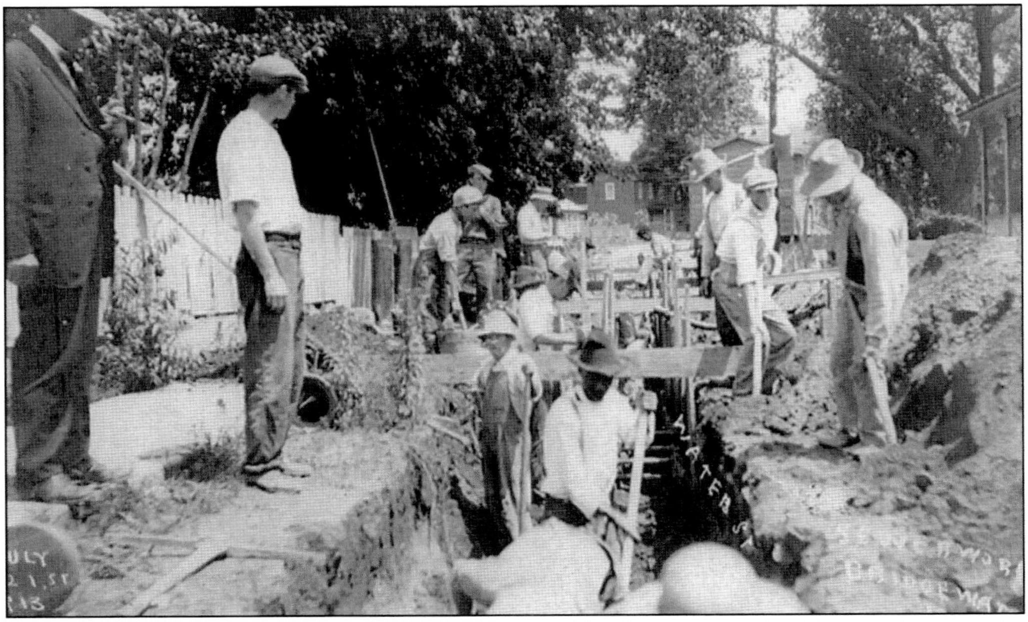


When it was time to extend water and sewer lines in 1913, there were no backhoes or dump trucks available, so all lines had to be installed by pick and shovel. Dozens of men would be used for this backbreaking labor, and progress was slow even in the best of conditions.

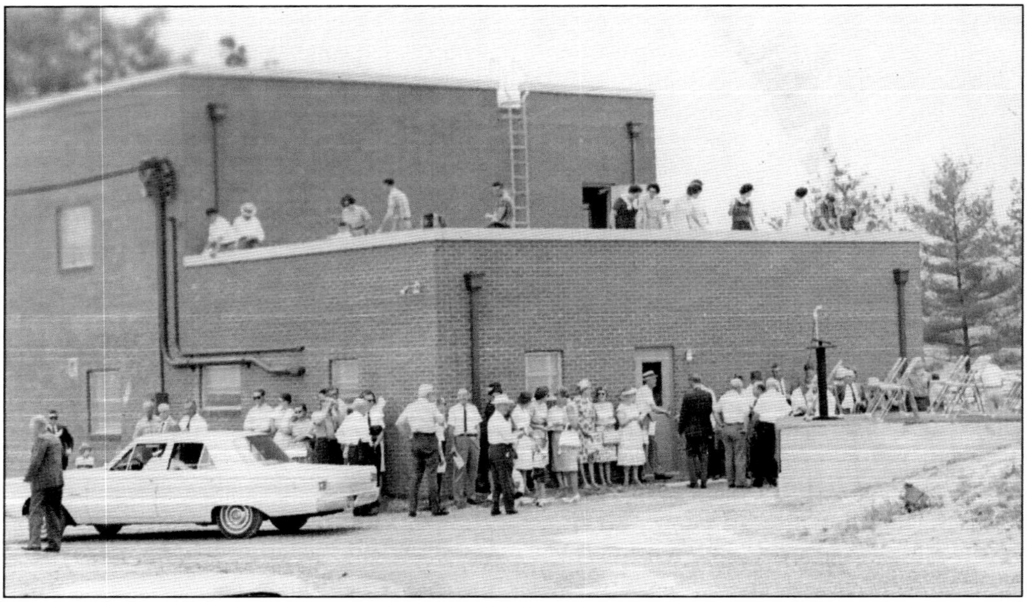

When the water-filtration plant opened in May 1966, more than 250 citizens attended the grand opening. This was indeed a time for celebration, since the old spring serving the town had failed. For quite a while, the only water Bridgewater citizens had available was from a portable treatment system loaned to the town by the U.S. Army Corps of Engineers.

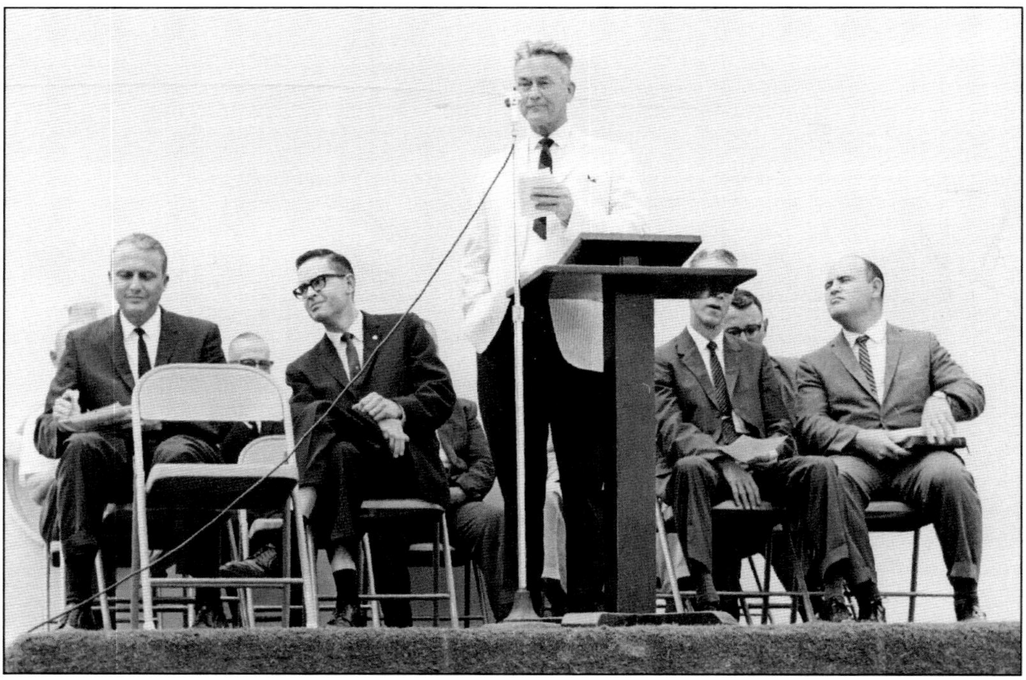

Mayor C. E. May introduces Congressman John Marsh (far left) at the dedication ceremony for the water-filtration plant in 1966. Congressman Marsh went on to become secretary of the U.S. Army during the Reagan administration.

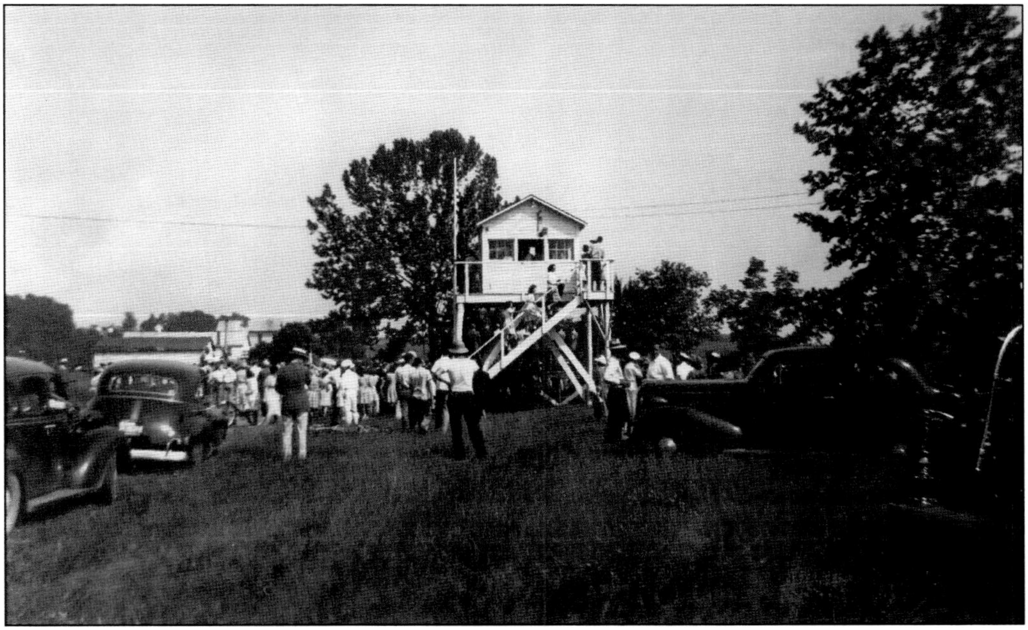

World War II was probably one of the more unifying events in the nation's history. Communities supported the war effort by buying bonds, saving scrap metal, and sacrificing in their everyday life in order to support the troops. Another task undertaken at the local level was a nightly blackout with local citizens acting as sentries in lookout towers such as the one shown above at the corner of Dinkel Avenue and Third Street.

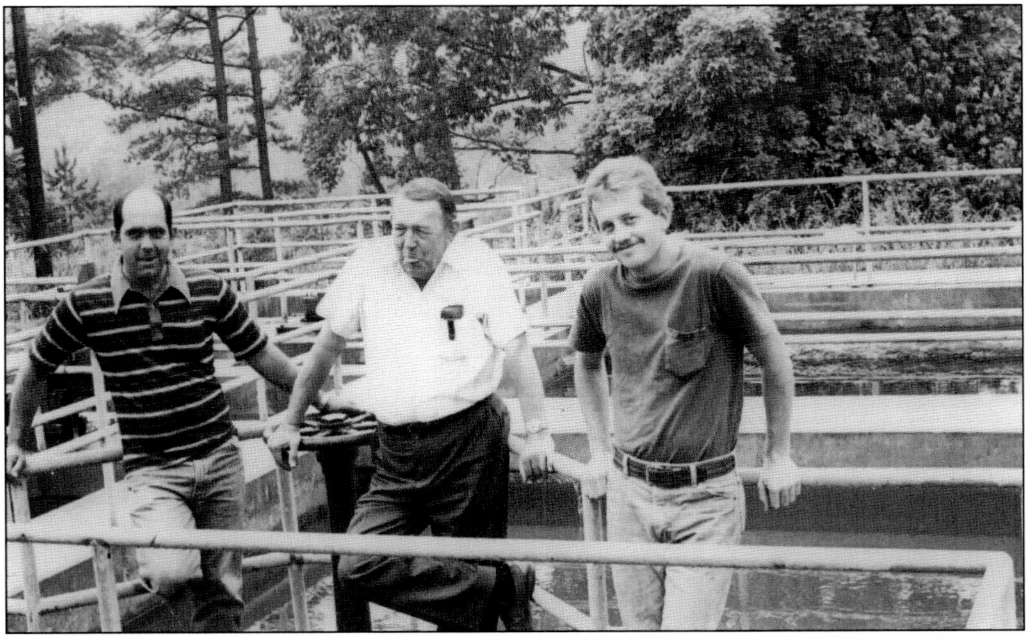

The caption for this photograph could be titled "The Three Chiefs." When the water-filtration plant was opened in 1966, Bill Hisey (center) served as chief operator. He was followed by Ron Shirkey (left) for several years. When Mr. Shirkey was appointed director of utilities for the town, he was succeeded by Charles Smith (right), who served until his retirement in 2006. Between them, they had nearly a century of experience in water treatment.

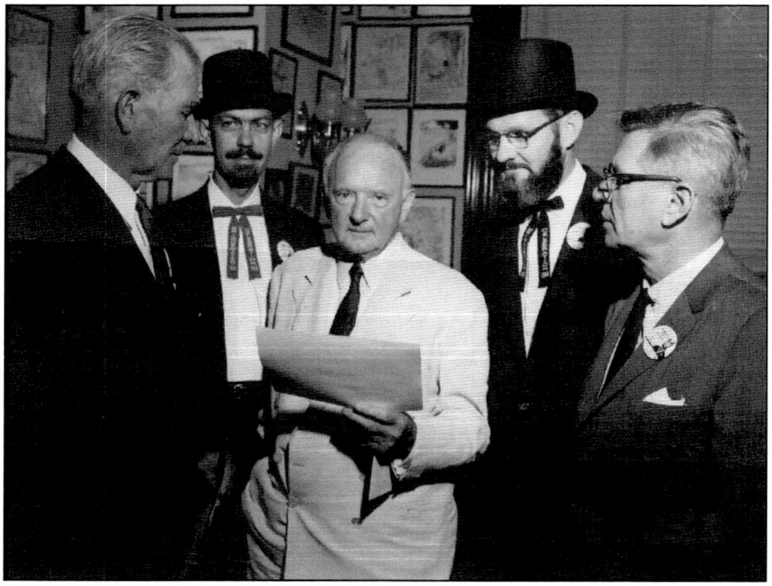

The 125th celebration of the founding of Bridgewater (1960) brought out the dignitaries. From left to right are U.S. senator Willis Robertson, John Flory, U.S. senator Harry F. Byrd Sr., Homer Miller, and Congressman Burr Harrison.

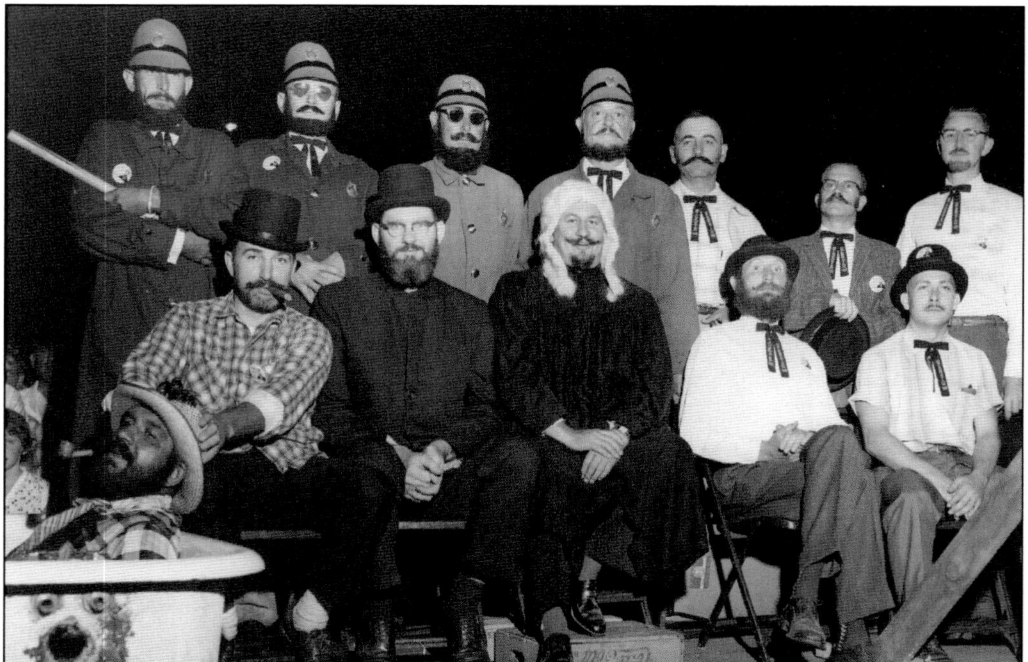

In 1960 (125th celebration), most of the men in the community grew beards or mustaches and dressed as their ancestors might have. Those that did not were punished by the Kangaroo Court shown above. Not everyone in this photograph can be identified, but Harold Shirkey is occupying the bathtub, and town attorney Don Litten is in the first row, far right.

For a brief time in 1960, Bridgewater reverted to horse-and-buggy days. The 125th celebration of the founding of the town was a highlight of community life for most of its citizens.

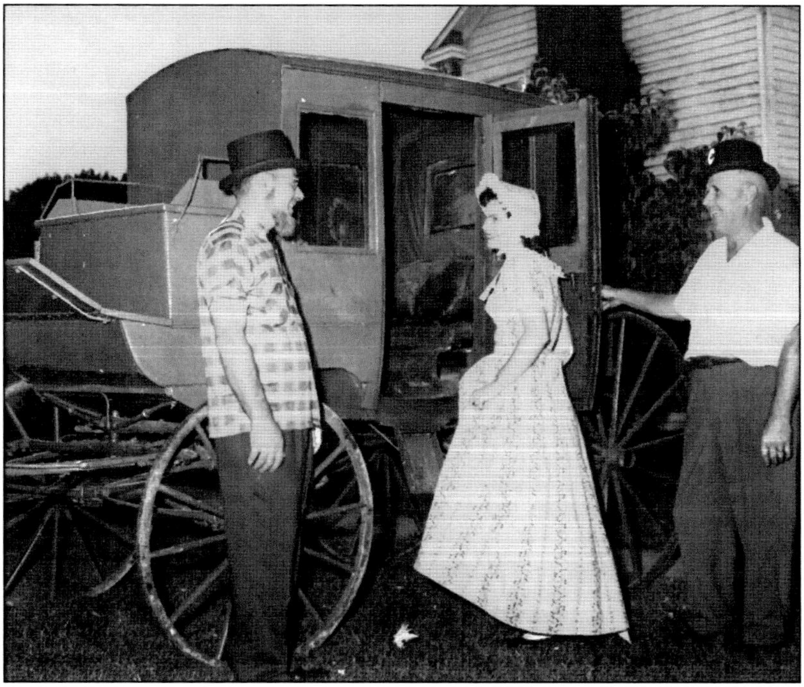

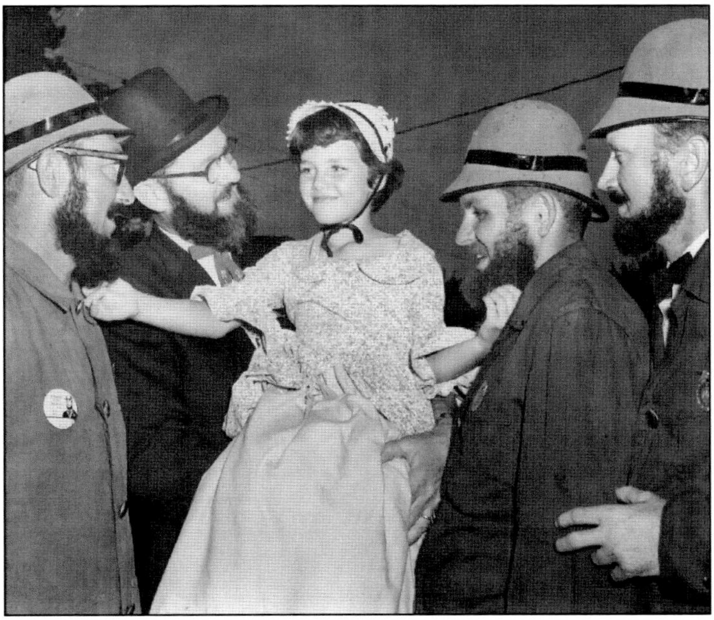

During the 125th celebration in 1960, Bridgewater's version of the "keystone cops" made many bogus arrests, but they were all in good fun. Men could be arrested for not having a beard or mustache, while women faced charges for dressing too modern. Pictured here from left to right are Harry Whitmore, Homer Miller, Ron Metzger, and Dal Hensley taking a break from their duties to entertain young Karen Miller, who is Homer's daughter.

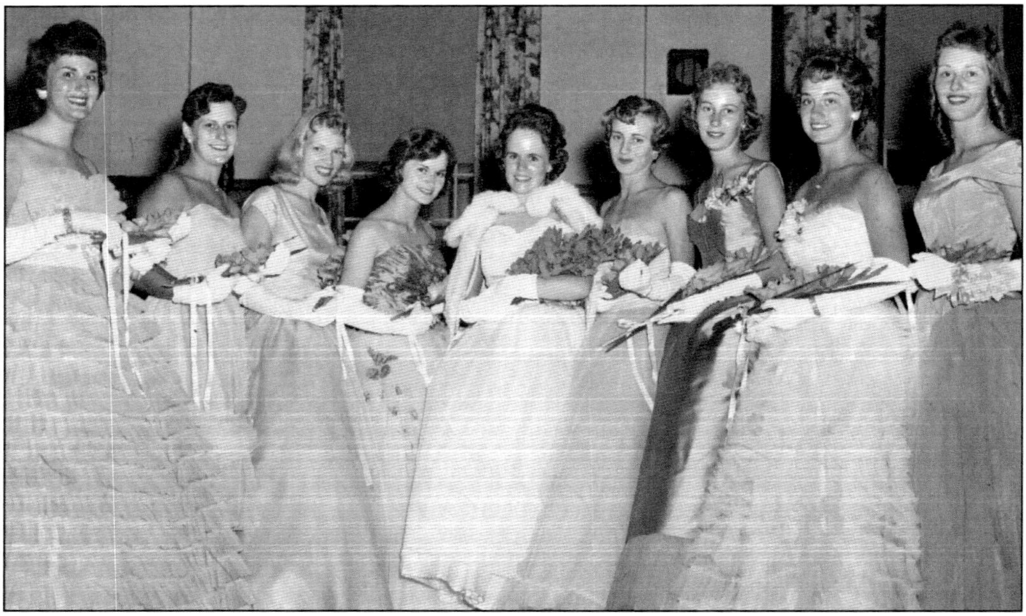

The queen and her court at the 125th celebration represented the town in many events during the celebration of the town's founding. Pictured from left to right are Pat Riddle Early, Joyce Wright, Linda Miller McDonald, Evelyn Jordan, Judy Row Galang (queen of the 125th celebration), Bea Brunk Miller, Barbara Whitmore Colona, Sue Grove Botkin, and Bonnie Miller Eckard.

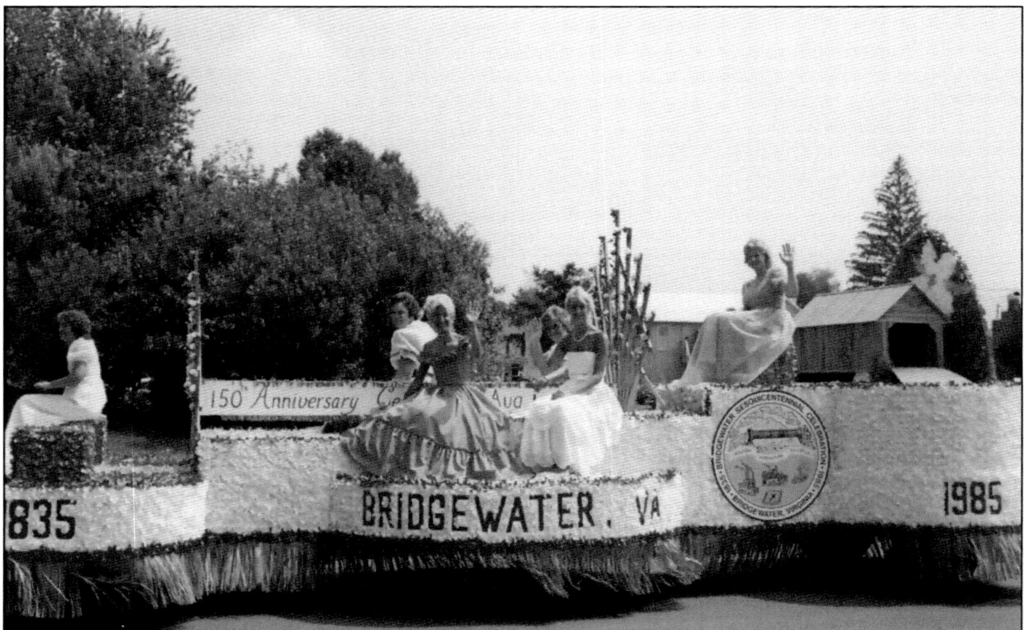


It seems that no celebration is complete without a float. In the 150th celebration (1985), the citizens constructed this float and included a model of the wooden bridge and seats for the celebration queen and her court. It appeared not only in Bridgewater parades but up and down the Shenandoah Valley wherever parades were held.

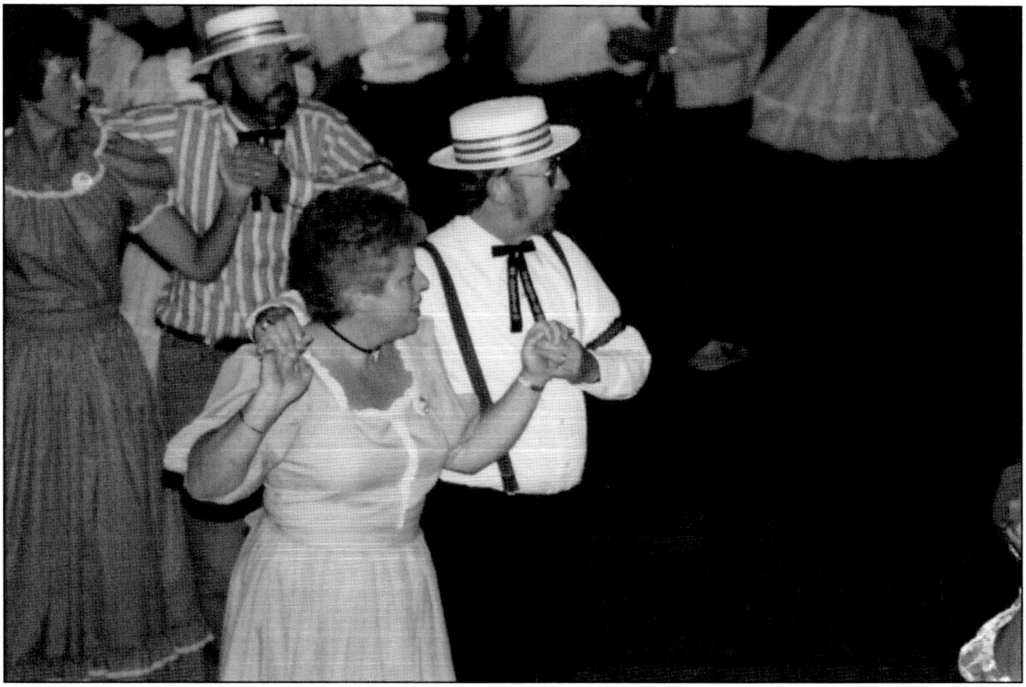

Louise and Pete Huffman join hundreds of others at a street dance during the sesquicentennial celebration in 1985. Street dances are rare today but often occurred in the summer, when the town council would close off a block, invite a band, and welcome citizens and guests to a summer evening dance.

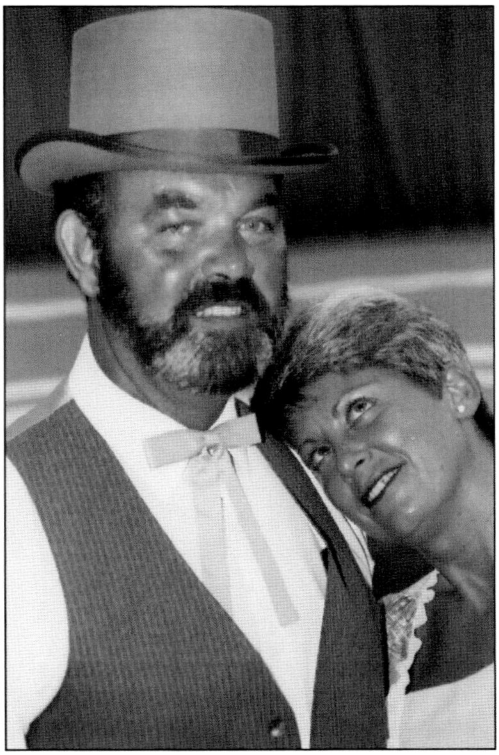

Larry and Ann Smallwood attended the 1960 celebration as children. This picture was taken in 1985 when they participated in the sesquicentennial celebration with their son and daughter. In 2010, they will likely bring their grandchildren to celebrate the 175th founding of Bridgewater. This epitomizes the continuity of the Bridgewater population. Generations settle here instead of simply passing through town.

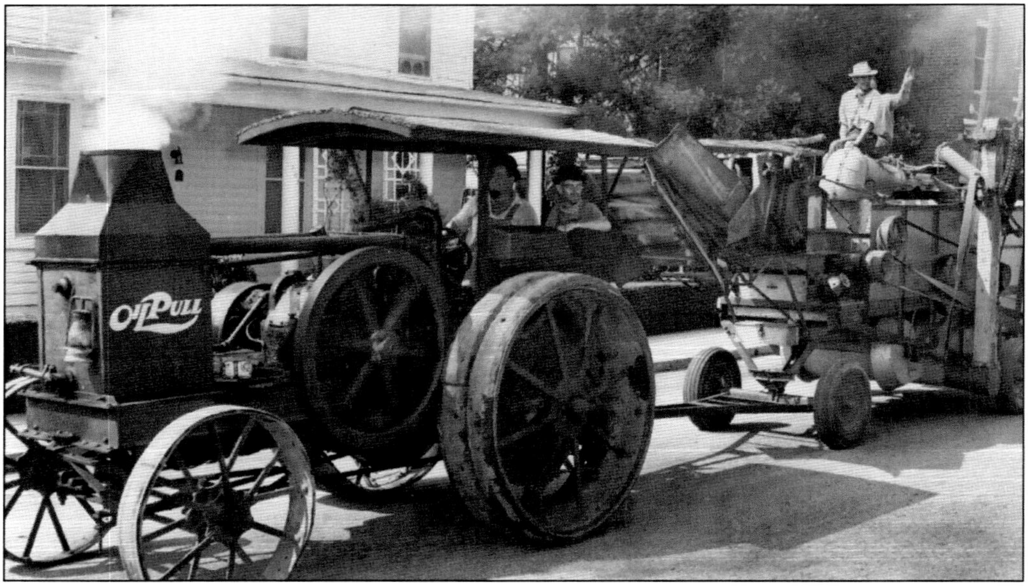

Parades occur every summer in Bridgewater during the firemen's lawn party. Antique farm equipment and steam engines are some of the most popular items in the parade. This photograph was taken a long time ago, but a similar scene can be observed each year during the third week in July.

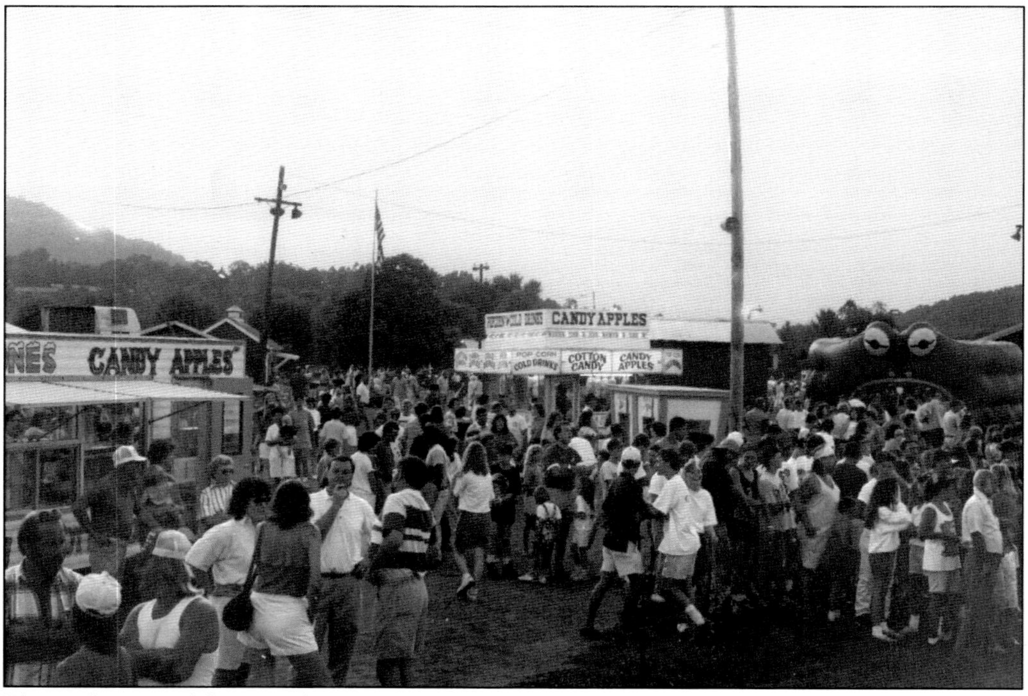


This is the annual firemen's lawn party as it looked in the past. It has grown to a four-night event that can bring out a crowd of 10,000 on a good evening. A large percentage of the annual fire department budget is raised through this special event.

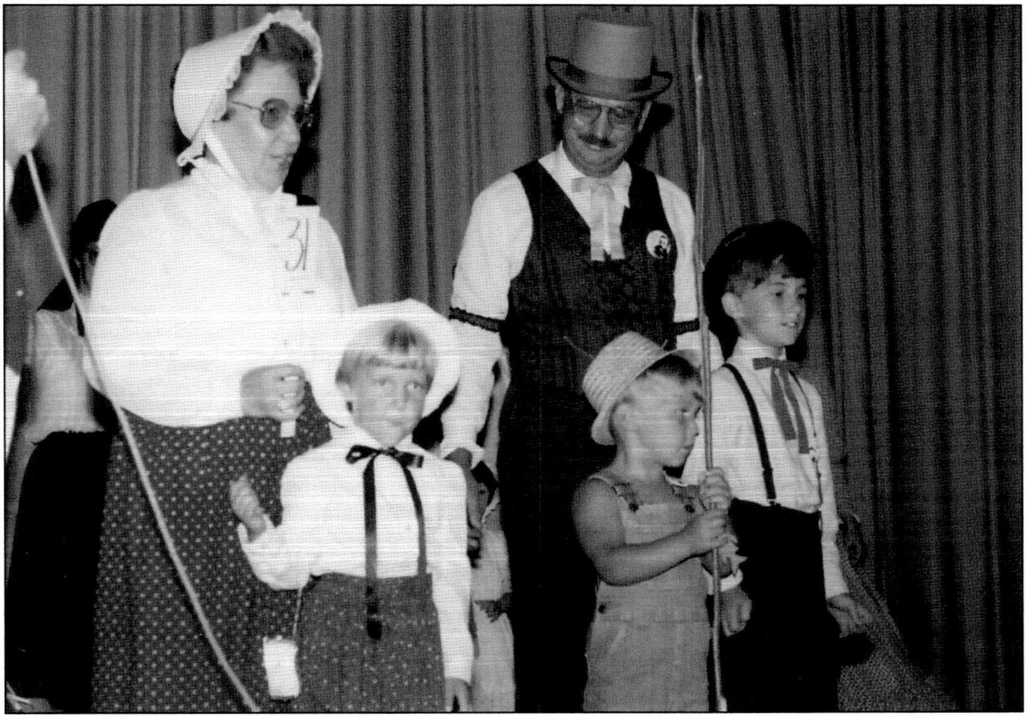

Jean and Bud Fulton celebrate the sesquicentennial with their grandchildren. Even children were dressed as they might have appeared in early American times.

Mayor Hallie Dinkel welcomes President Clinton to the Bridgewater area in 1999. The theme of this chapter is continuity in the midst of change, which is reflected by the very fact of Mr. Dinkel's election as mayor. He is a direct descendent of John Dinkle, one of the founders of Bridgewater. Note that over the years, the spelling of "Dinkel" changed from "le" to "el."

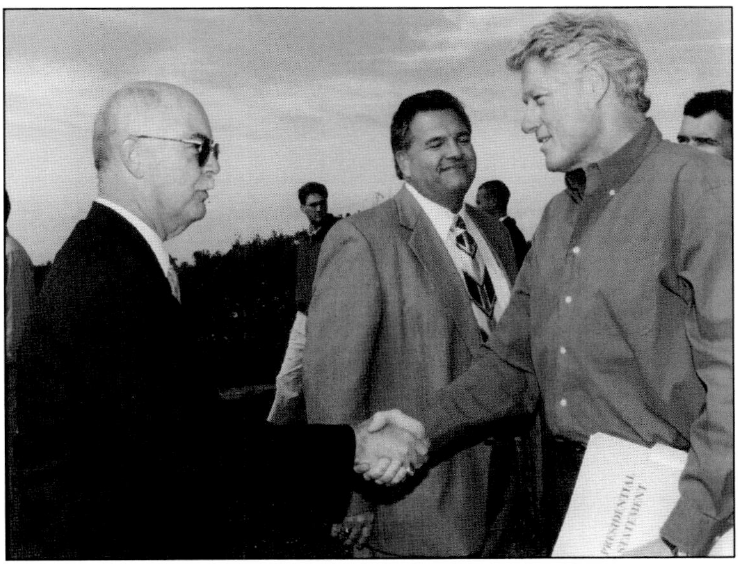

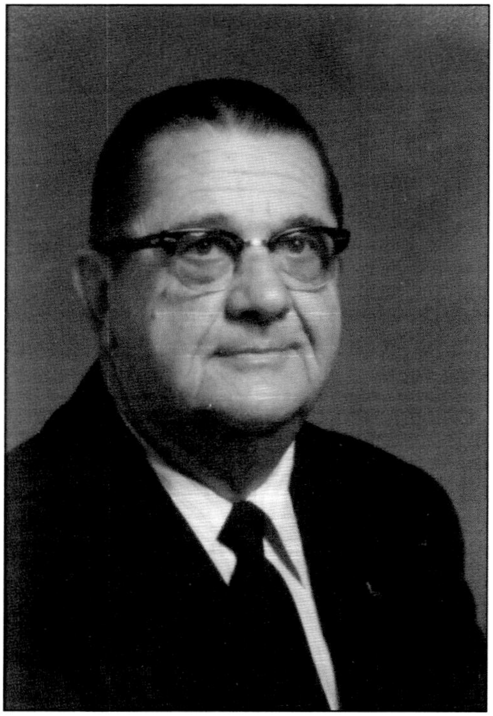

The late Roland Z. Arey served 40 years on the Bridgewater Town Council, with the last 20 of those years as mayor. His ancestor George Aehrig (Arey) arrived in the same generation as the founders and helped establish St. Michael's Church.

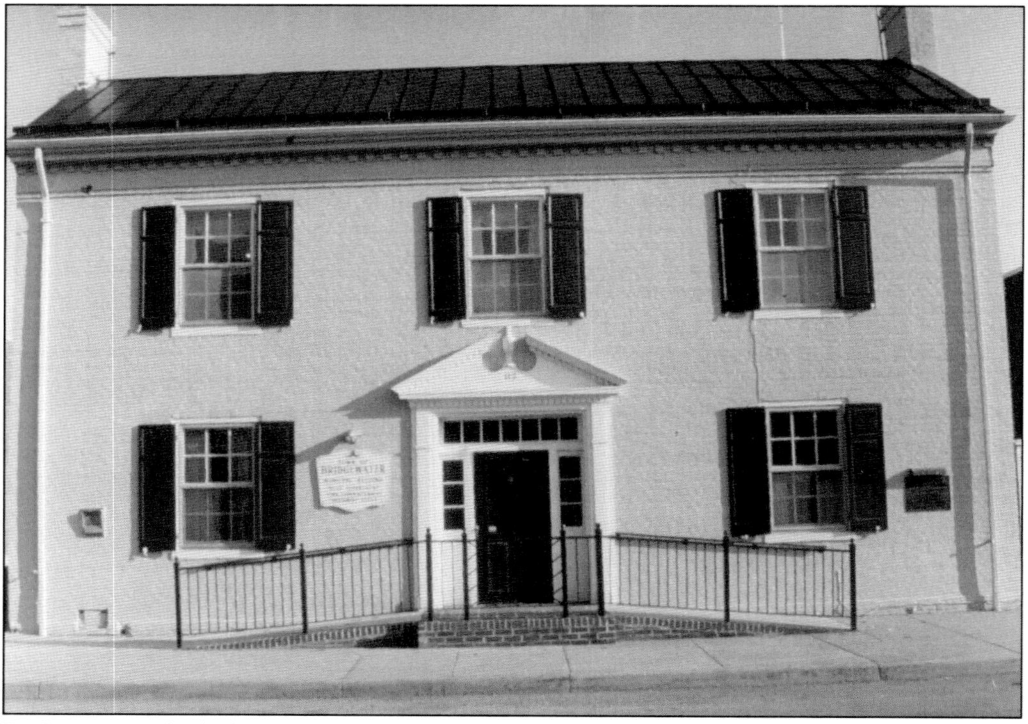


Dr. J. G. Miner built this house at 112 North Main Street a few years before the Civil War. When the war came, it was converted to a military hospital. Almost 100 years later, it was purchased by the Town of Bridgewater for use as a town hall during the period of 1956 to 1993. Today it is part of a complex of buildings known as the Crimson Inn.

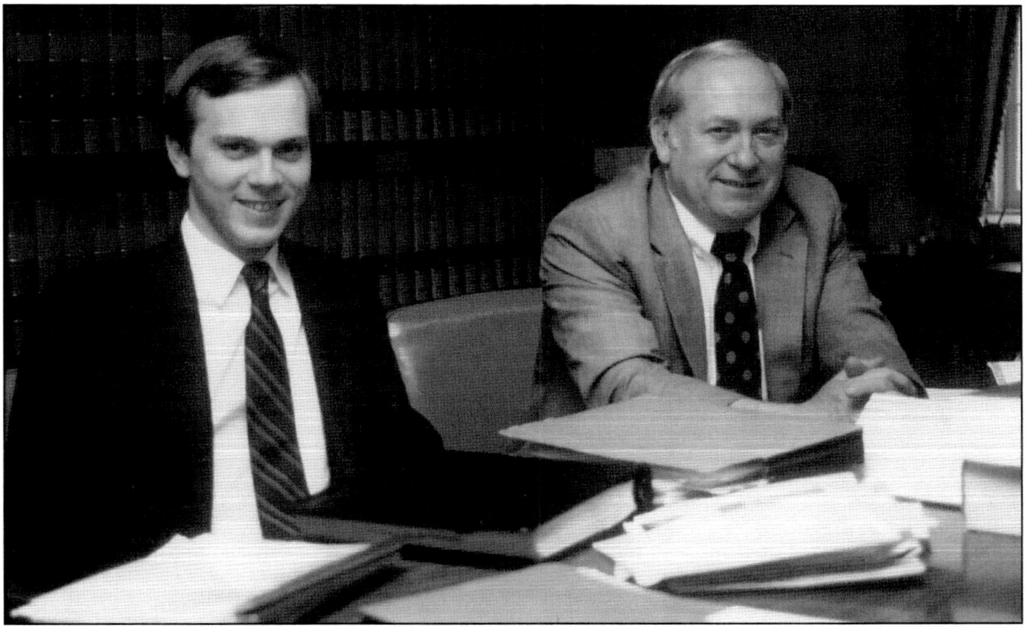

Since 1956, the position of town attorney has been filled by a member of the Litten family. It would be difficult to find two attorneys who equalled Jay and Don Litten in both their legal skills and personal commitment to the town. They have guided Bridgewater through annexation struggles, litigation, and day-to-day issues needing their advice and expertise.

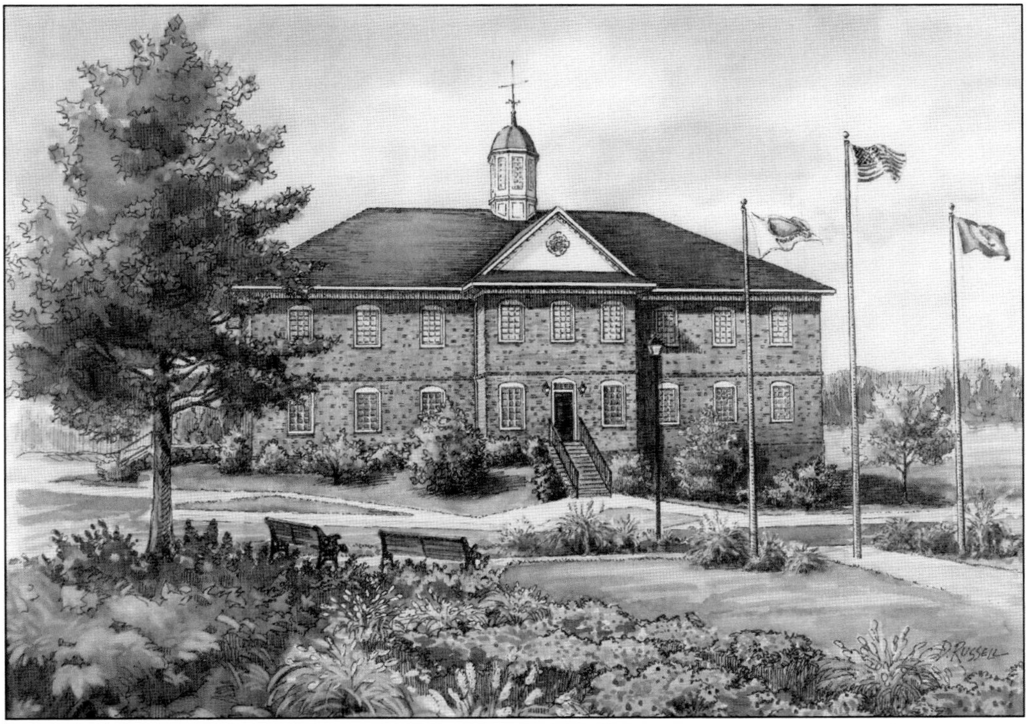

In February 1996, the town council and staff moved to this attractive structure on Green Street. It was modeled after the first mental hospital constructed in Williamsburg, Virginia, which some have claimed is very appropriate for a government office building.

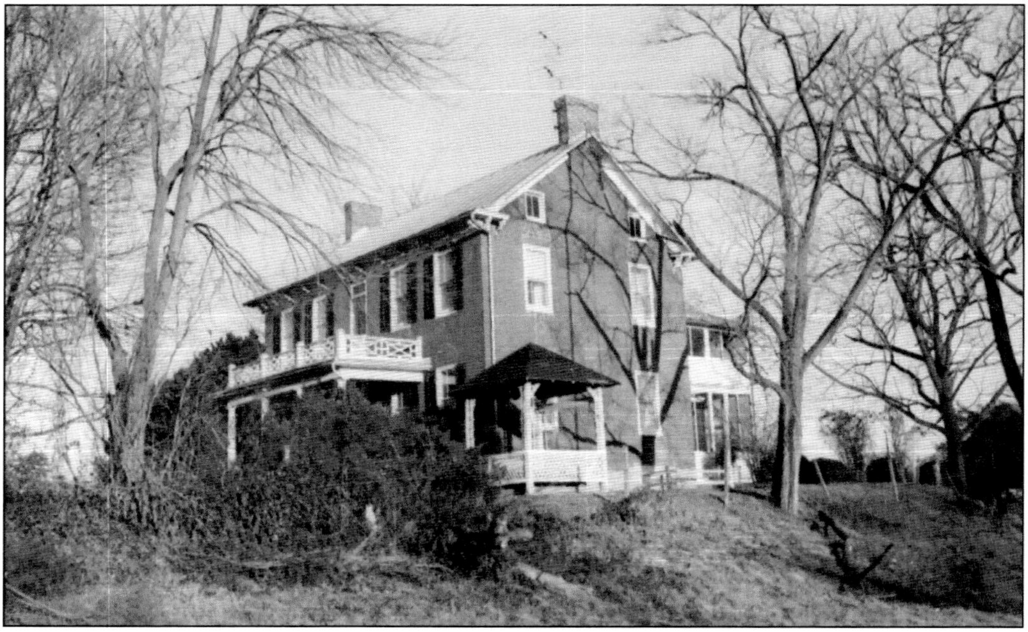

A few years after Jacob Dinkle built his home on Main Street, his brother John Dinkle constructed this beautiful Federal-style house on Wynant Place. Brick-jack arches still top the windows, but the wooden cornice and three-bay porch are later alterations. The interior contains a central passage plan with much of its elaborate woodwork and mantels remaining. Today it is the home of former state senator Nathan Miller and his wife, Kim.

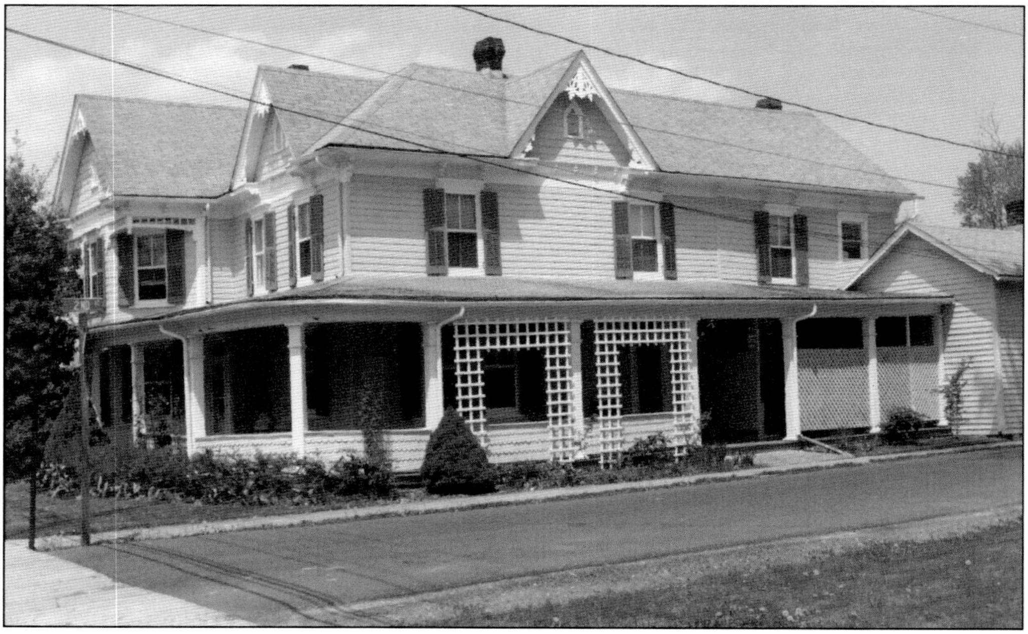

William H. Sipe was a prominent local merchant and civic leader. He, along with Mr. Arey, first purchased the Sanger Brothers Store in the late 1800s and called it the Sipe and Arey Department Store. Later Mr. Sipe bought out Mr. Arey's share and renamed the establishment the W. H. Sipe Company, Inc. He had this home at 210 East College Street built in the 1890s, and it still stands.

# *Two*

# CHURCHES

Churches tie generations together. They also provide a stabilizing influence to any community. It is not unusual for travelers to come to Bridgewater in search of their roots, and there are few better places to find them than at the churches their ancestors attended.

It is unknown which congregation arrived first, but a Lutheran minister named Peter Schickle came to Bridgewater around 1838 and organized the Trinity Lutheran congregation. Records indicate that the Methodists were also conducting worship services in the area at about the same time, but they did not become affiliated with the Methodist Episcopal Church of the United States until 1841.

The founders of Bridgewater, Jacob and John Dinkle, were instrumental in the establishment of both churches. Jacob donated land to the Methodists, while John deeded a lot to the Lutheran church. Both buildings still stand, although neither has been used as a church for many years.

Even though churches were not established until 1838 or later, religion still played a part in the lives of early settlers. Please remember that life in the early 1800s was not easy. Roads were generally in poor condition, and transportation was limited to horse and buggy. Churches did exist in larger communities, but getting to them was not an easy task. Quite often, religious services were held in home churches, and on occasion, a traveling minister would come to town to officiate weddings and deliver a message to all who would listen.

After the Civil War, African Americans were free to form their own churches and established branches of both Methodist and Baptist denominations. North River Baptist Church still stands.

Other churches that came after the War Between the States included the Bridgewater Baptist church in 1873 as well as the Presbyterian and the Church of the Brethren denominations that arrived around 1878.

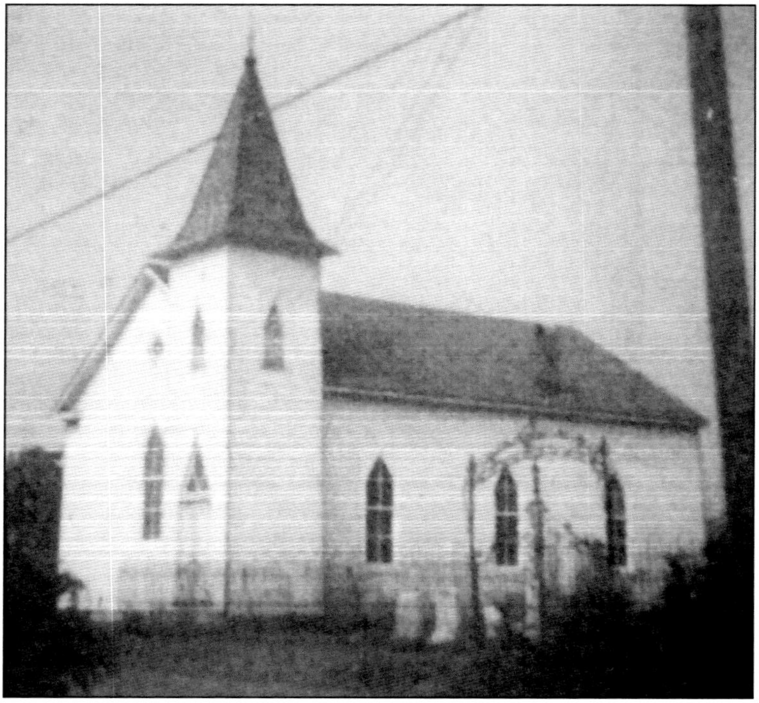

The African Methodist Episcopal Church, known as "AMES," stood in the cemetery behind the Bridgewater United Methodist Church for many years. It is interesting to note that the separation of the white church from AMES physically was a matter of a few feet, but culturally the gap was much wider. As times changed, the need for churches separated by race disappeared, and the sanctuary was torn down.

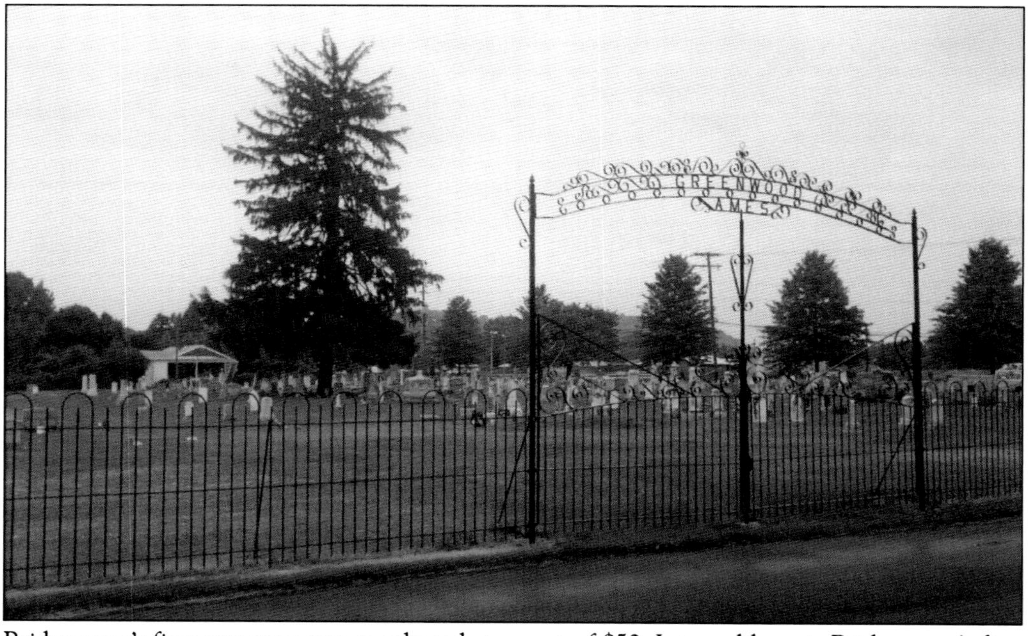


Bridgewater's first cemetery was purchased at a cost of $50. Interred here is Bridgewater's first mayor, Adam Radar, and many others who played a prominent role in the development of the town. For many years, the cemetery was segregated by race and housed the African Methodist Episcopal Church (AMES), which was used exclusively by the African American community.

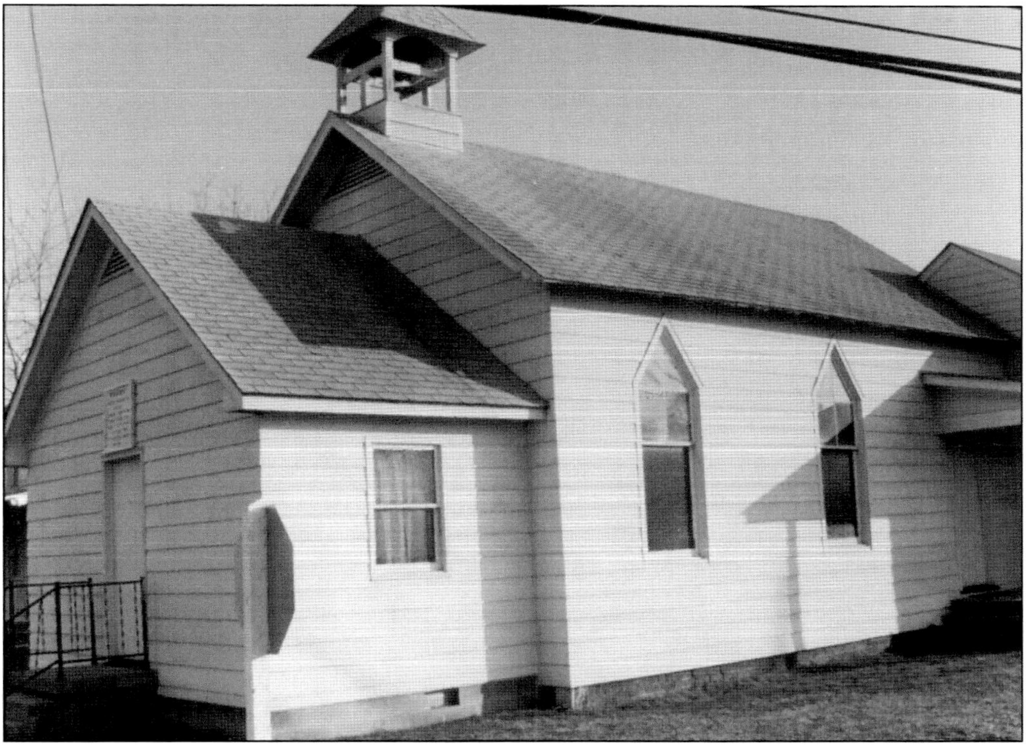

Around the 1880s, North River Baptist Church began meeting for worship in the Bridgewater area. By 1902, this congregation had built its present church on Mount Crawford Avenue.

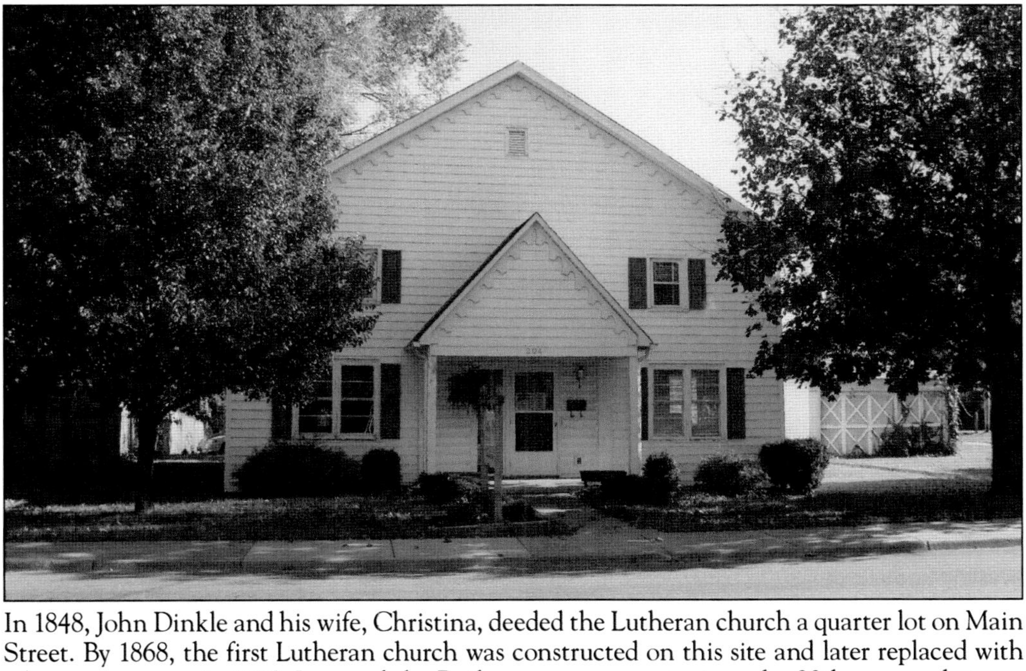

In 1848, John Dinkle and his wife, Christina, deeded the Lutheran church a quarter lot on Main Street. By 1868, the first Lutheran church was constructed on this site and later replaced with a larger sanctuary in 1883. It served the Bridgewater community into the 20th century but was eventually purchased and used as a dwelling by a local school teacher. Today two businesses operate out of the building shown here.

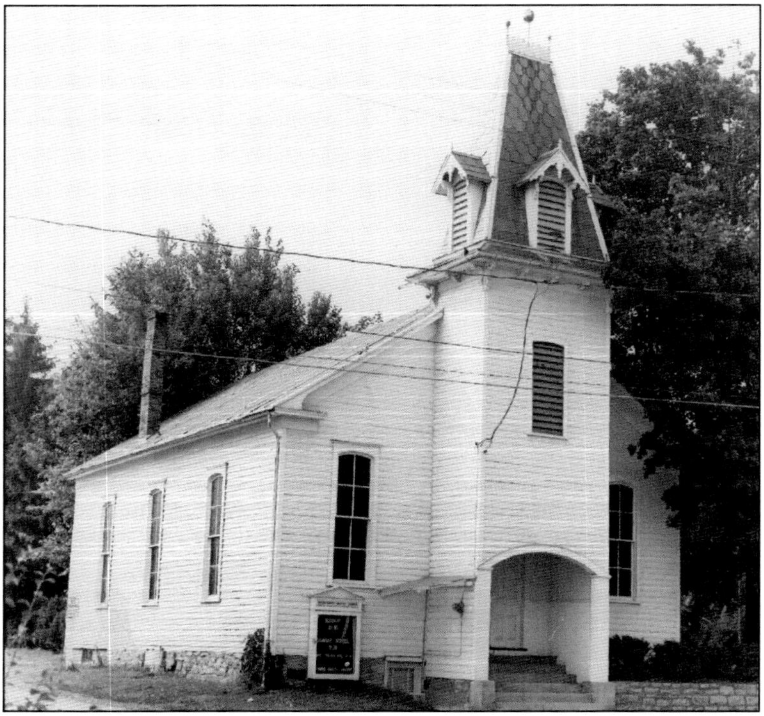

Around 1855, Bridgewater Baptist Church purchased an old meetinghouse on this lot at 117 South Main and spent considerable money remodeling and enlarging it. In 1882, a major renovation took place, adding some of the ornate touches seen in this picture. Changes in more recent times have removed much of the 1882 decorations.

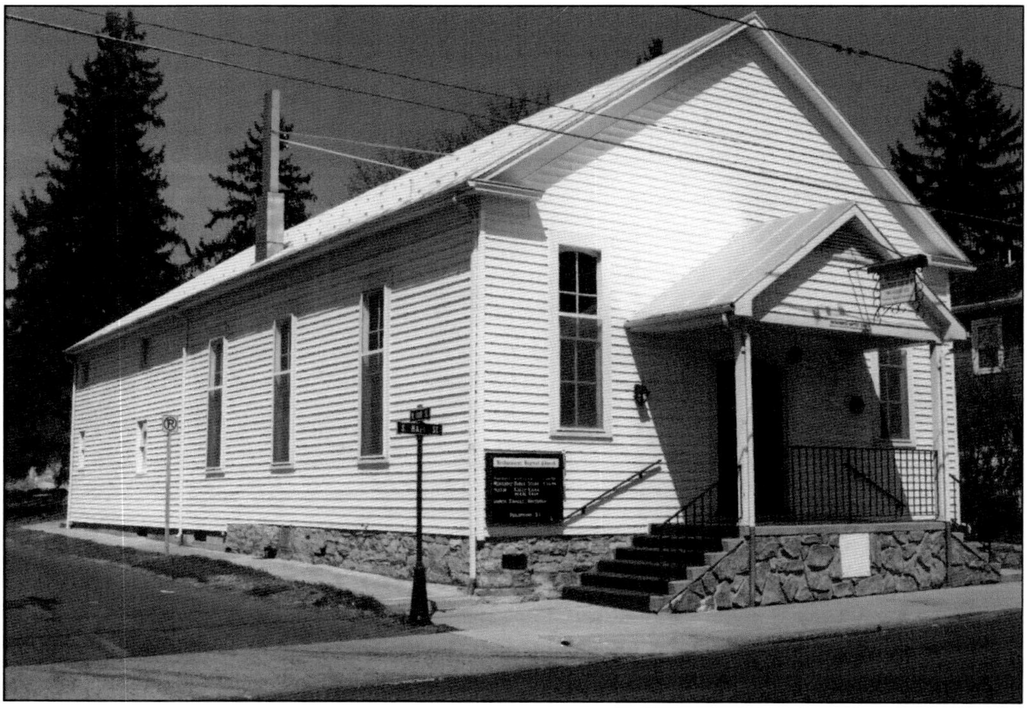

Since the 1882 renovations, the sanctuary has been enlarged twice, but many of the ornate touches installed a century ago have disappeared.

A small group of 14 organized the Bridgewater Presbyterian congregation in 1878. For the next 11 years, they met in various places, but in 1889, they completed a church of their own on East College Street. The church was noted for its unusually high steeple. Around 1900, the steeple was hit by lightning and destroyed. At that point, the congregation decided it should be replaced with a much shorter one. (Sketched by Glenn Felix.)

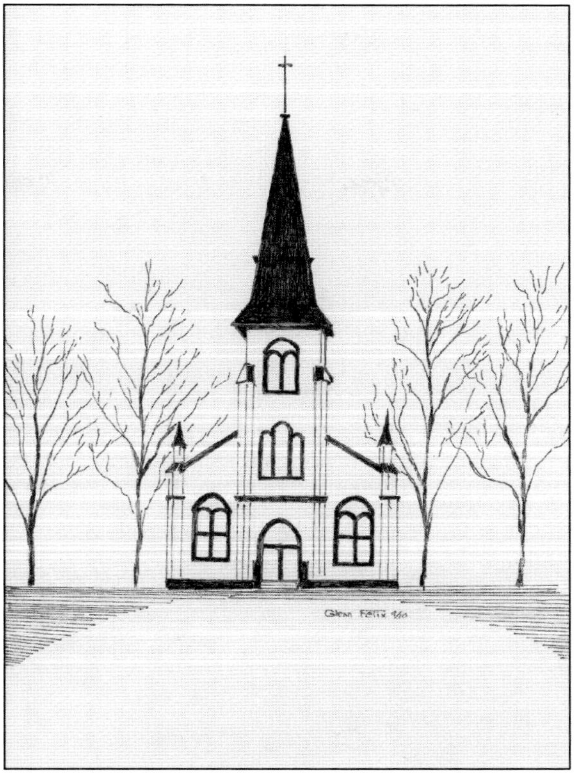

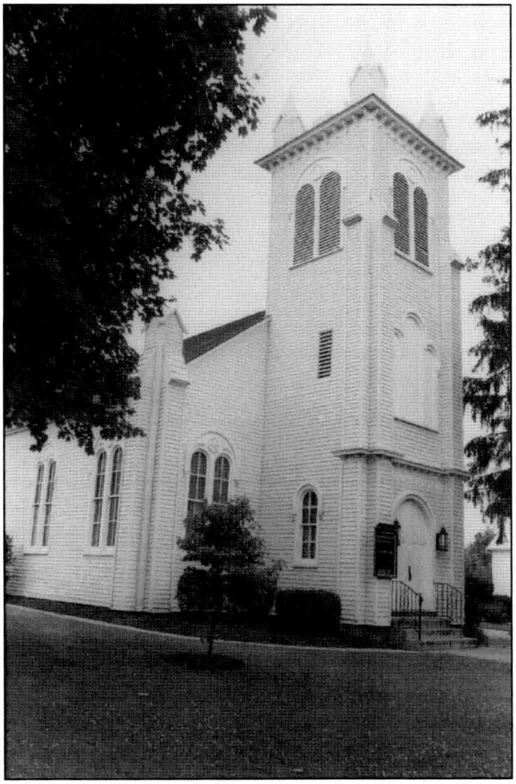

Today's version of Bridgewater Presbyterian Church lacks only the unusually high steeple that was a part of the original design.

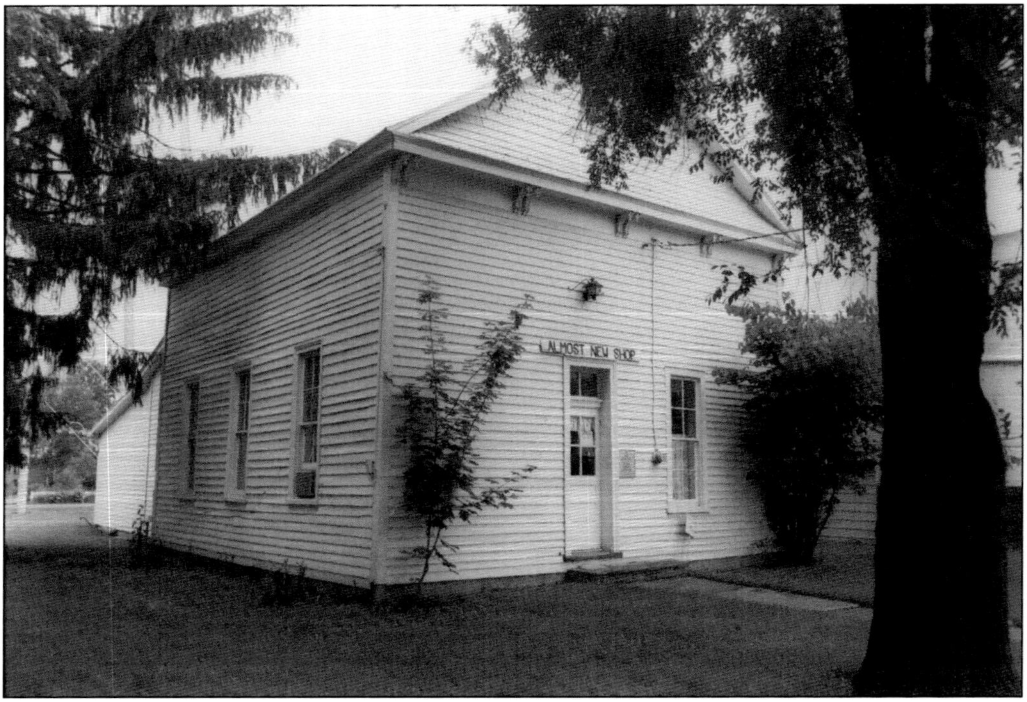


This innocent-looking building was the center of controversy prior to the Civil War. It was deeded to the Methodist Episcopal Church of North America on the condition that it became the property of the town should the local church ever leave the parent organization. With the coming of the war, the church broke into north and south branches, thus transferring ownership of this building to the Town of Bridgewater.

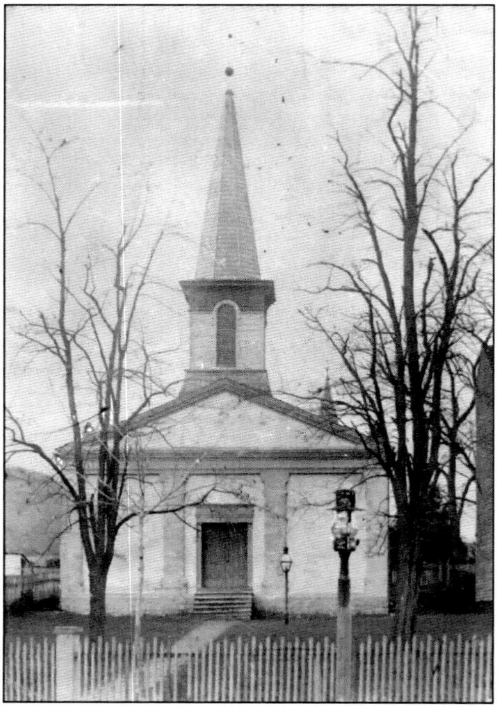

William Rice was a well-to-do member of the Methodist Church. When he died in 1852, he stipulated that part of his estate would go towards the construction of a new Methodist Episcopal Church South in Bridgewater. The church trustees purchased 1 acre of land on Main Street in Bridgewater at the cost of $100 and completed their new church by 1855.

In 1904, the Methodist church underwent a major renovation. The structure was faced with brick, and two south towers were built. Stained glass windows were added and oak pews installed.

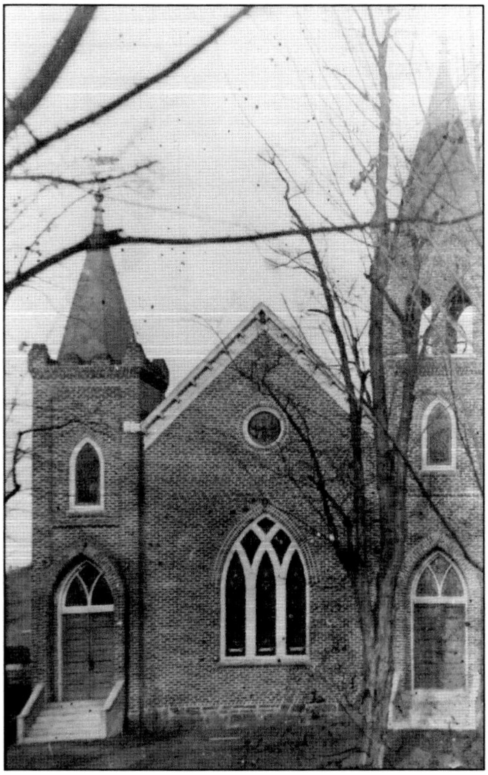

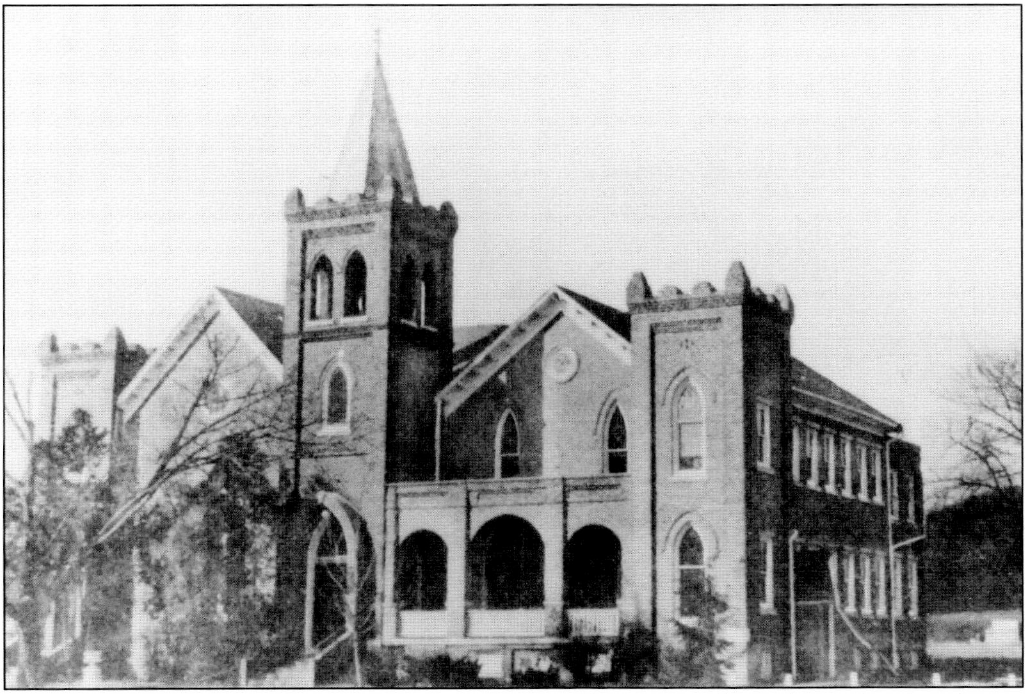

Further changes occurred in 1925, 1992, and 2002. The picture above shows the church as it looked prior to the 1992 addition. Today Bridgewater United Methodist Church has nearly 600 members.

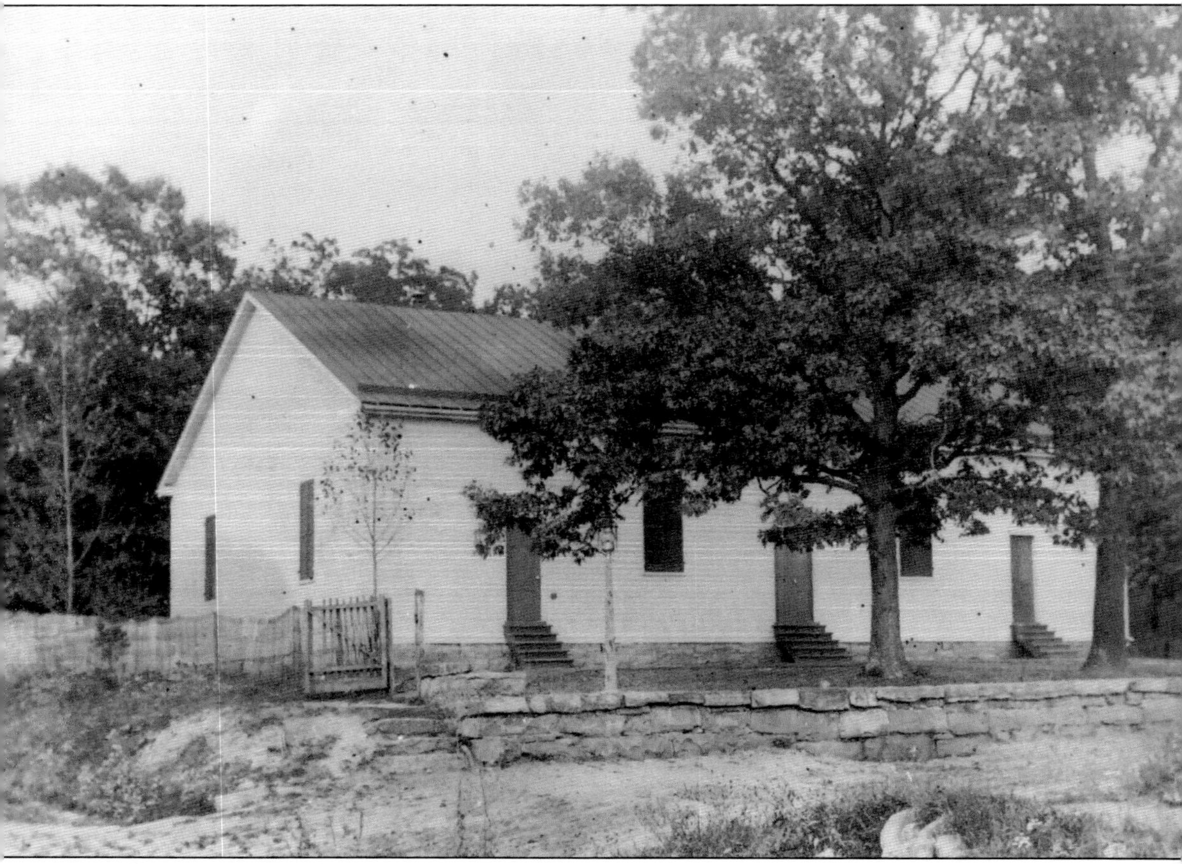

The first Brethren church in Bridgewater, erected in 1878, was located at the intersection of Main Street and Oakwood Drive. It was a wooden structure, 60 feet by 80 feet, which could accommodate a large congregation. Elder Solomon Garber preached the dedication sermon, and an estimated 3,000 gathered on August 25 for this occasion. Please note the separate entrances for men and women. Another anomaly not common today was baptismal services conducted in open water by immersion. It is reported that in 1894, four inches of ice had to be cut from the North River to open a site for baptismal services for 41 members. The church was torn down in 1937, when the congregation moved to a larger sanctuary located on East College Street.

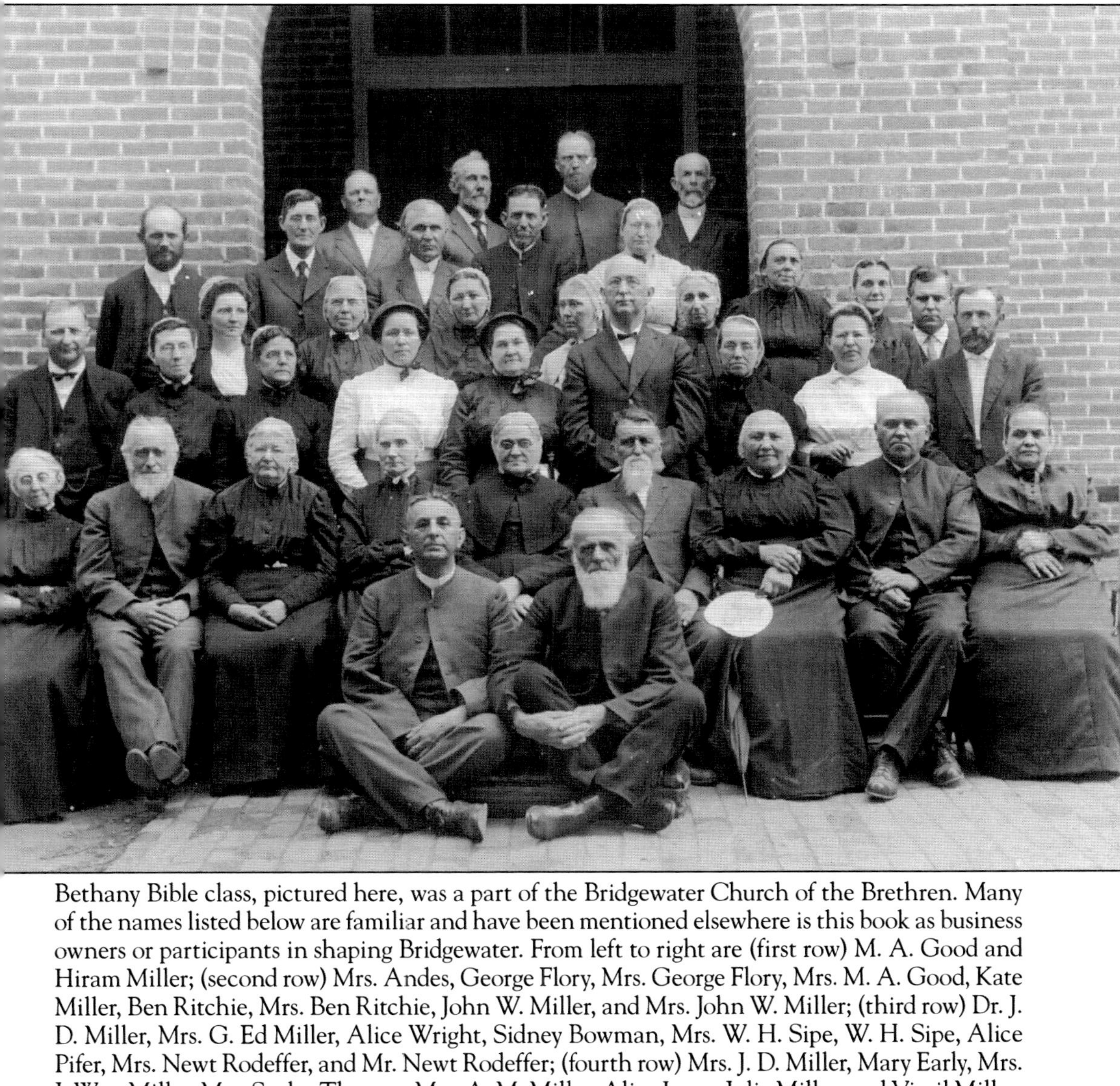

Bethany Bible class, pictured here, was a part of the Bridgewater Church of the Brethren. Many of the names listed below are familiar and have been mentioned elsewhere is this book as business owners or participants in shaping Bridgewater. From left to right are (first row) M. A. Good and Hiram Miller; (second row) Mrs. Andes, George Flory, Mrs. George Flory, Mrs. M. A. Good, Kate Miller, Ben Ritchie, Mrs. Ben Ritchie, John W. Miller, and Mrs. John W. Miller; (third row) Dr. J. D. Miller, Mrs. G. Ed Miller, Alice Wright, Sidney Bowman, Mrs. W. H. Sipe, W. H. Sipe, Alice Pifer, Mrs. Newt Rodeffer, and Mr. Newt Rodeffer; (fourth row) Mrs. J. D. Miller, Mary Early, Mrs. J. Wm. Miller, Mrs. Saylor Thomas, Mrs. A. M. Miller, Alice Long, Julie Miller, and Virgil Miller; (fifth row, order unknown) J. W. F. Miller, Will Miller, Sam Garber, John Wine, Ben Bowman, D. S. Thomas, Mrs. B. Bowman, James Wright, and one unidentified.

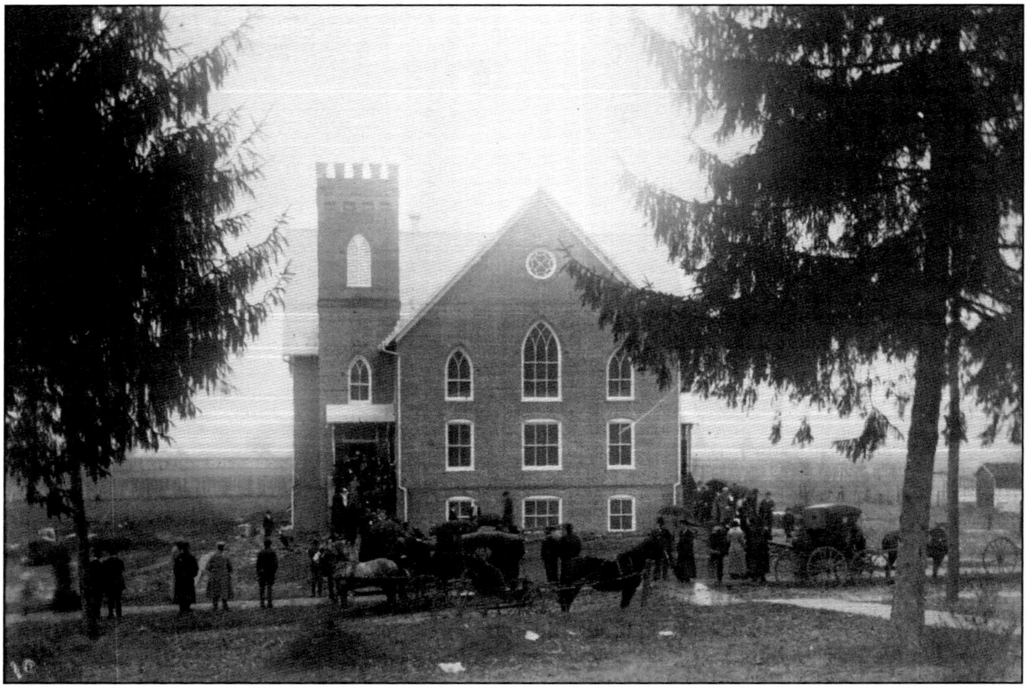

This picture, taken in 1937, shows the sanctuary on East College Street shortly after completion. It housed the Brethren congregation for many decades and became part of the Bridgewater College campus when the new church was constructed in 1998.

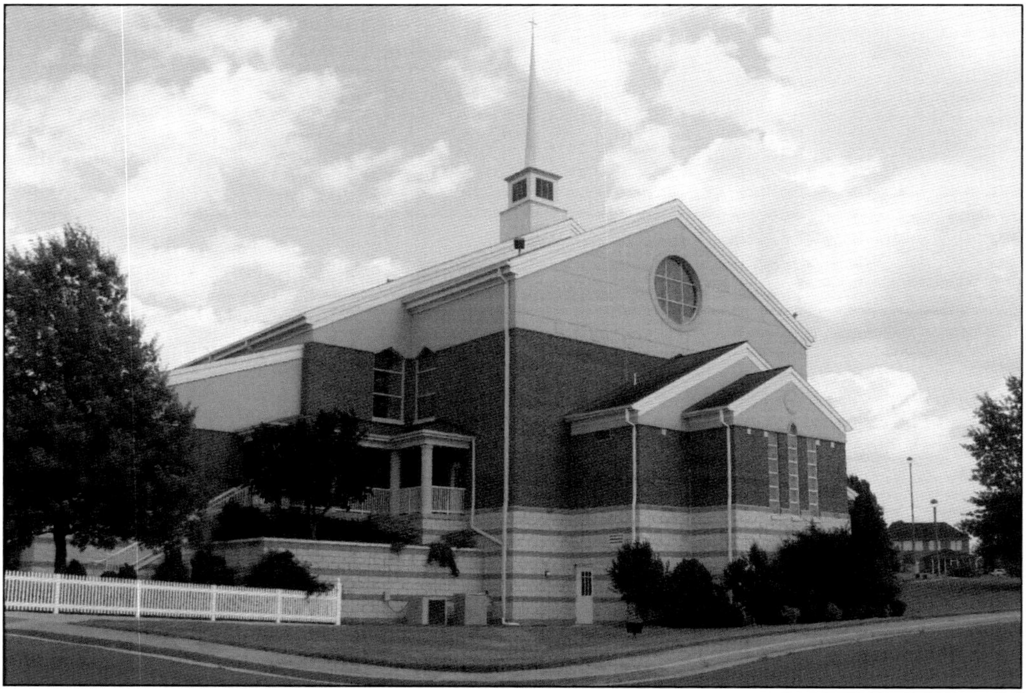

By the 1990s, the congregation was outgrowing the site on East College Street, and the decision was made to construct a new church complex on College View Drive. The site selected was on a hill overlooking both the college as well as the entire town of Bridgewater.

# *Three*

# Education in Bridgewater

One of the greatest changes after the Civil War was the establishment of public schools. In 1870, the general assembly passed a bill creating a uniform school system supported by taxes and free to all. By 1871, Bridgewater had one of two public schools in Rockingham County. A principal and two teachers taught 86 children over a nine-month term. The first schoolhouse was a four-room building constructed in 1874 that was used until 1911 for all classes.

The law mandated that schools were "free and open to all," but races were segregated where education was concerned. An African American school was built at the same time as the white school. From the outside, there did not appear to be any differences, but inside was another story.

Around the same time, D. C. Flory organized Spring Creek Normal School and Collegiate Institute a short distance outside of town. By 1882, he relocated to Bridgewater and later changed the name to Bridgewater College. From that day forward, Bridgewater College has played an integral role in the progress of the community.

In a matter of two decades, education in Bridgewater changed from private schools educating the elite to public schools available to all and a college within its boundaries giving the opportunity for higher education.

Today Bridgewater houses public and private elementary schools, a public high school, and Bridgewater College, all located within the borders of this small town of 6,000.

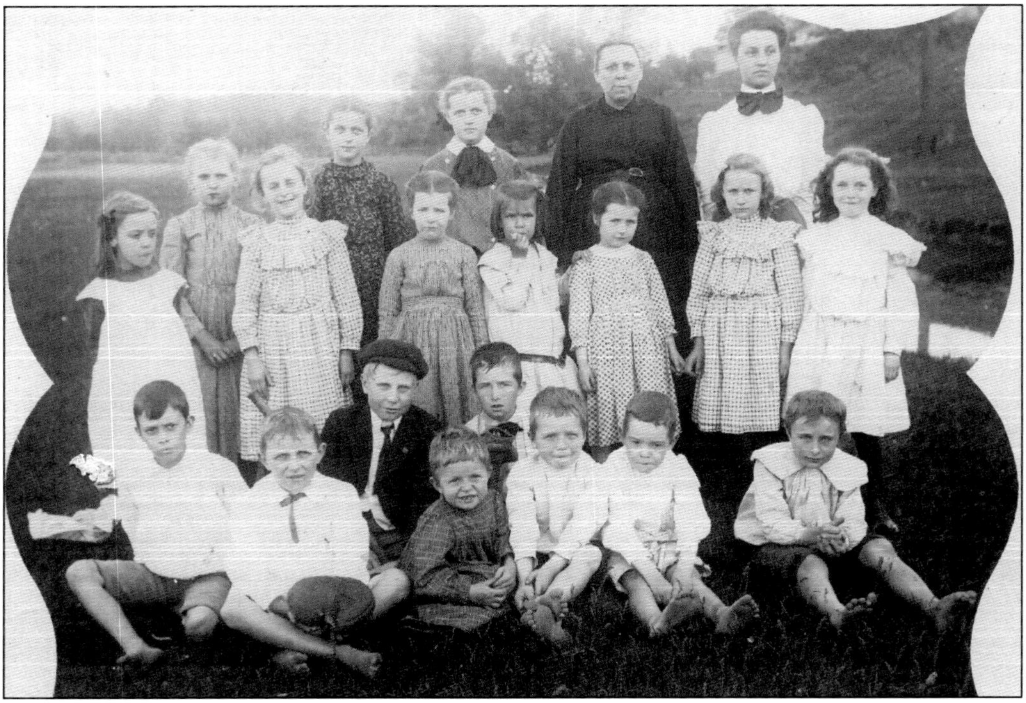

Bridgewater had several private schools in the late 19th century. Kate Long's private school was located at West College Street. Unfortunately the names of the children and adults are not available. Another private school was one operated by Colonel Barbee's daughters Mollie Barbee and Gabie Terrell. The Reverend W. H. Tinkle and the Reverend G. W. Holland, both Lutheran ministers, established the Bridgewater Female Institute in 1867 and operated it for several years. W. T. Scott, W. S. Kennedy, and John Barb leased the town hall for private high schools between 1865 and 1871.

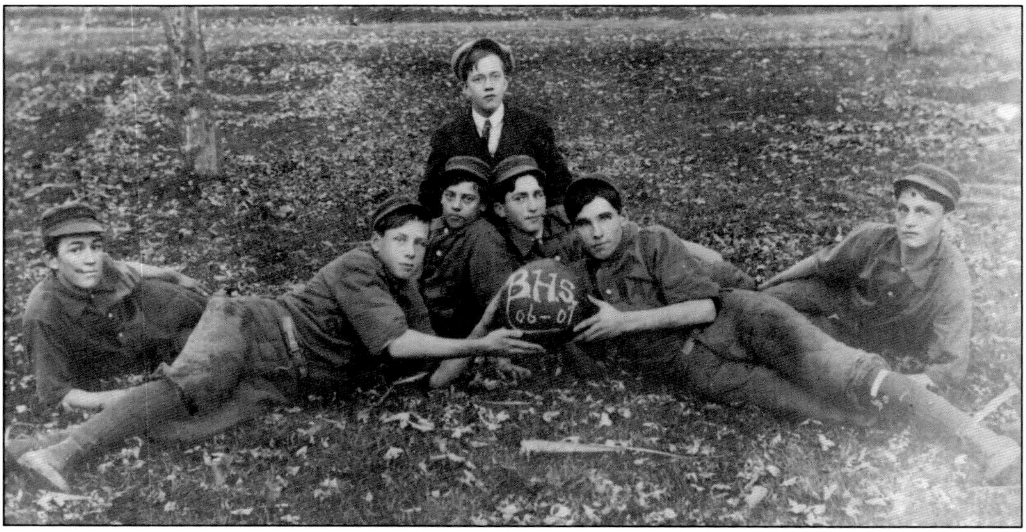


Shortly after the founding of a public school system was the addition of high school athletic programs. While baseball was probably the most popular sport in Bridgewater, the school eventually fielded basketball and football teams as well. The picture here shows one of the first basketball teams at Bridgewater High School.

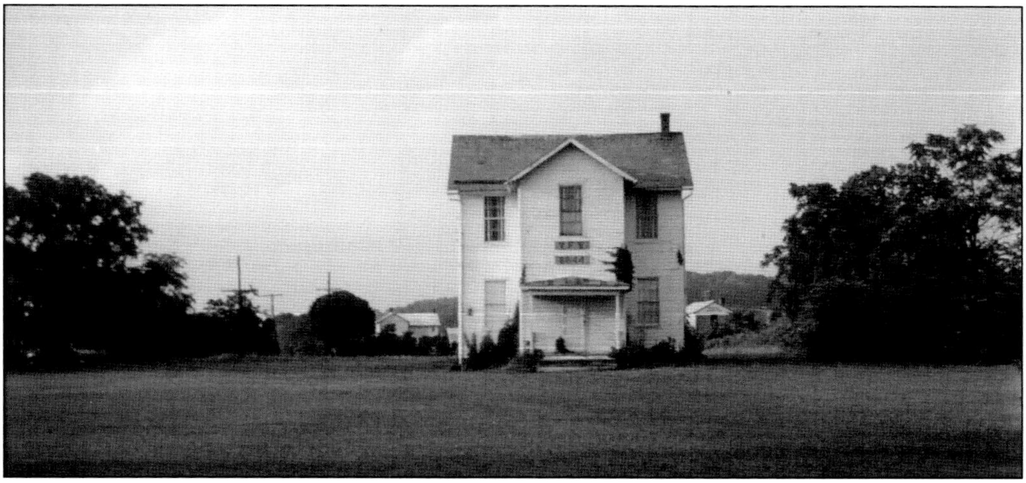

When public education came to Virginia in 1870, it was not measured out equally to both races. African American students were relegated to separate facilities. Councilman Roscoe Burgess remembers that the school was heated by wood or coal. Older boys came early on cold mornings to make sure the fire was started. Of course there was no indoor plumbing; those facilities were provided by an outhouse. A full-time African American teacher came every day from Harrisonburg. In addition, Bridgewater College students came at least one day a week to tutor and entertain the younger children. Pictured below is the school for whites that was built about the same time and used until 1911 for all public school classes. It, too, lacked indoor plumbing and was heated by wood or coal. As years went by, parents complained that the building was overcrowded and poorly ventilated. It stayed in service for 26 years, after which it was replaced by a more modern school.

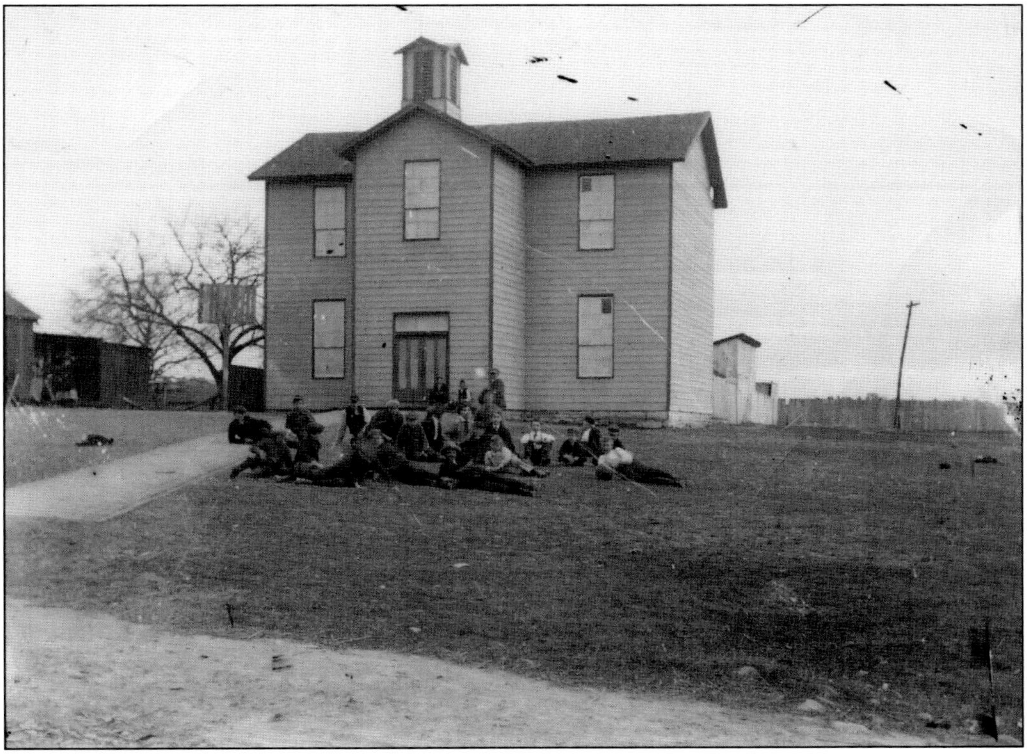

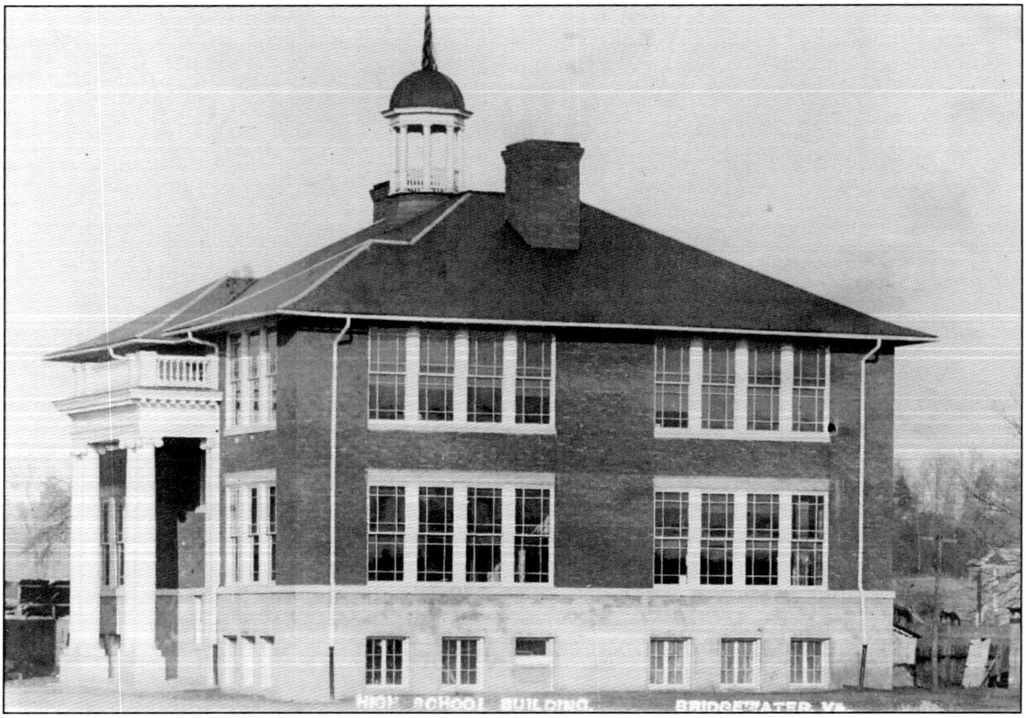


In 1911, the school shown above (presently Blue Ridge Christian School) was constructed. On opening day, the faculty and staff welcomed 20 high school and 187 elementary school students. High school offered a three-year course in 1911 and a four-year course in 1916.

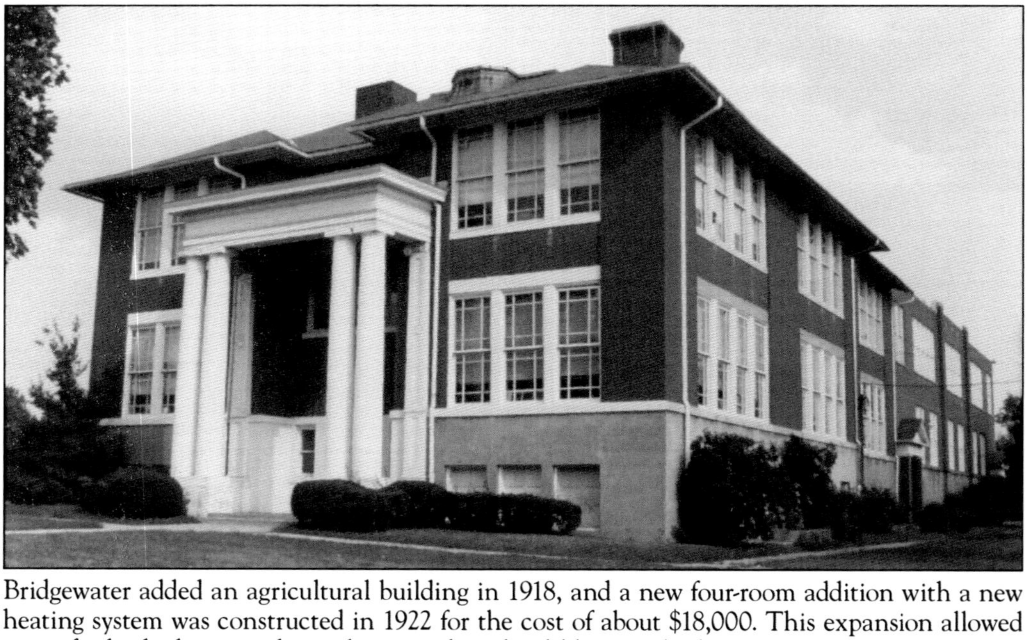

Bridgewater added an agricultural building in 1918, and a new four-room addition with a new heating system was constructed in 1922 for the cost of about $18,000. This expansion allowed space for both the agriculture classes and a school library. The last major construction at the Bridgewater school was in 1933–1934. By 1955, the last class had graduated from this building, and local students began attending the new Turner Ashby High School that fall. Today this structure is home to Blue Ridge Christian School, a private institution.

At the age of 26, D. C. Flory started Spring Creek Normal School, which eventually became Bridgewater College. In addition to being an educator and minister, he was a surveyor who helped to organize telephone lines and mail service in neighboring communities. He founded the Staunton Church of the Brethren and was their first pastor. He died at age 60 during a preaching mission in Indiana. (BCAMML.)

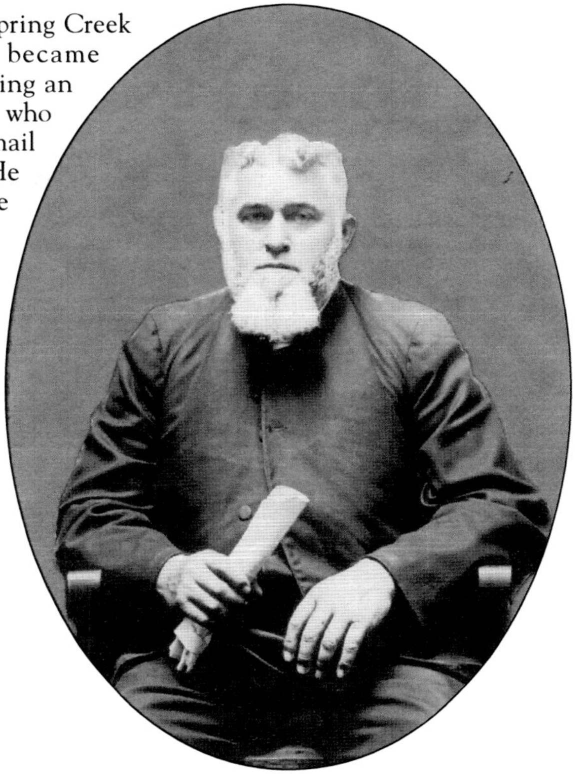

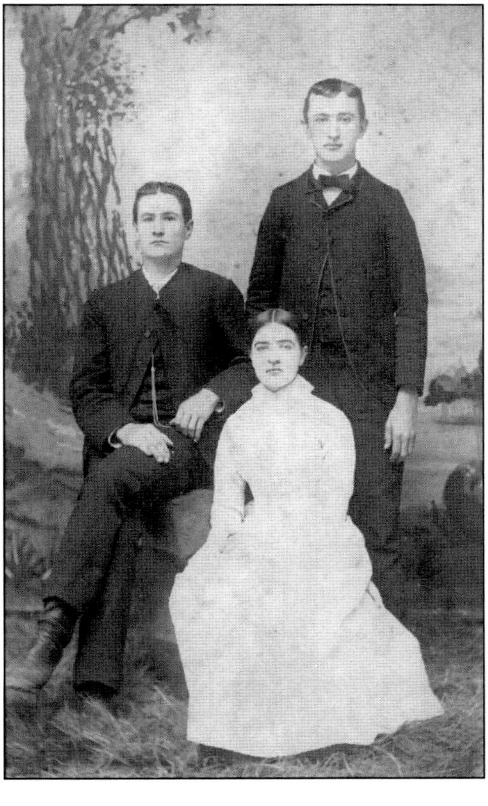

Pictured here are D. C. Flory's first graduates. When opened in 1880, Flory's school was known as Spring Creek Normal School and Collegiate Institute. Nine years later, it became Bridgewater College. (BCAMML.)

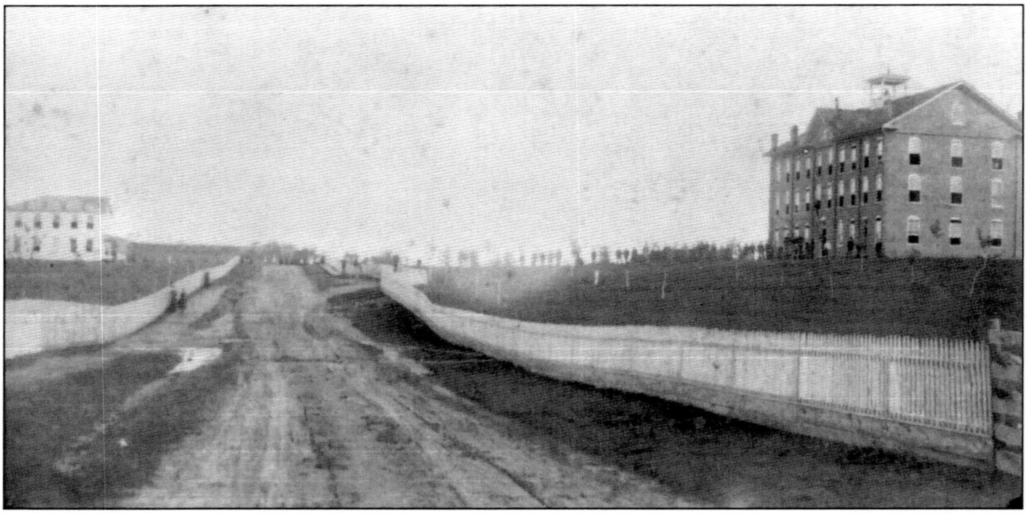

The Virginia normal school that started in Spring Creek moved to Bridgewater in 1882 and evolved into Bridgewater College by 1889. Its founder, D. C. Flory, moved the school because of the accessibility to Warm Springs Turnpike and the anticipation of railroad service. The cost of a 40-week session was $122.50. This included tuition, board, room, and other expenses. The school also opened an elementary branch for the children in Bridgewater at a tuition cost of about $12 for a three-term session.

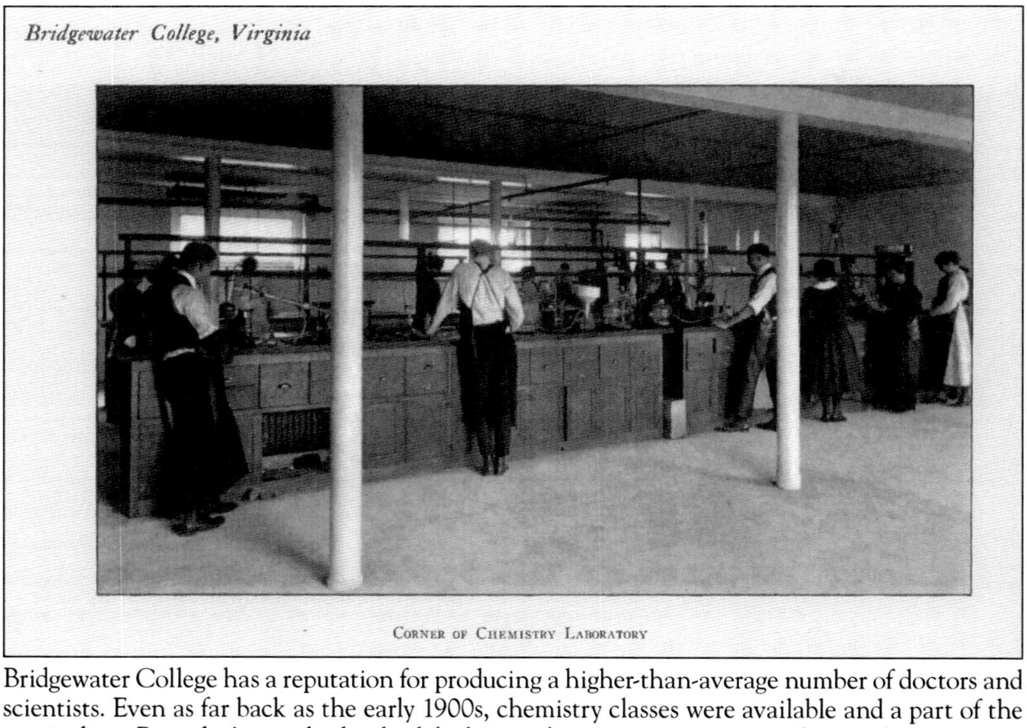


Bridgewater College has a reputation for producing a higher-than-average number of doctors and scientists. Even as far back as the early 1900s, chemistry classes were available and a part of the curriculum. By today's standards, the lab shown above is quite primitive but at that time was probably state-of-the-art to those learning the intricacies of physical matter. (BCAMML.)

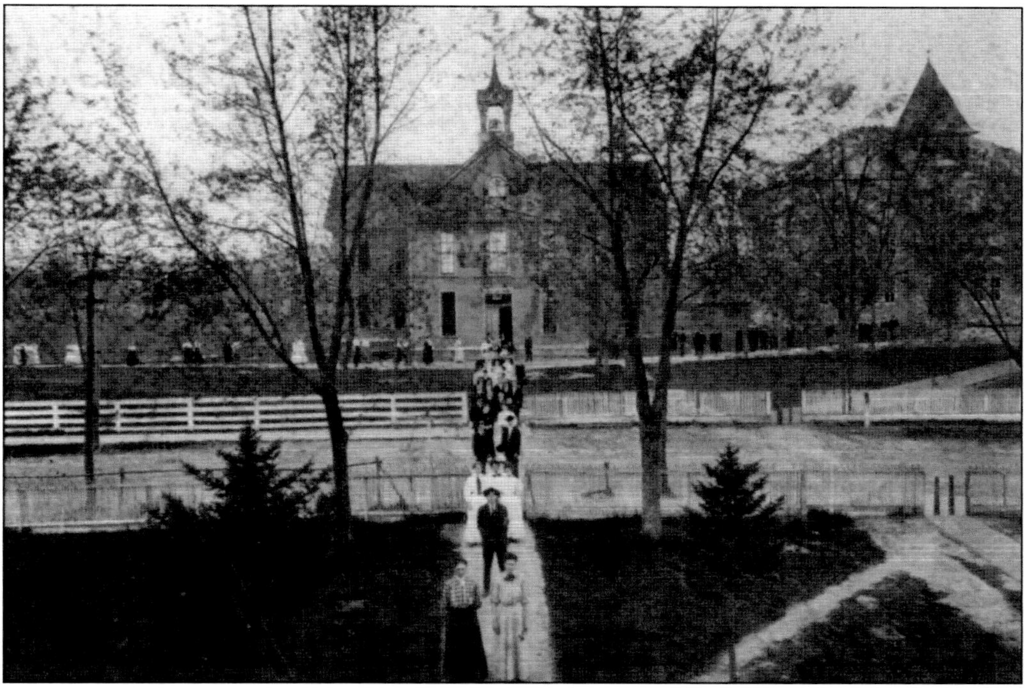

The picture of Memorial Hall at Bridgewater College was taken in 1907. By this time, Bridgewater had grown to 201 students. Unlike many colleges of that day, both male and female students were admitted.

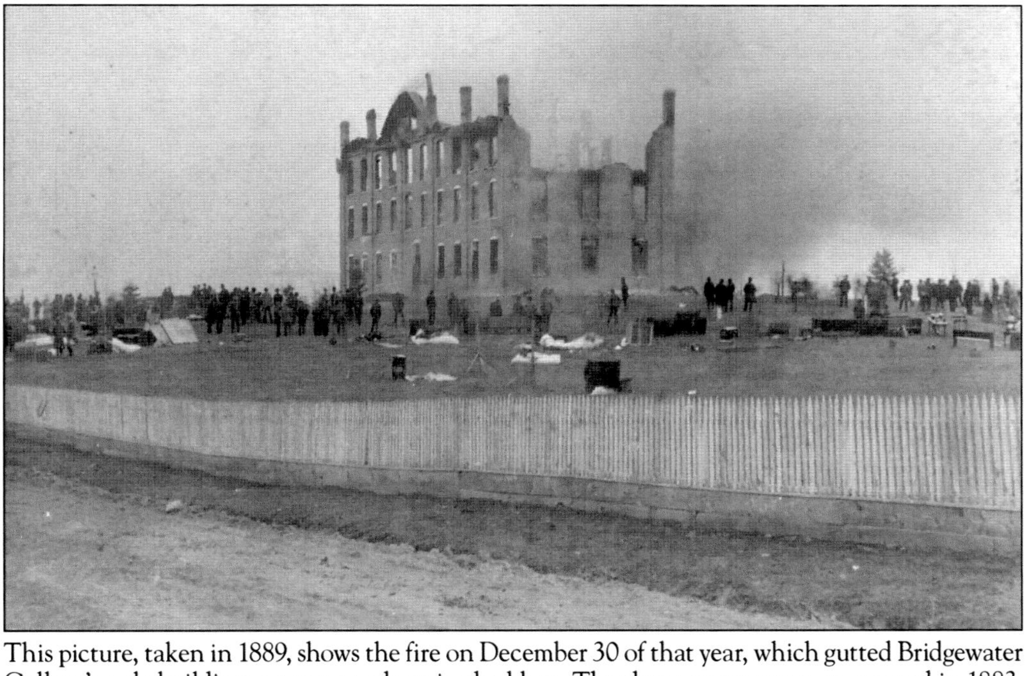

This picture, taken in 1889, shows the fire on December 30 of that year, which gutted Bridgewater College's only building; no one was hurt in the blaze. The three-story structure, erected in 1883, housed the school's library, classrooms, chapel, and administration on the first floor. Students lived on the second and third floors. After the fire, classes were held in rented quarters throughout town. (BCAMML.)

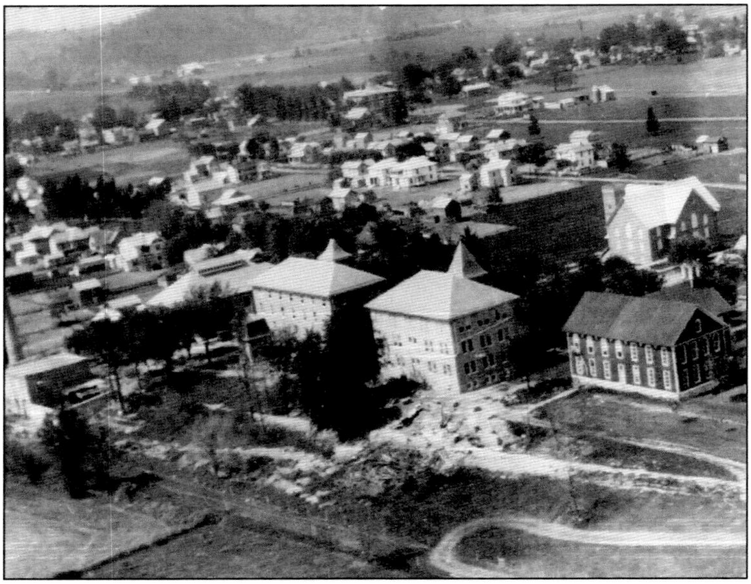

This is an aerial view of the campus taken in 1960. All of the buildings shown are actively used today, but it is safe to say that the campus has doubled in size just as the student population has. (BCAMML.)

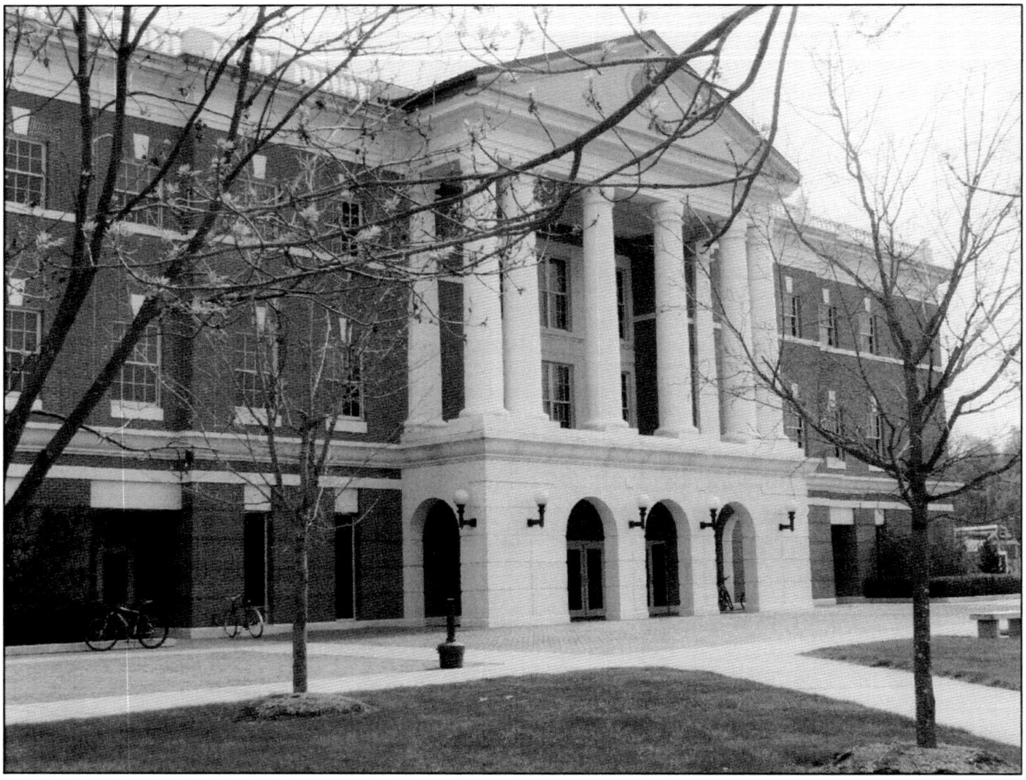

The growth of Bridgewater College is due to many factors, one of which is the generosity of alumni. The building above, named the McKinney Center, was constructed in part from contributions by Dr. Robert M. McKinney and his wife, Mary Engler McKinney. Dr. McKinney, a research chemist at the Dupont Corporation, graduated from Bridgewater College in 1924. In 2010, the college finished a campaign called "One Student, One Commitment" that brought $43 million in funds for endowed scholarships and other long-range purposes.

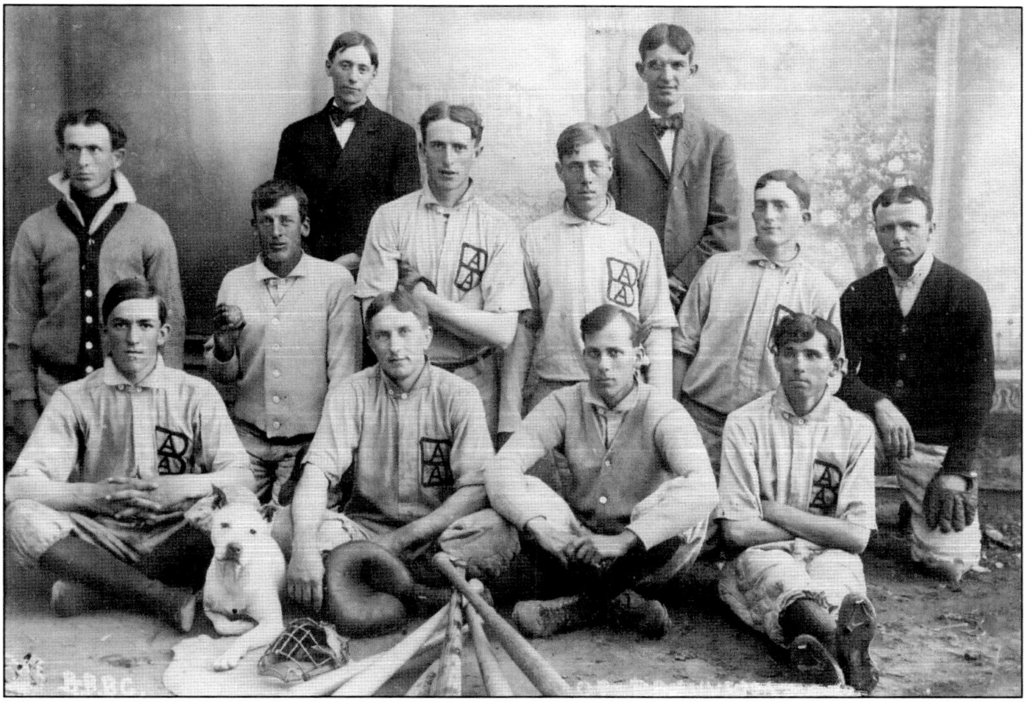

Sports were a part of college life almost from the beginning. This picture shows the 1910 Bridgewater College baseball team. Many of the players shown are ancestors to those living in Bridgewater today. While not all of the team members in the picture are identified, it is known that Hallie Dinkel (not the mayor), Gleaves Turk, Wythe Sellers, Cliff Riddel, Ed Sipe, and Homer Anderson were on the team.

Nelson T. Huffman was a professor of music at Bridgewater College and served as mayor of Bridgewater during the 1949 flood. The flood so devastated the finances of the town that no money could be found to put up Christmas decorations. Undaunted, Mayor Huffman initiated the decoration of a tree on Main Street in an effort to promote Christmas spirit and provide hope for the town's citizens. (BCAMML.)

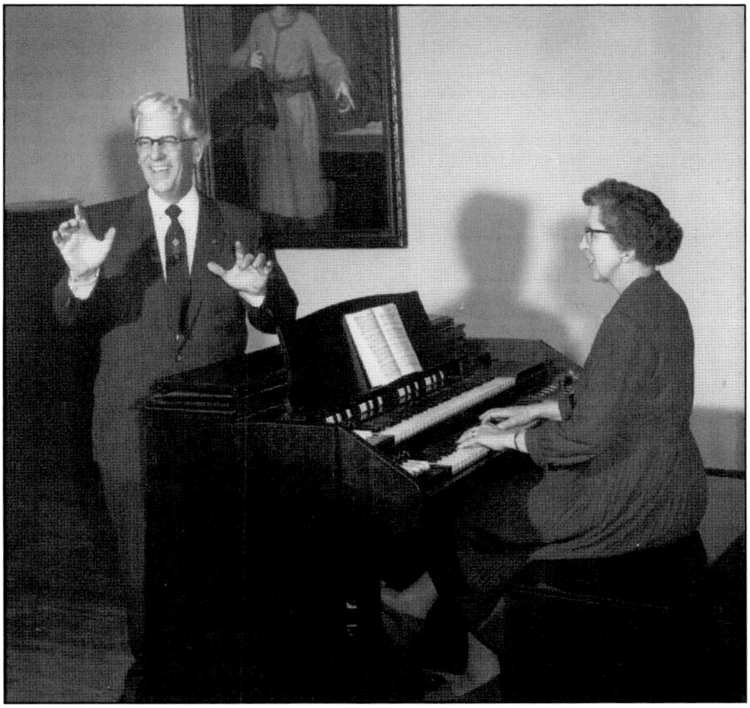

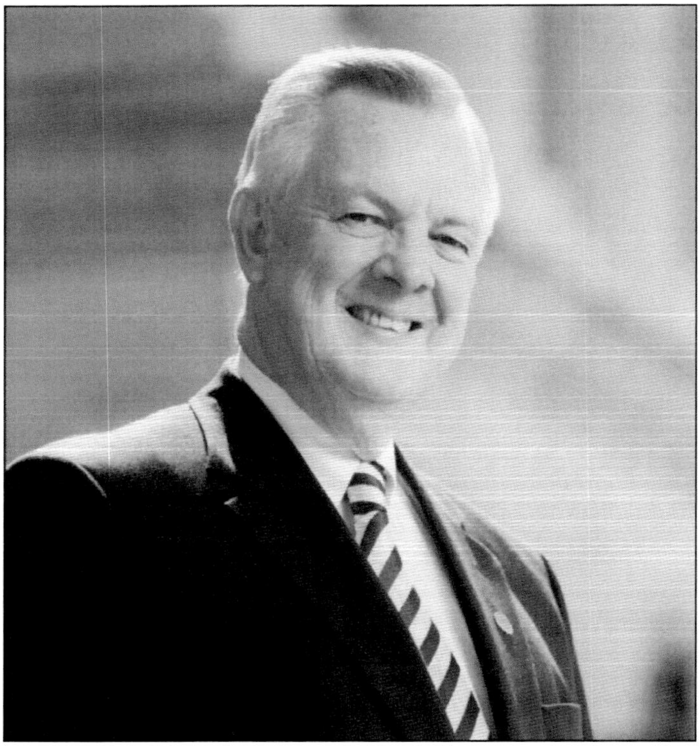

Phil Stone is a very talented man. He was senior partner at the law firm of Wharton, Aldhizer, and Weaver, is a renowned Lincoln scholar, and most important to this community, served 16 years as president of Bridgewater College. During his tenure as president, student enrollment doubled. At the same time, athletics and academics both prospered. Stone's life story is a classic American tale that began with humble beginnings only to end with success in many fields of endeavor. (BCAMML.)

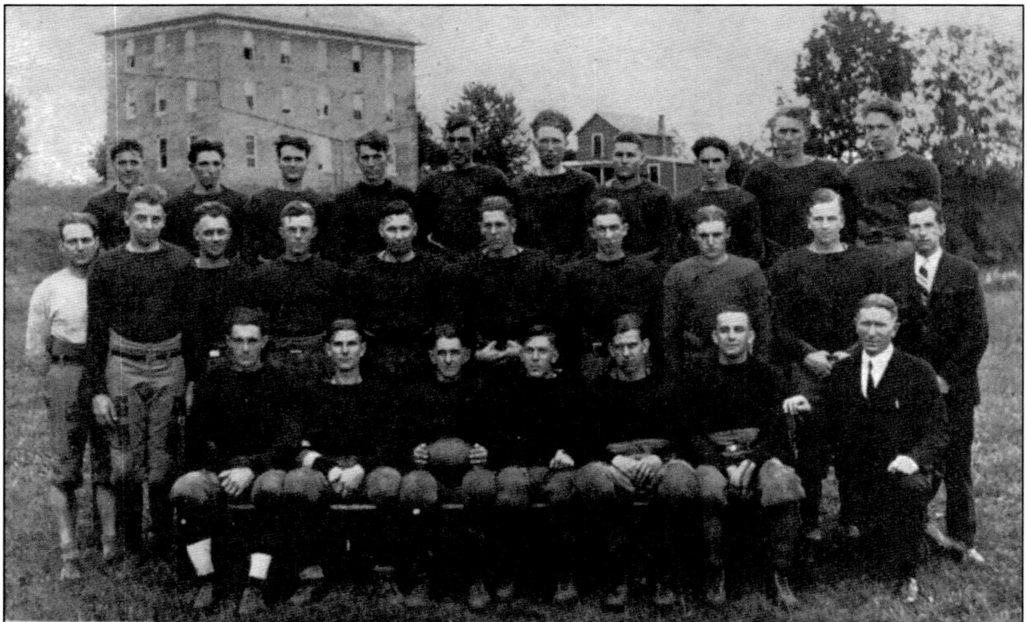

Bridgewater College Football Squad, 1926

Football has been a part of college life for many generations. The 1926 version of the Bridgewater Eagles played a rugged brand of the game with only leather helmets and limited padding for protection. Bridgewater College did not have great success in football until the hiring of coach Mike Clark in 1995, which led to division championships and the chance to play for the Division III national title.

# *Four*

# The Ebb and Flow of Business

It sounds contradictory to say the only constant of Bridgewater's businesses is change, but that can also be said for life in general. The job one might have had in 1840 in no way compares with a job the typical Bridgewater resident would have today.

By the time of its incorporation in 1835, many new businesses were opening on Main Street. One such proprietor was Henry Smals, who made and repaired shoes for more than 50 years. Smals was the exception. While some men may have had the luxury of operating a store or business of their own, most men of this time would have worked backbreaking jobs cutting and milling lumber or working on flatboats to haul such products to larger markets. Women, of course, would have worked at home, because they had not yet found acceptance in the workplace.

Perhaps the heyday of business in Bridgewater was the era from 1900 to the start of the Great Depression. Main Street was filled with every type of store a small community would want. It would be fascinating to go back in time and walk the length of Main Street to visit the businesses along that route. All of this changed, however, with the arrival of the automobile. Previously every small town needed grocery stores, department stores, and the like, because travel to larger cities was difficult and for most, impractical. As more and more families purchased cars, it was easier to drive to the shopping mall or discount stores where better prices and variety could be found.

A walk down Main Street today would reveal many of the buildings that stood a century ago, but none of the businesses remain. New ones have taken their place and provide the services expected by the modern world. As previously stated, the only constant in business is change. Such is the story of Bridgewater.

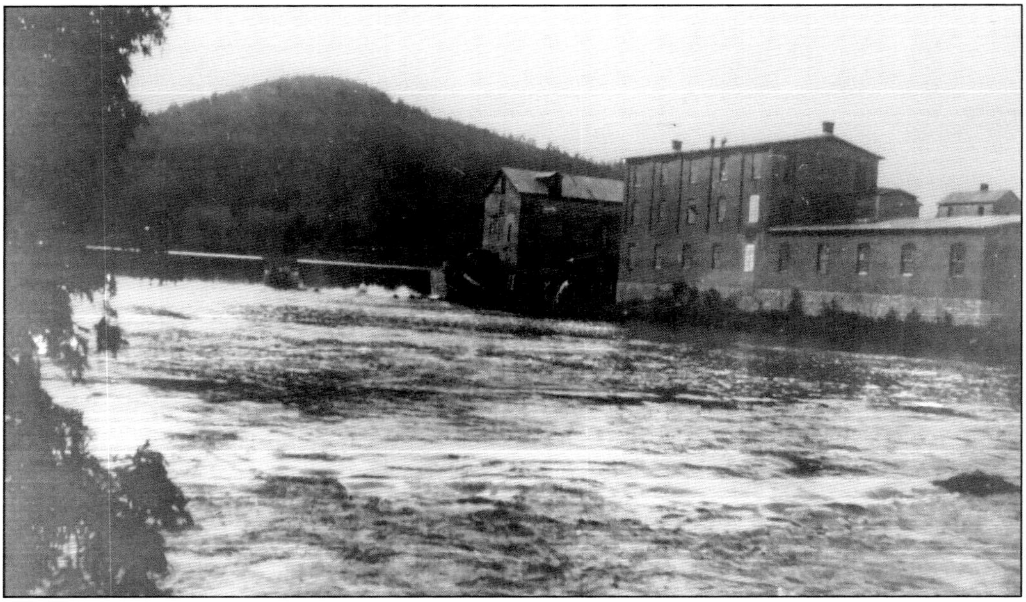

Farmer's Mill was organized in 1877 as the North River Manufacturing Company to make woolen goods, fertilizers, agricultural implements, and castings. It subsequently became a flour mill and burned in 1935.

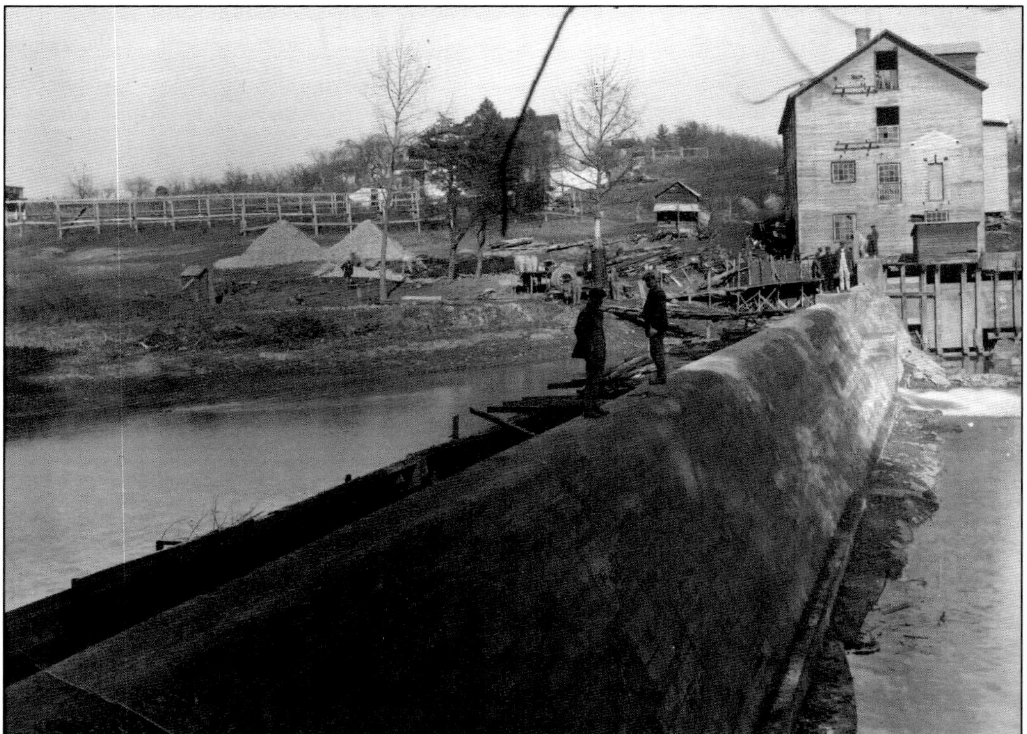

The concrete dam at Wildwood Park is the second such structure at this site. Amazingly it has stood the test of time serving the community for more than 100 years. It stands as a tribute to the workmanship of our ancestors and the quality of materials they used.

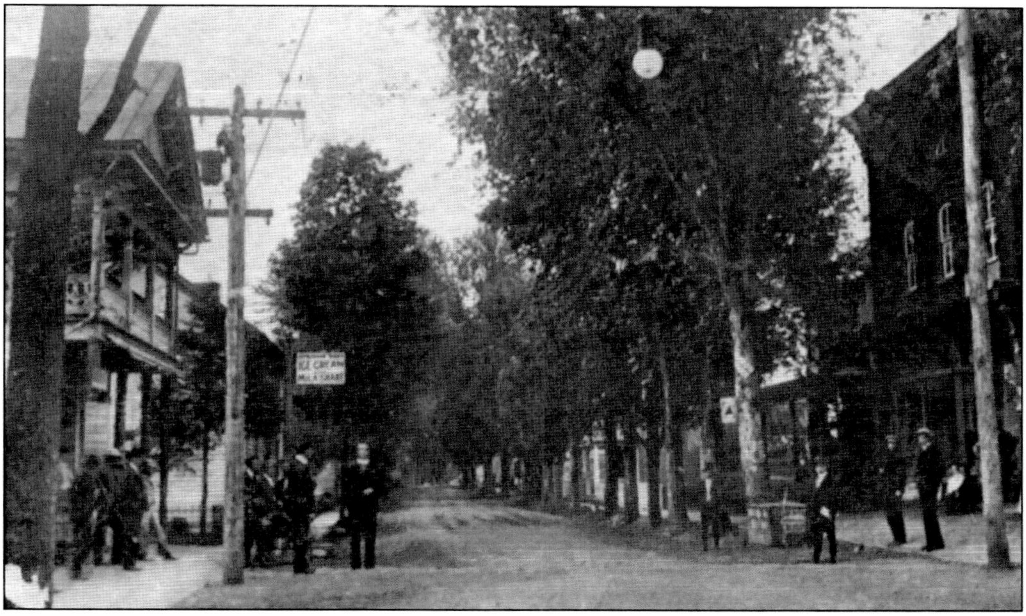

For most of the nation's history, Main Street has been the center of commerce for any town or city. Bridgewater was no exception to this rule. At one time, the stores of Bridgewater would purchase fresh produce, hams, poultry, and beef from nearby farms to sell to its citizens. In return, the local mercantile might pay cash, but more often the farmer would receive sugar, flour, or other dry goods needed to sustain their life on the farm.

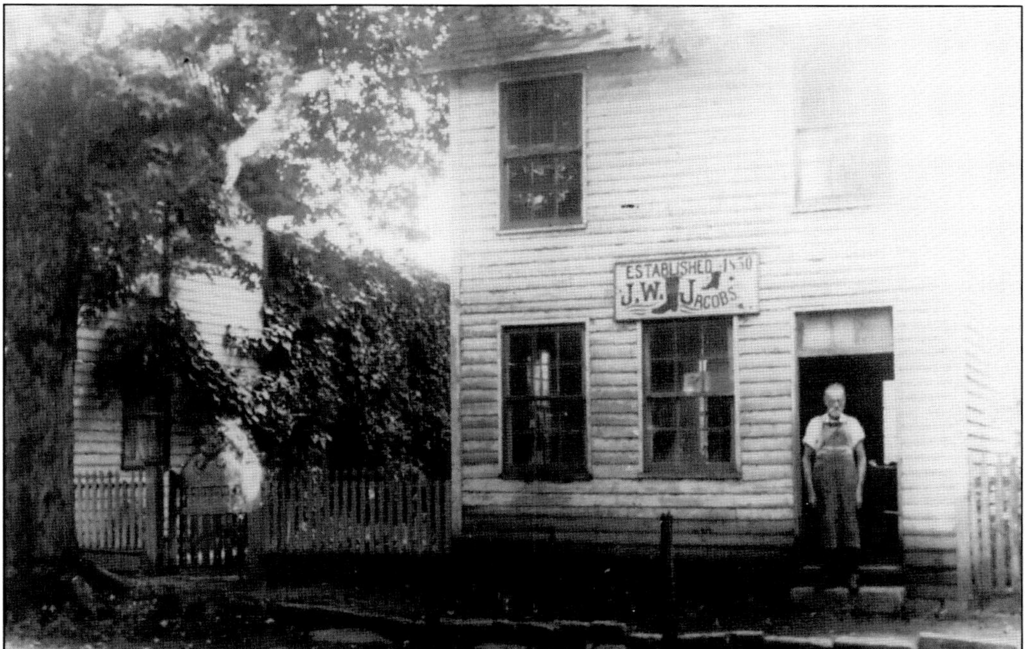


J. W. Jacobs opened a shoe repair shop in 1850 near where Fisher Auto Parts is located today. Jacobs was in business until his death in 1908. Raymond Spitler purchased the business and operated it until his death. His son then took over and continued until the late 1950s. It was torn down around 1970 to make way for the Fisher Auto Parts store.

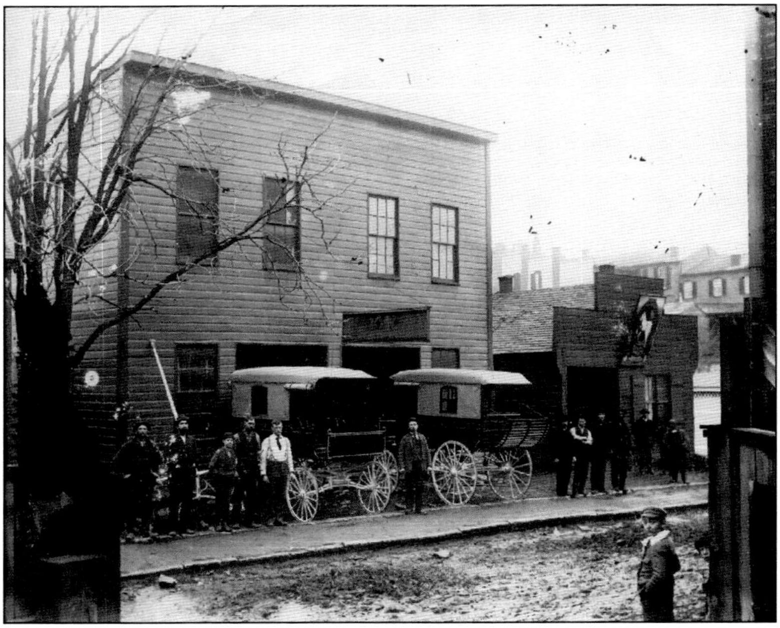

Located behind Robson's Store was a carriage shop operated by D. S. Thomas. He was involved in many Bridgewater businesses including the cannery, the plow factory, and eventually he opened a Pontiac dealership with his sons.

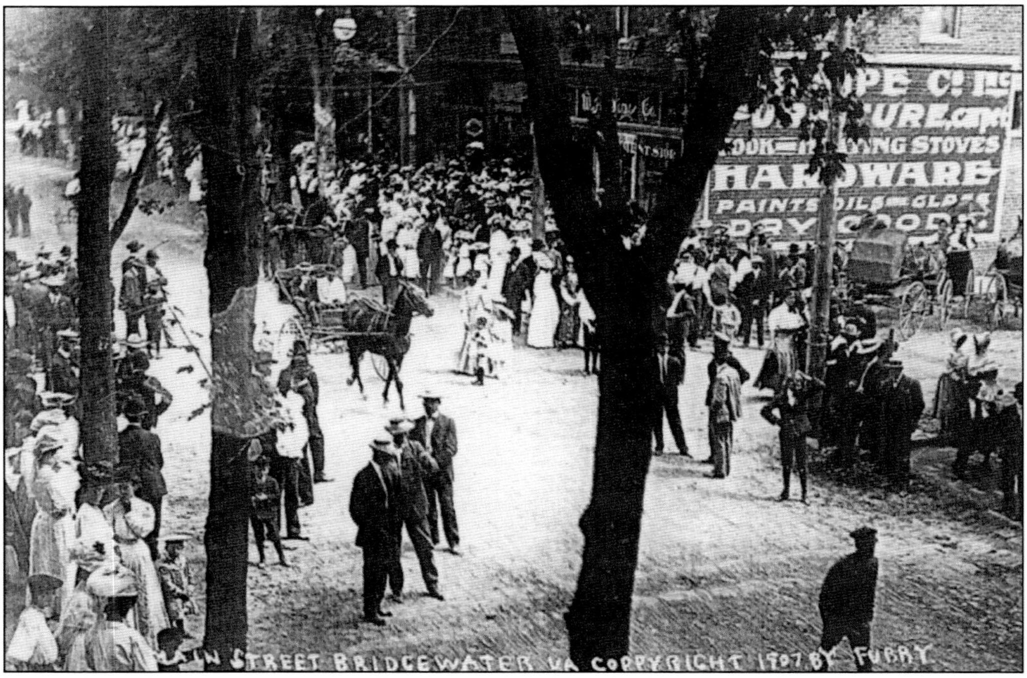


W. H. Sipe Company, Inc. was the largest mercantile retail establishment in all of Rockingham County. When a major sale was conducted, crowds like the one shown above would arrive. To these small-town residents, it must have seemed like they were standing in the middle of Times Square. With the growing popularity of the automobile, stores like this were gradually squeezed out by the appearance of shopping malls.

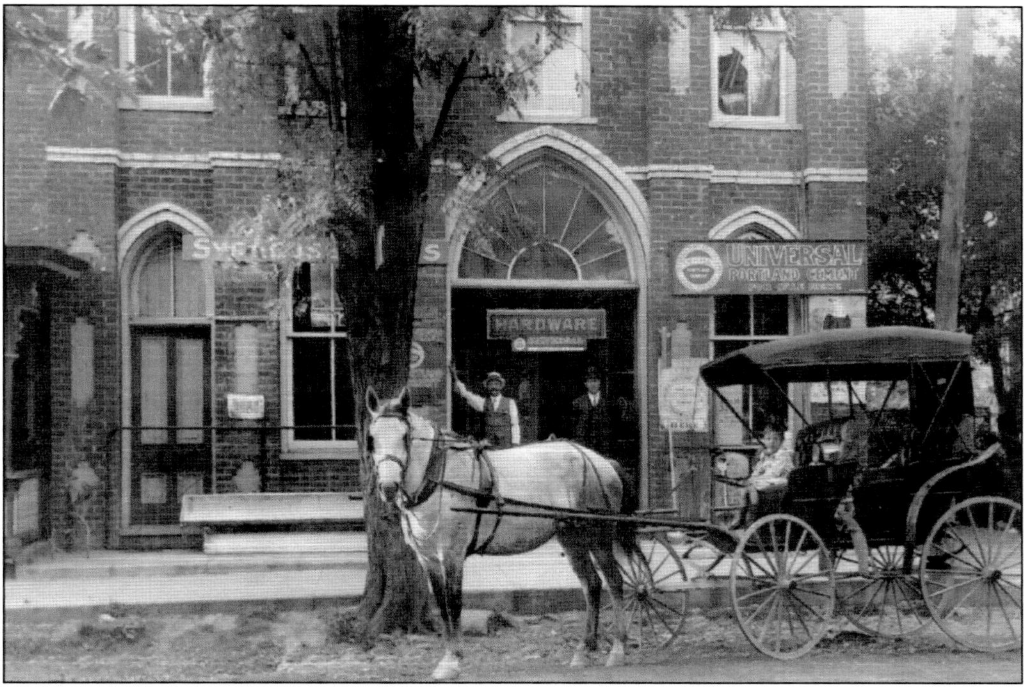


This photograph of the Bridgewater Agriculture and Implement Store was taken around 1917. The store was located on South Main Street in Bridgewater and was erected on the west side of the street next to the Rockingham Mill building. The proprietor of the store, C. W. Bowman, is standing at the entrance (left). Next to him is Virgil Miller, and Dick Bowman is the young lad in the carriage.

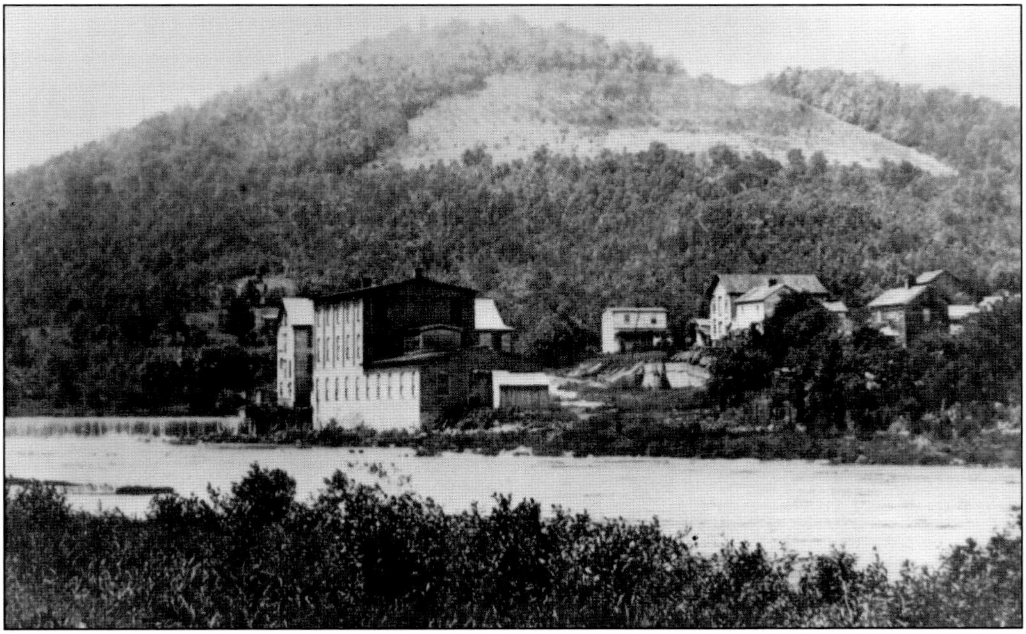

Bridgewater had five mills to grind flour and meal: George W. Berlin's mill at Berlinton, Isaac Marshall's mill east of the bridge, Farmer's Mill and Natural Falls Mill at Wildwood, and the Dry River Mill built by Adam R. Hollen in 1872 on Route 257 north of the Sandstone Subdivision.

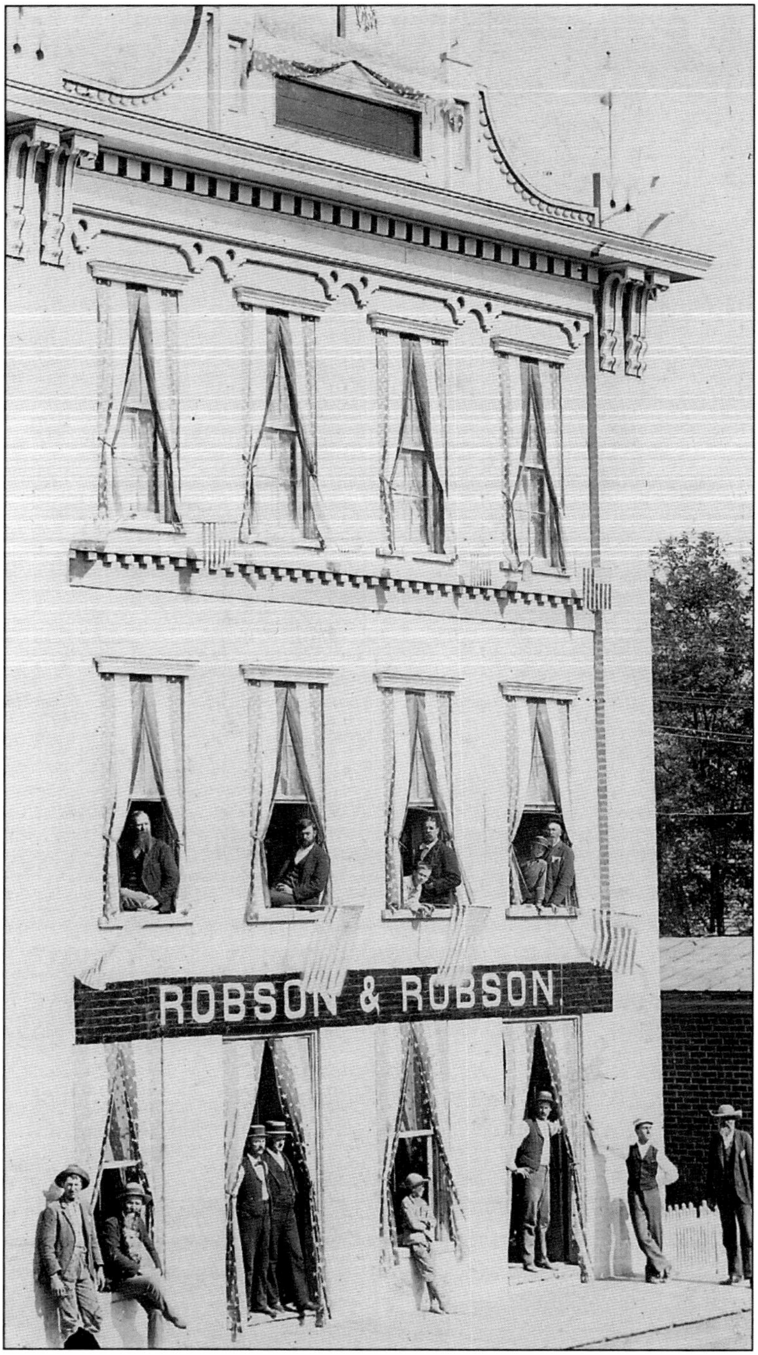


At the end of the Civil War, J. W. Allemong joined with members of the local Masonic Lodge in constructing this three-story building next to North River. The Masonic Lodge always occupied the third floor, but the remaining floors were used by a variety of mercantile establishments. Allemong had the first store in the building, but this site was best known as Robson and Robson. They sold groceries, books, shoes, floor coverings, china, glass, and tinware. They often took butter, eggs, poultry, and farm goods in exchange. It still stands today, but the Masons have moved on to larger and newer quarters. For many years, this site has been used for purely residential purposes.

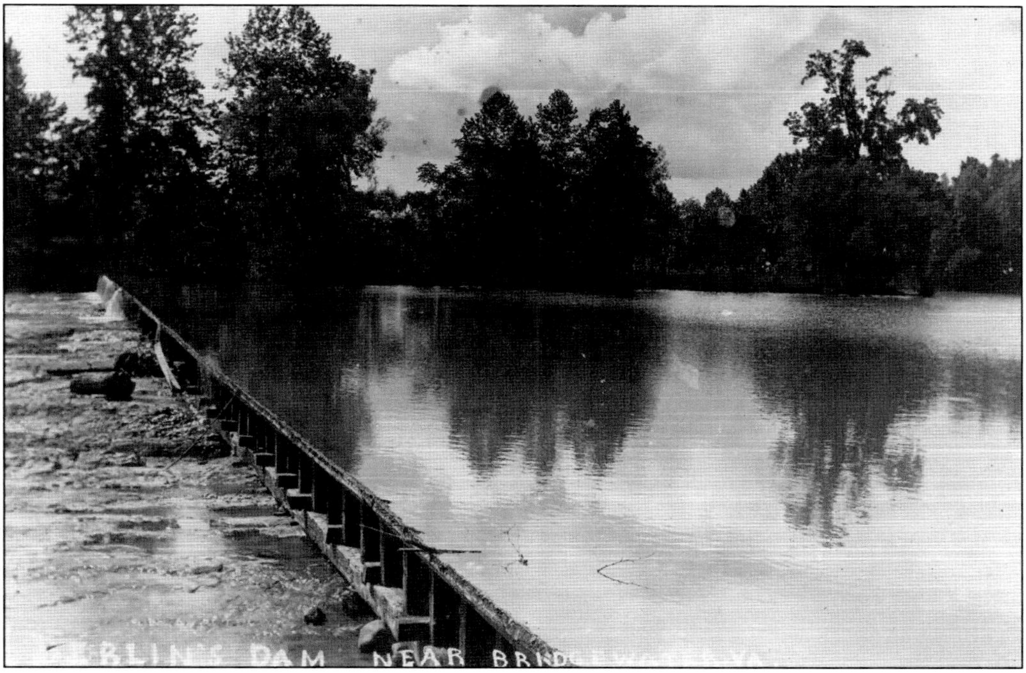


George W. Berlin was an attorney who moved to Bridgewater in 1865. He is best known for his business activities including the founding of a local newspaper, the construction and operation of Berlin Mill, and the production of electricity at the dam located on North River in the southeast portion of Bridgewater. He was so prominent that the area surrounding the mill became known as Berlinton and retained that name until it was annexed by Bridgewater in 1985.

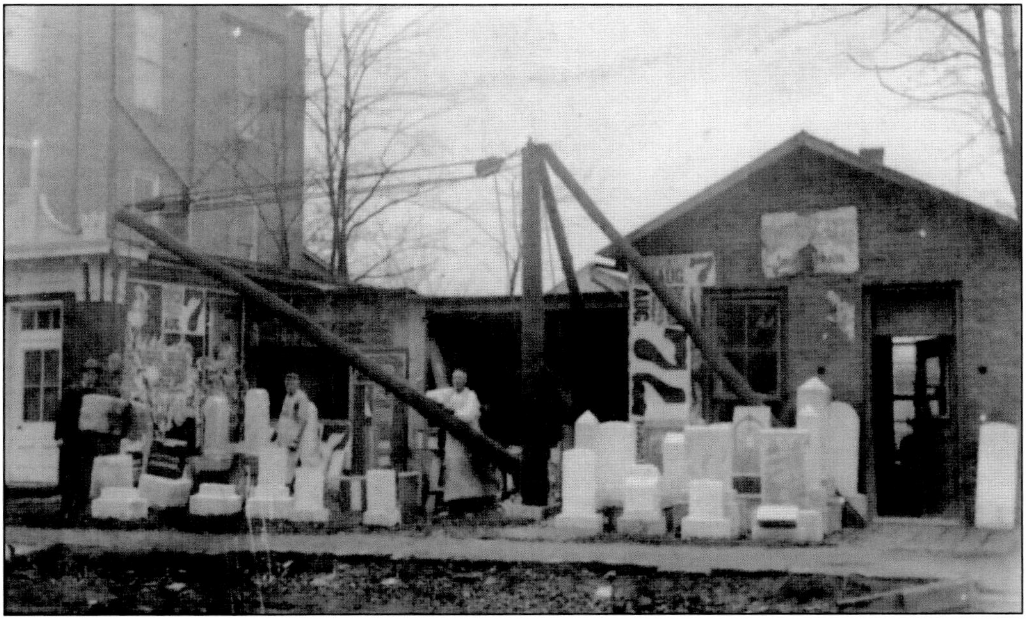

Rinker Brothers Marble Yard was located on South Main Street across from Rosenberger's Funeral Home. There are few families in Bridgewater and the surrounding area who have not been patrons of this enterprise at some point. Many of the tombstones in the area that date from 1885 to the era after World War I originated from this site.

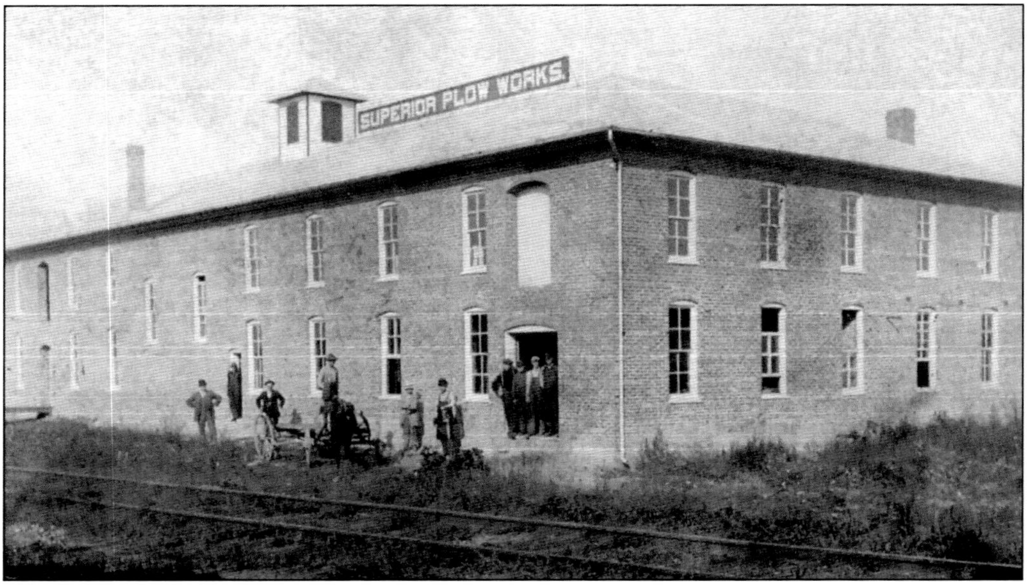


The Bridgewater Plow Corporation was founded by D. S. Thomas in 1908. This is the same D. S. Thomas who initiated the carriage shop, the cannery, and the Pontiac dealership. Over the first few years of operation, output grew from a few hundred plows annually to thousands that were shipped nationwide. By 1916, it was doing business as Superior Plow Works.

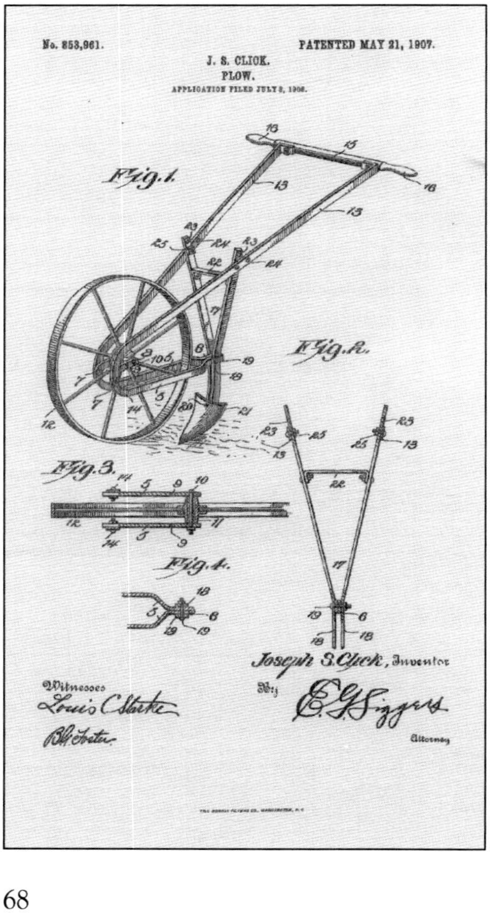


The Click hand plow is now a collector's item. Thousands were sold nationwide from the Superior Plow Plant in Bridgewater. Occasionally a home gardener in the Bridgewater area can be seen bringing one of these antiques from the storage shed each spring to work the soil in the same manner his grandfather might have years ago.

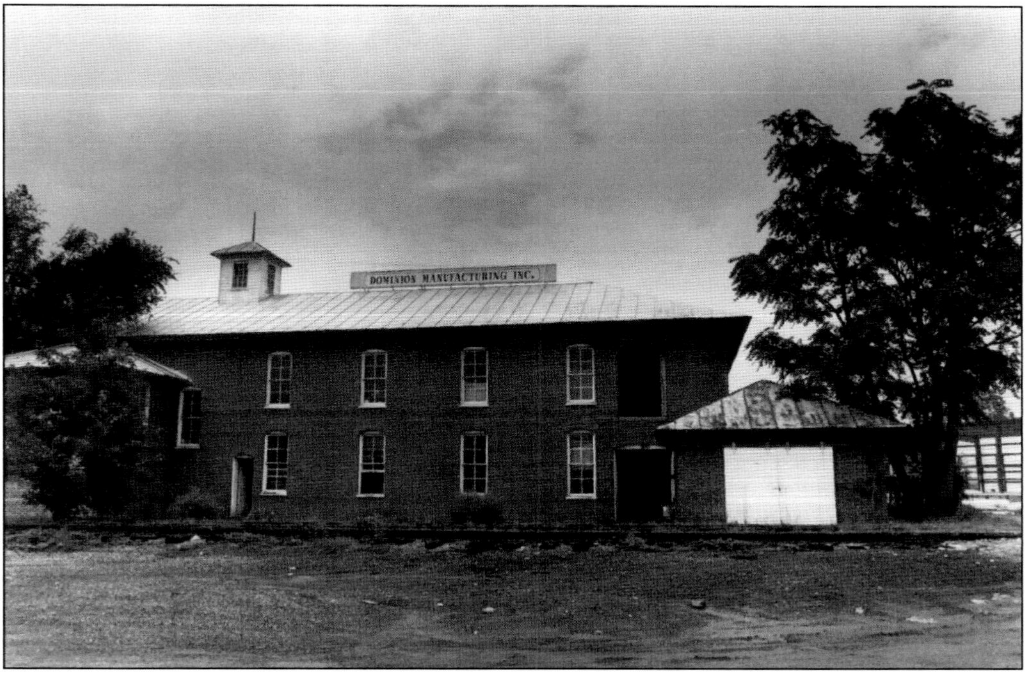


In 1956, John Flory and Stuart Baker purchased the company formerly known as Superior Plow Works and changed its name to Dominion Manufacturing. Prior to that time, their main commodity was hand-driven garden plows, which were losing popularity in a more mechanized world. By 1959, the new owners had diversified the line of garden and lawn tools to include gas-powered lawn tractors, rotary tillers, and field mowers. While they had many years of success, business eventually faded, and the doors of Dominion Manufacturing were closed.

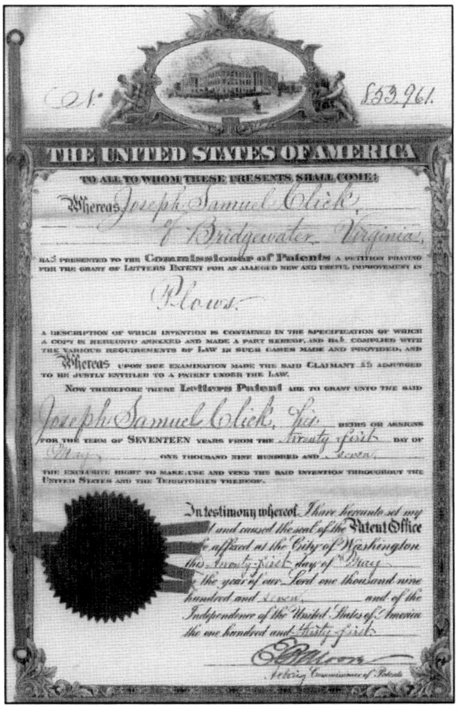
No. 853,961.

THE UNITED STATES OF AMERICA

TO ALL TO WHOM THESE PRESENTS SHALL COME:

Whereas Joseph Samuel Click, of Bridgewater, Virginia,

HAS PRESENTED TO THE Commissioner of Patents A PETITION PRAYING FOR THE GRANT OF LETTERS PATENT FOR AN ALLEGED NEW AND USEFUL IMPROVEMENT IN

Plows.

A DESCRIPTION OF WHICH INVENTION IS CONTAINED IN THE SPECIFICATION OF WHICH A COPY IS HEREUNTO ANNEXED AND MADE A PART HEREOF, AND HAS COMPLIED WITH THE VARIOUS REQUIREMENTS OF LAW IN SUCH CASES MADE AND PROVIDED, AND

Whereas UPON DUE EXAMINATION MADE THE SAID CLAIMANT IS ADJUDGED TO BE JUSTLY ENTITLED TO A PATENT UNDER THE LAW.

Now THEREFORE THESE Letters Patent ARE TO GRANT UNTO THE SAID Joseph Samuel Click, his HEIRS OR ASSIGNS FOR THE TERM OF SEVENTEEN YEARS FROM THE twenty-first DAY OF May ONE THOUSAND NINE HUNDRED AND seven, THE EXCLUSIVE RIGHT TO MAKE, USE AND VEND THE SAID INVENTION THROUGHOUT THE UNITED STATES AND THE TERRITORIES THEREOF.

In testimony whereof I have hereunto set my hand and caused the seal of the Patent Office to be affixed at the City of Washington this twenty-first day of May, in the year of our Lord one thousand nine hundred and seven, and of the Independence of the United States of America the one hundred and thirty-first.

E. B. Moore
Acting Commissioner of Patents.

While Dominion produced many different garden-related products, the most popular item was the J. S. Click hand plow that originated at the Bridgewater plant. The patent has stayed with the family and is currently in the possession of Click's great-niece Liz Bodkin.

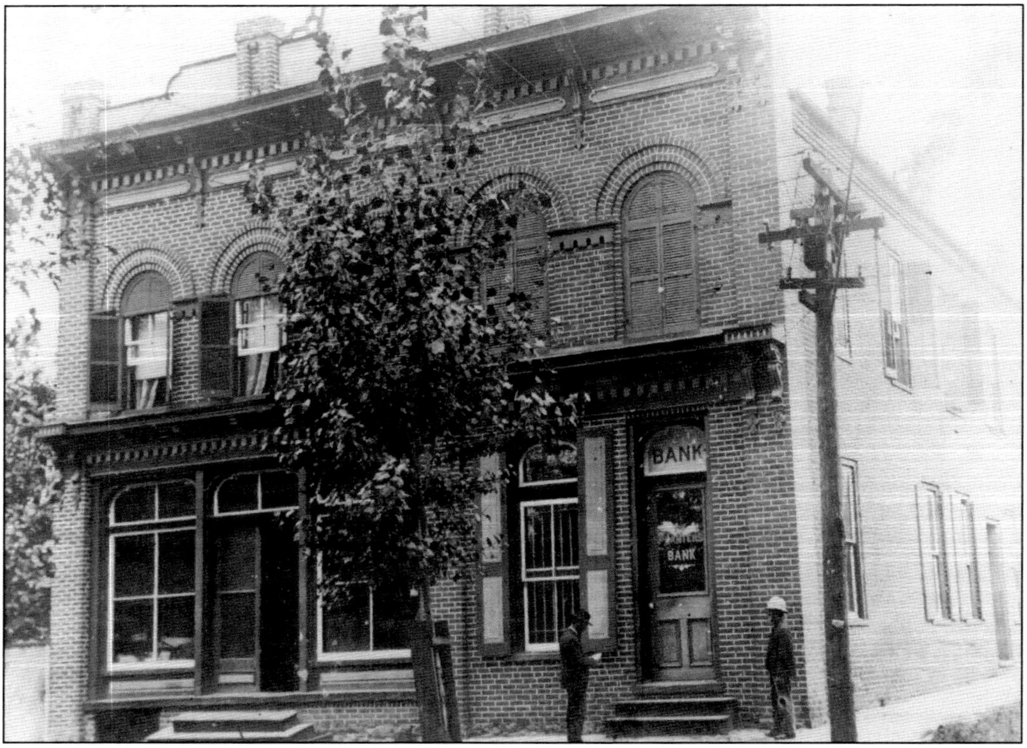


Farmer's Bank was established in 1878 and was led by J. W. F. Allemony, who served as president. Even though this building has been converted to residential use, it still contains a large bank vault on the first floor.

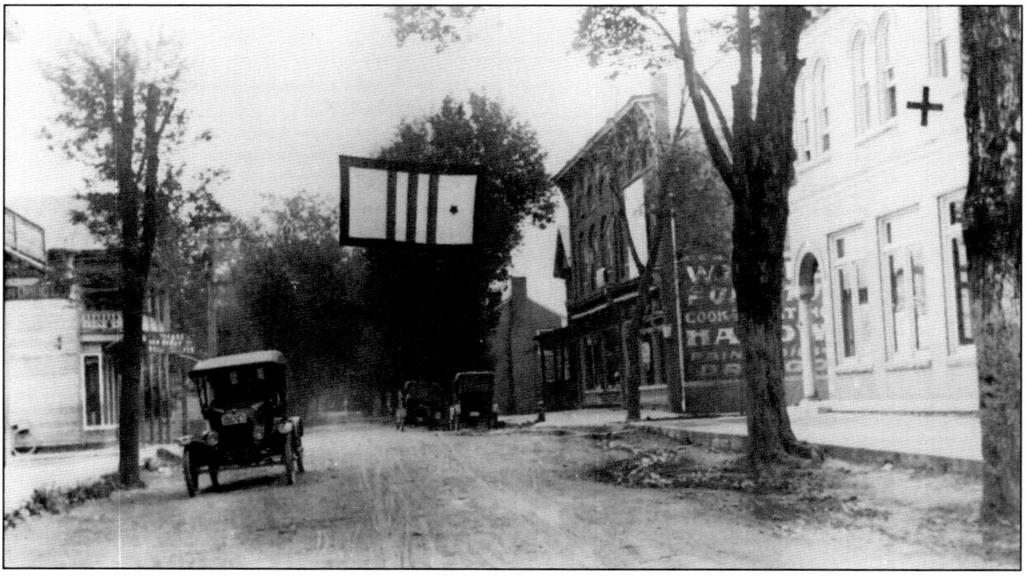

The flag suspended across Main Street had special meaning during World War I. The three vertical blue stripes on a white interior bordered in red indicated it was the third "Liberty Loan" endeavor to support the war effort. A community or bank that exceeded the prescribed sales quota of "Liberty" bonds received this flag. The star seen on it indicated that bond sales were double the prescribed quota.

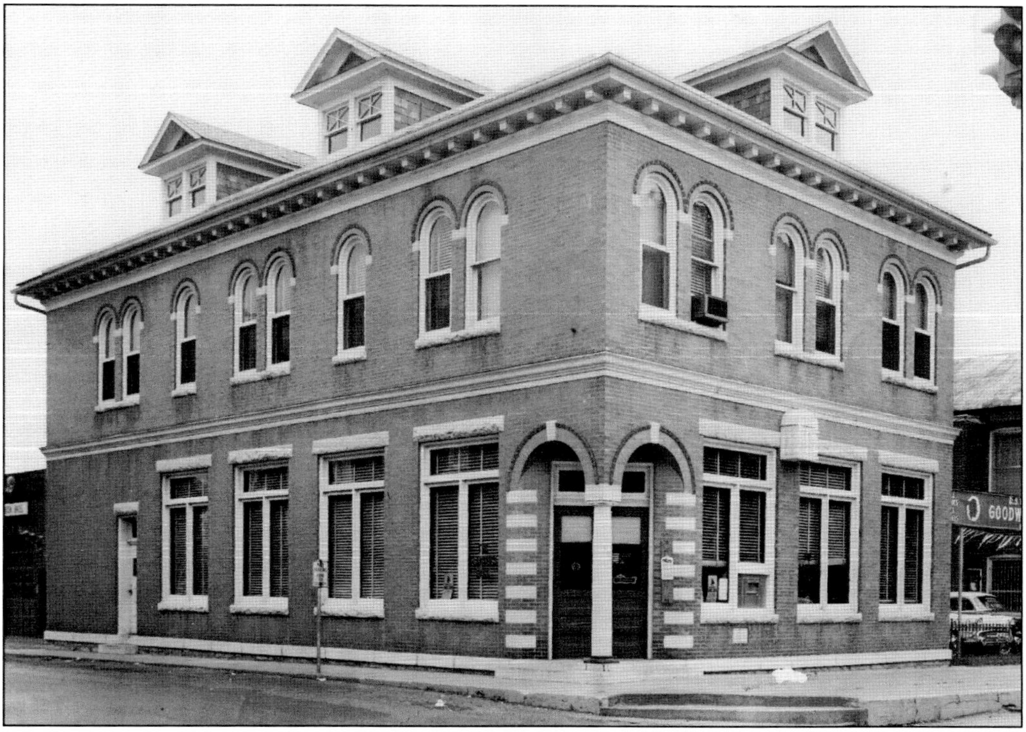

In 1898, Planters Bank of Bridgewater was opened on the southeast corner of Main and East College Streets. It operated at this location for 77 years, at which time it moved to a new building one block north.

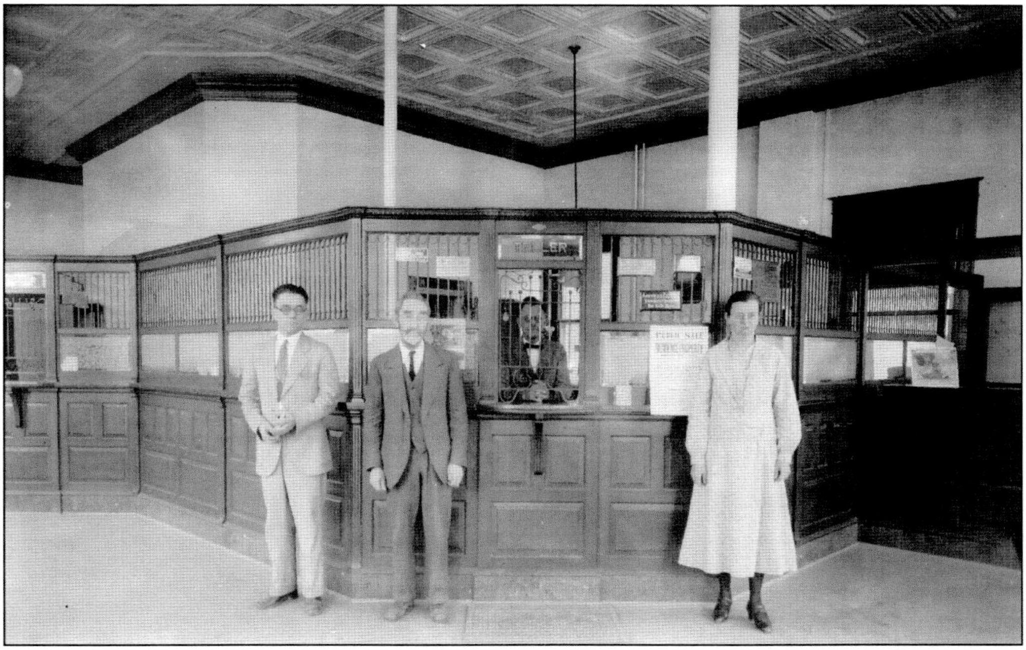

When Planters Bank opened in 1898, the board of directors selected J. H. Craun as president, James R. Shipman as cashier, and S. H. W. Byrd as assistant cashier. The woman to the right is believed to be Lizzie Thomas.

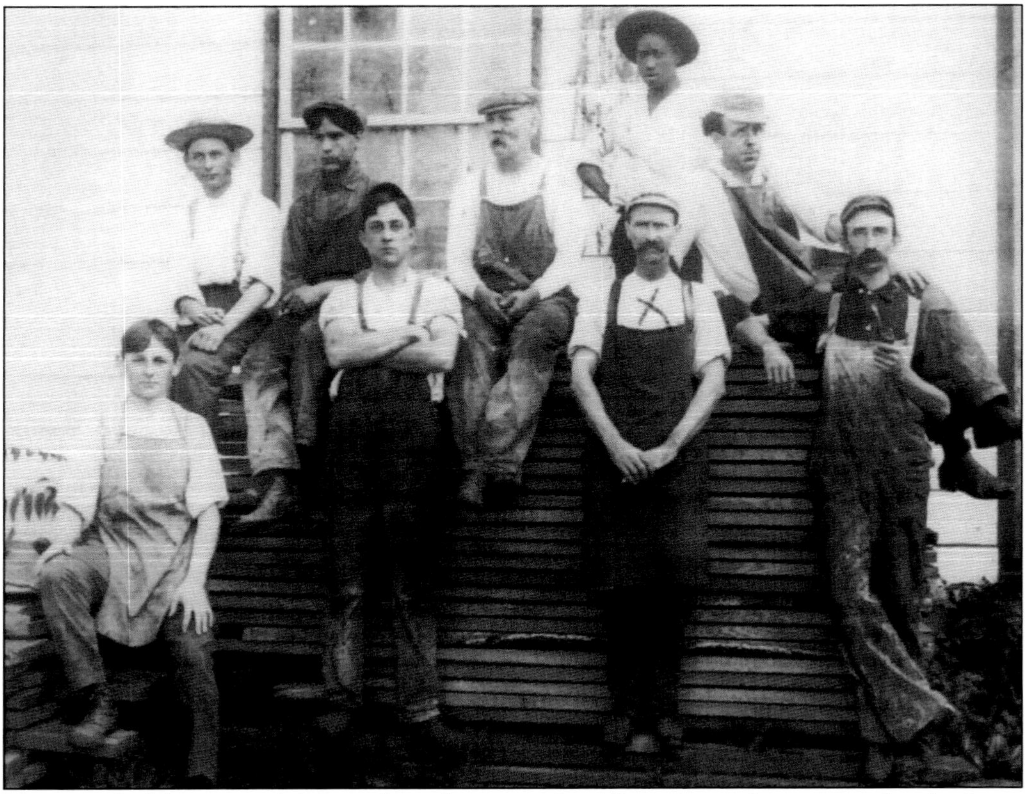

The arrival of the automobile brought with it new jobs. All mechanical equipment breaks down, and the automobile is no exception to that rule. By 1925, Thomas Garage was opened. This picture shows the staff taking a break from their daily routine.

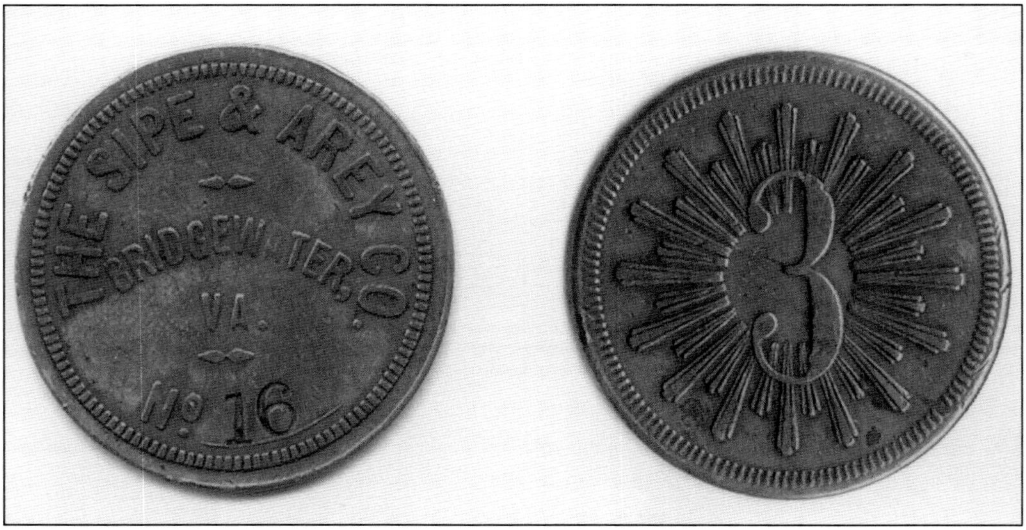


It is a little-known fact that at one time stores issued their own tokens or coins. Most stores in Bridgewater at the dawn of the 20th century took part in this practice. Often the tokens could be purchased at less than face value, which provided the consumer a discount. Of course, the drawback was that it could only be used at the store issuing the token.

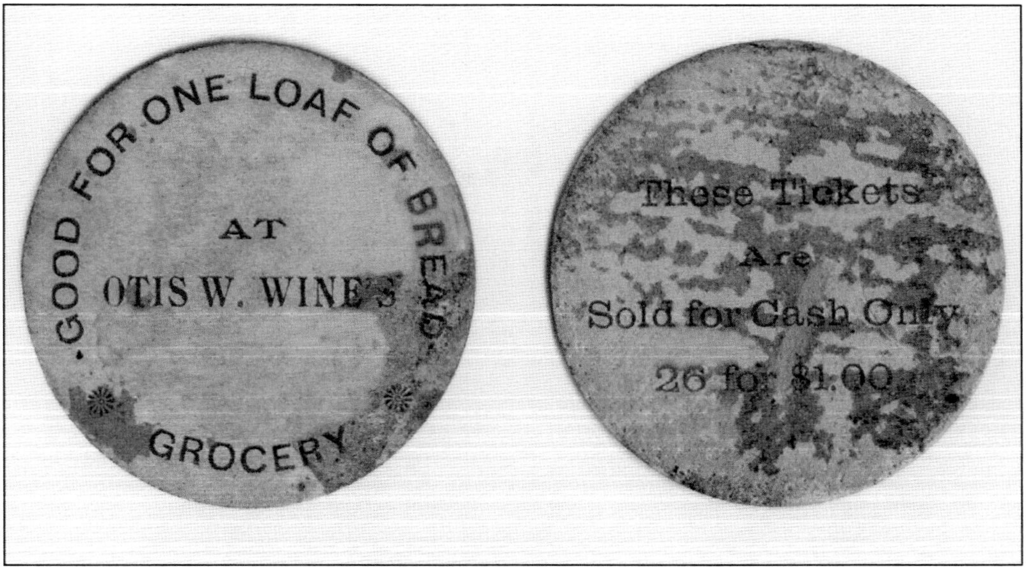


Otis Wine issued a unique token at his grocery store. It was good for a loaf of bread, and one could purchase 20 tokens for $1, which meant the cost of a loaf of bread was 5¢.

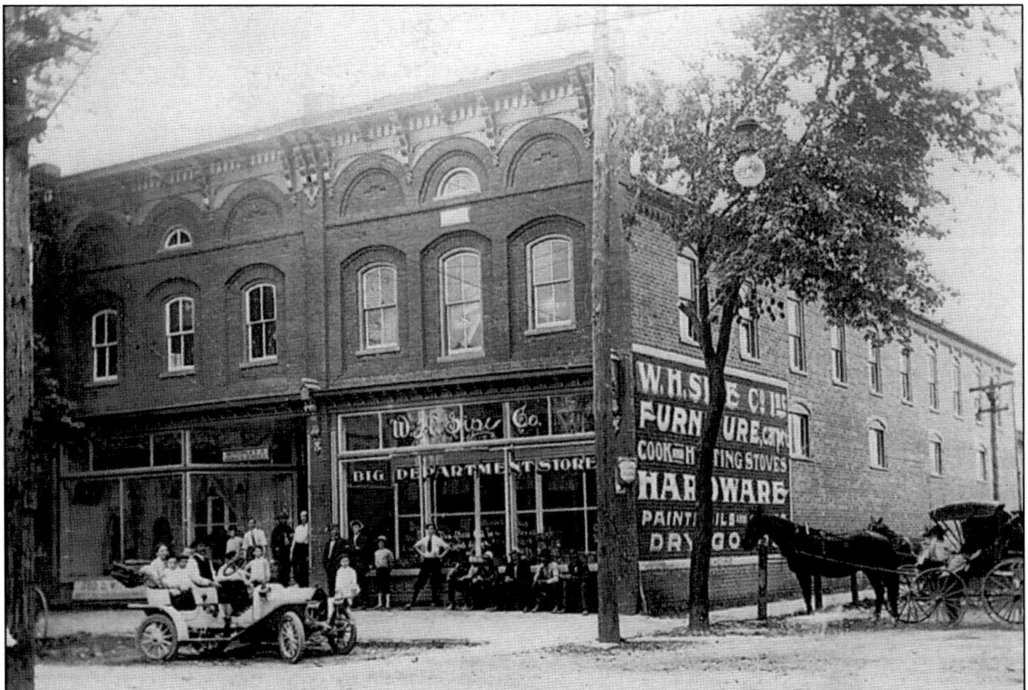


W. H. Sipe Company, Inc., located at 100 North Main Street, was the largest store in Bridgewater. It started during horse-and-buggy days and lasted long after the arrival of the automobile. Like most general stores of that time, it sold virtually everything a family could want. In later years, this building was used as a post office, hardware store, and office complex.

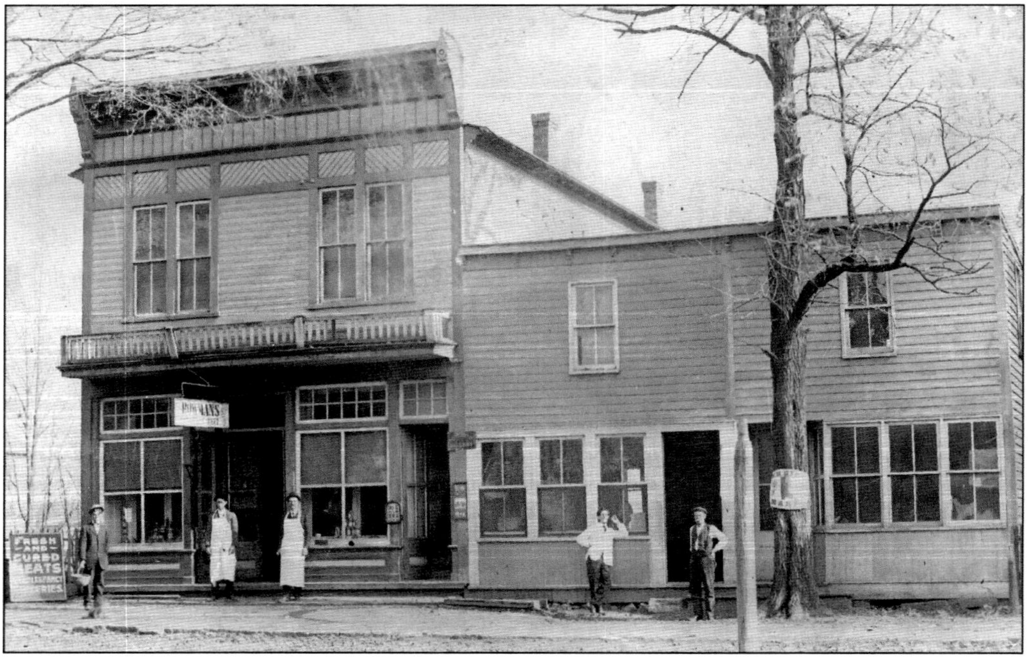


Bowman's Meat Market was located at the intersection of Main and College Streets just south of today's BB&T bank. It was not uncommon for a town of Bridgewater's size to have several grocery and hardware stores as well as specialty shops such as a butcher. Eventually this site became Mick or Mack Grocery. Today Francesco's Restaurant occupies this space.

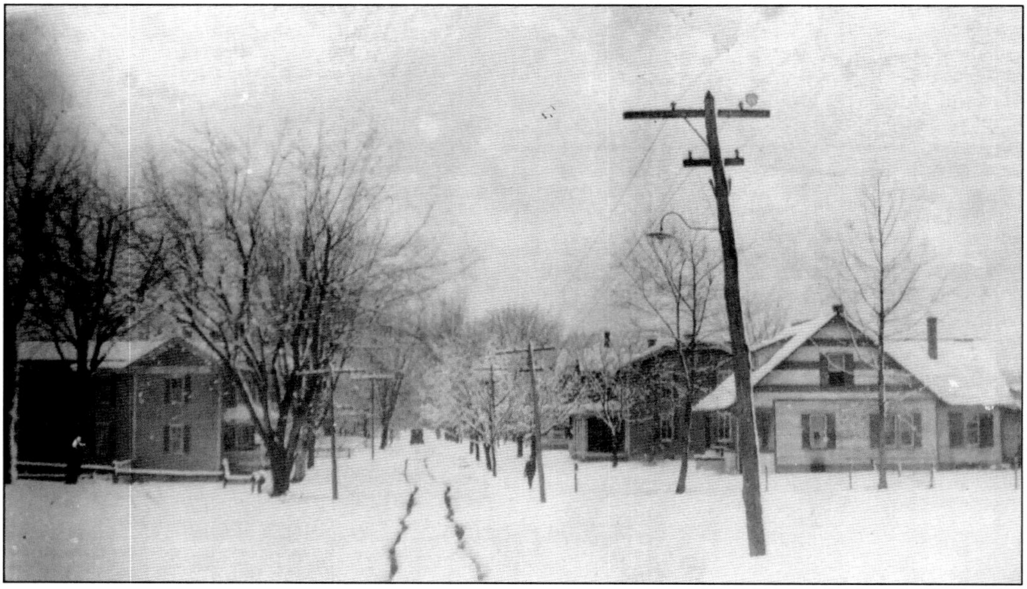

It is hard to imagine that most roads were unpaved a century ago, but that is the case. Horse and buggies traveling East College Street would have to deal with snow-covered streets, such as this one in the winter, and mud puddles in the spring, because road maintenance was a concept unheard of at this time. It would not be uncommon for the home owner to dump cinders from the fireplace into potholes to keep the surface passable.

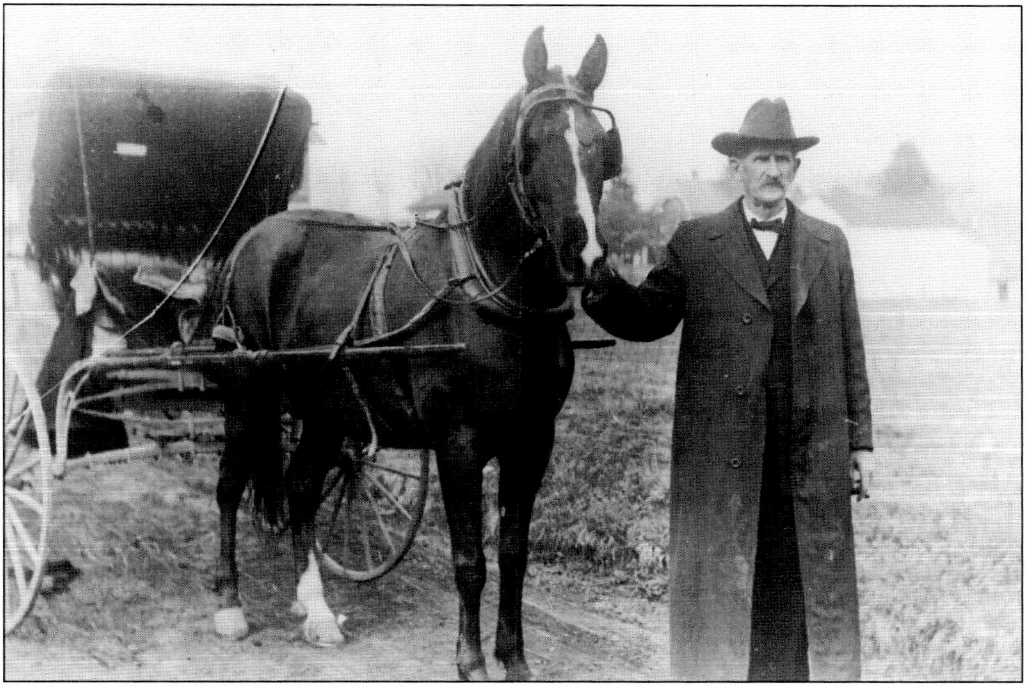

Dr. B. H. Beydler opened his medical practice in Bridgewater in 1909. It is believed that he delivered over 3,000 babies during his career. The charge was $25 per baby. Many people in those days could not pay cash, so Dr. Beydler would accept hogs, hams, eggs, or homegrown food in lieu of cash. In October 1936, Dr. Beydler answered a late-night call seeking his medical expertise for a patient at the local hospital. En route he was struck head-on by a drunk driver and died a few months later at the relatively young age of 64.

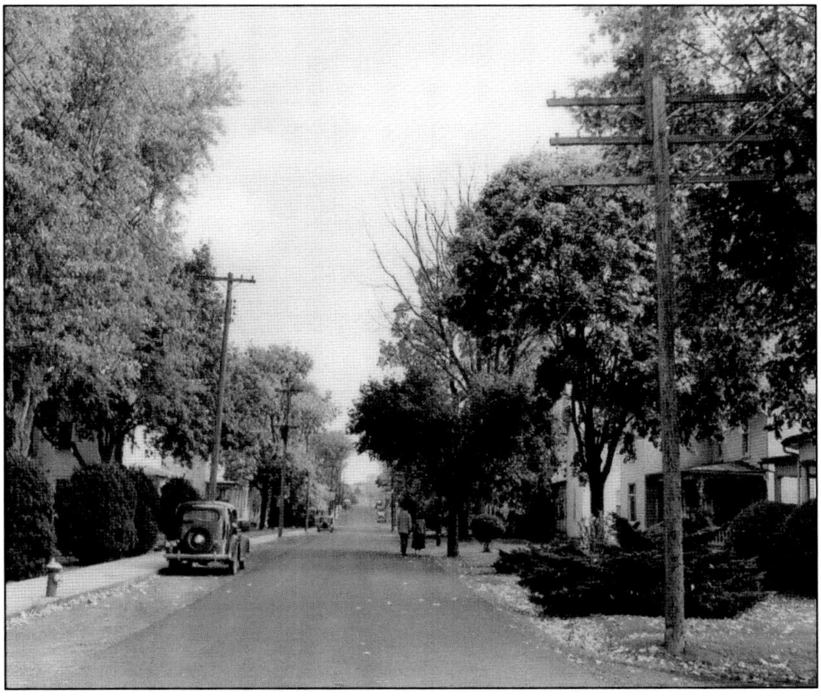

East College Street was paved by the middle of the 20th century, making it much more passable in inclement weather. Trees still line the street, and many of the houses are the same as those a century ago.

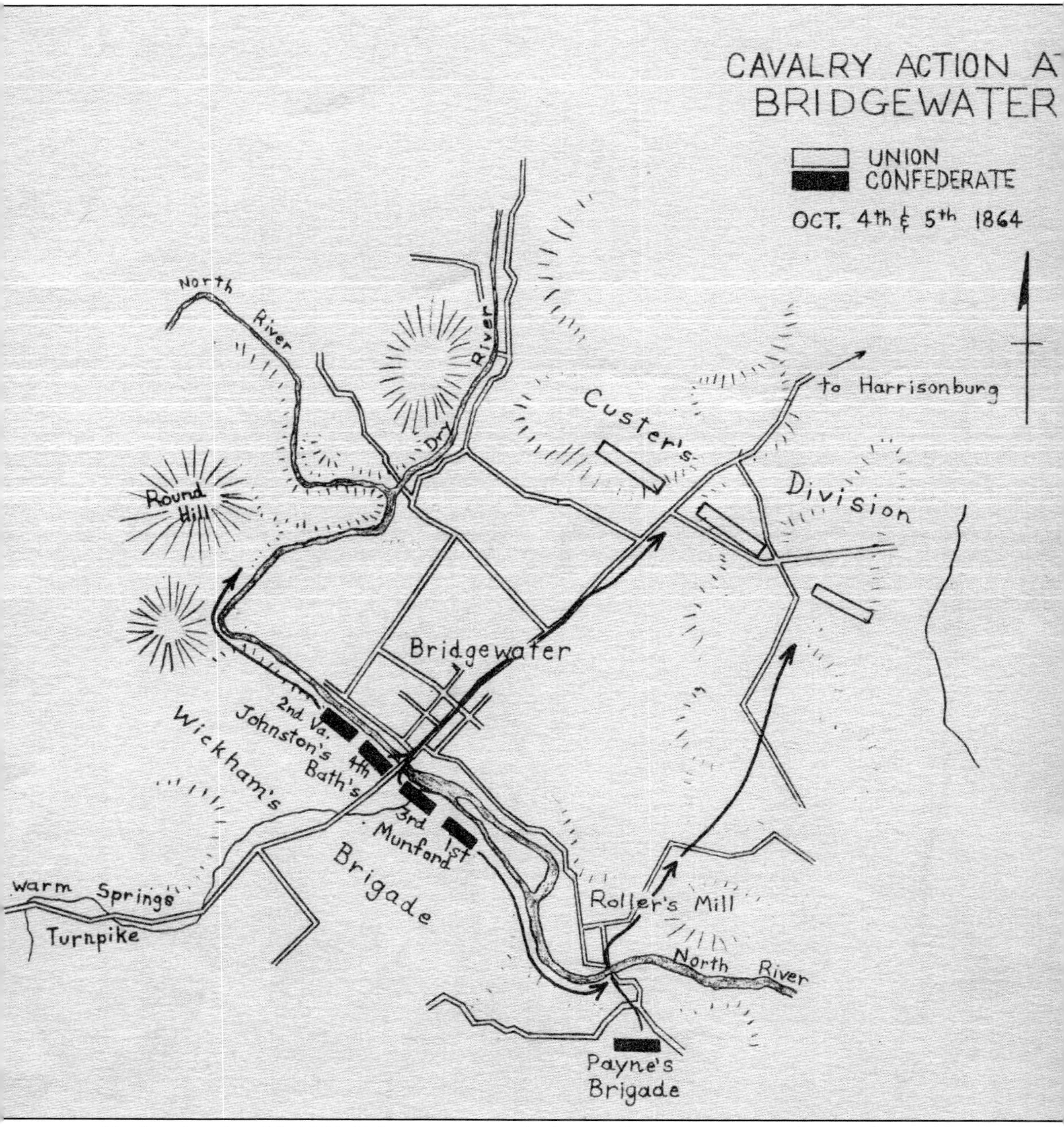


On October 4 and 5, 1864, Calvary action took place in Bridgewater. Gen. George Custer's division was on the Bridgewater side of the North River facing Col. Thomas Munford to the south. There was no bridge at this time, because Stonewall Jackson had burned it earlier in the war to prevent Federal troops from advancing. General Custer is rarely remembered for his visit to Bridgewater but is certainly well known for "Custer's Last Stand" at Little Big Horn.

Civil War reenactments are still popular nearly a century and a half after the war ended. In 1960, citizens dressed as both Blues and Grays to recreate these pivotal moments in their history. (BCAMML.)

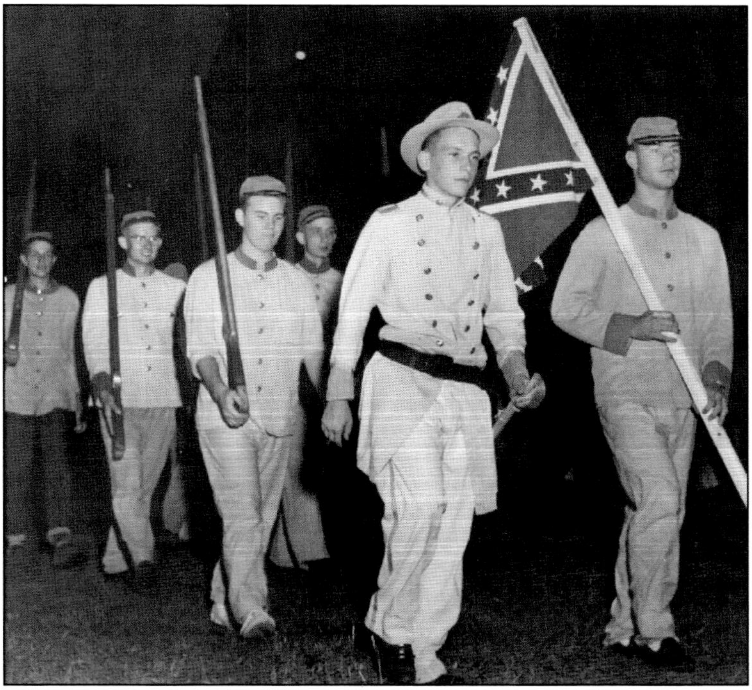

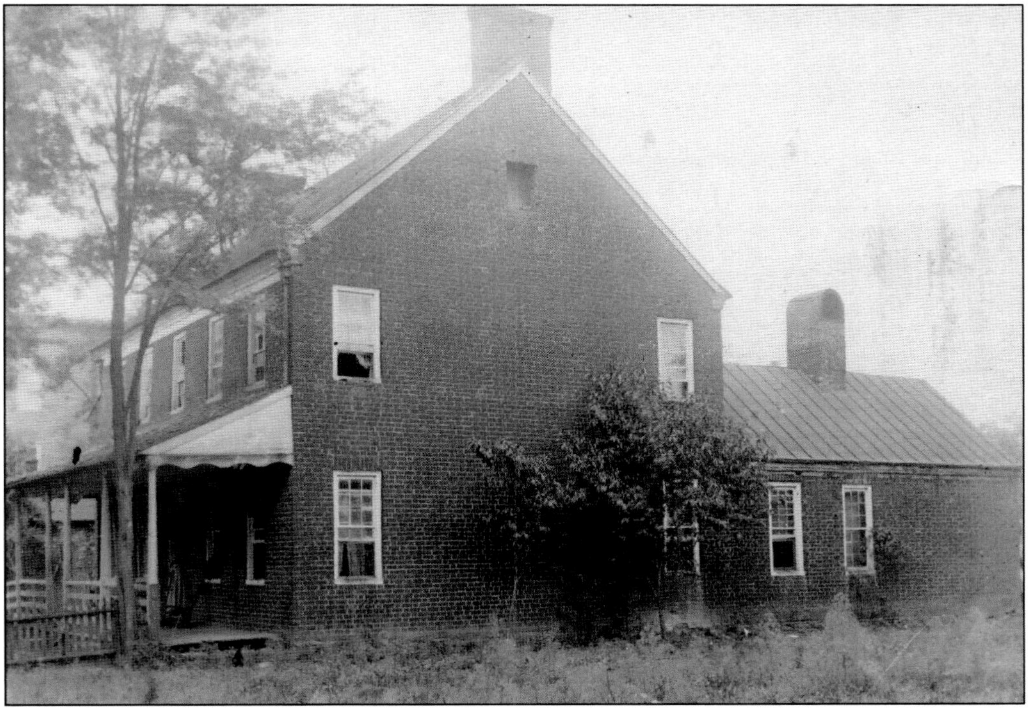

Dinkle Tavern was open and in use during the Civil War. Records indicate that Stonewall Jackson passed by the tavern after defeating Fremont at the Battle of McDowell in Highland County. This is probably how the tavern looked at that time.

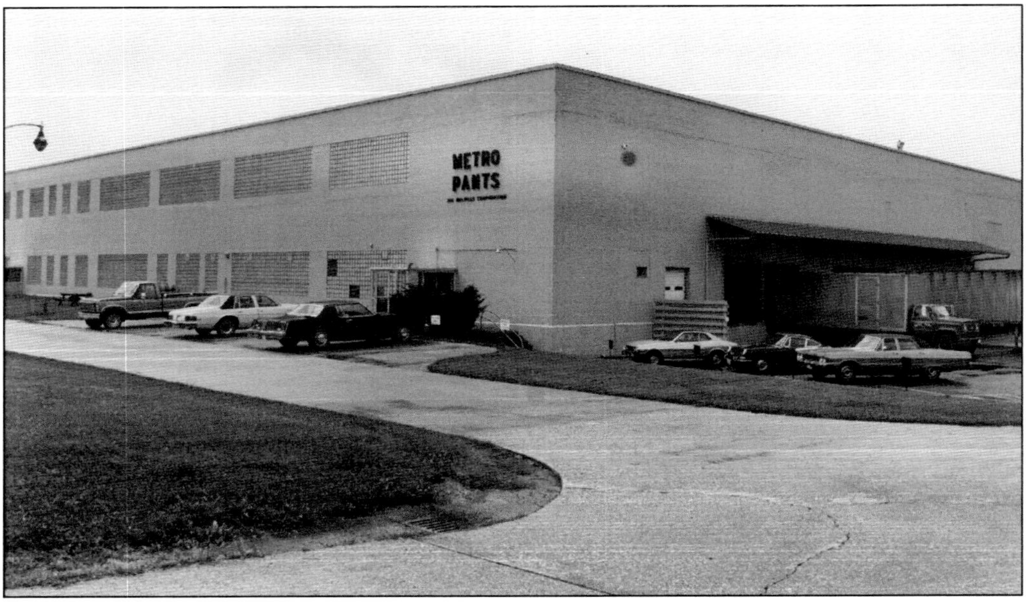


Metro Pants was a division of Melville shoes of Andover, Massachusetts. At their peak, they employed nearly 400 and were known primarily for making uniforms. By the 1970s, the textile business in the United States was dying, and Metro disappeared with many of their compatriots.

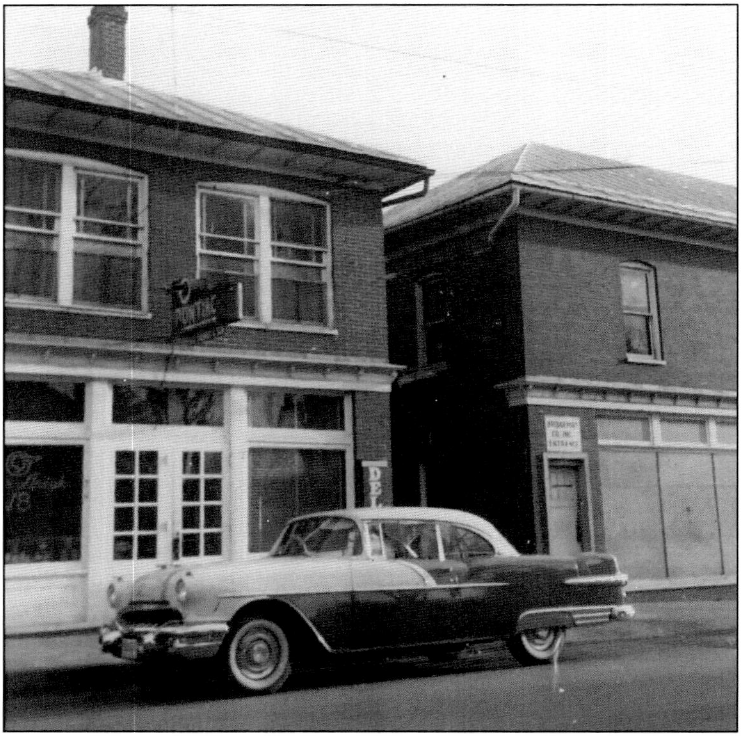

After World War II, new car dealerships sprung up across the land. Even towns the size of Bridgewater would often have a General Motors or Ford dealership. When D. S. Thomas opened at this site, he used both buildings shown in this picture to sell Pontiacs to the Bridgewater community. The trend of small town dealerships soon faded. In response to declining business, Mr. Thomas first reduced the dealership to one building housing only a few cars but eventually closed the doors permanently.

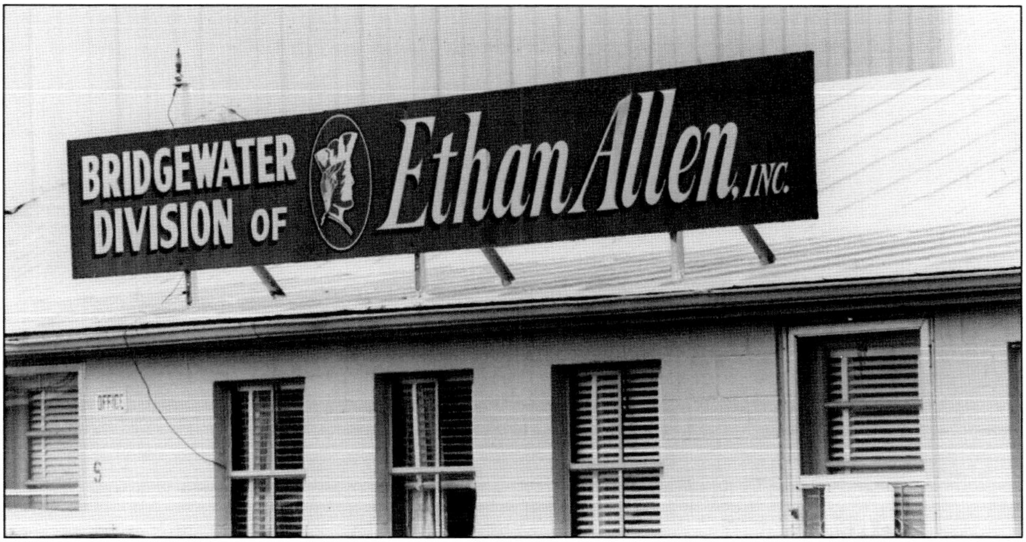


While the name changed several times, Ethan Allen provided gainful employment to area residents for nearly 100 years. The original enterprise started as Thuma and Dovel Woodworking and was located near the woolen mill on North River. Following a serious fire, the operation was moved to Chesapeake Avenue where the building still stands. At that time, they sold furniture to Ethan Allen, but a few years later, Ethan Allen purchased the operation and renamed it.

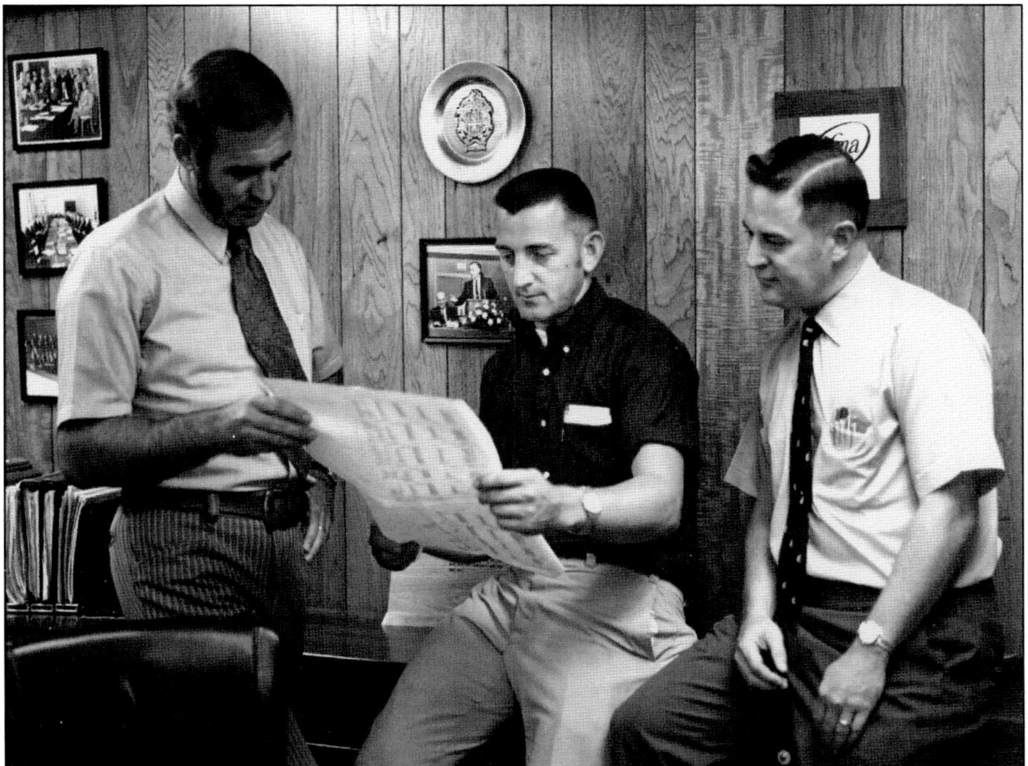

After World War II, Ethan Allen had 36 employees but could produce 5,000 to 6,000 tables in a week. Pictured here from left to right are Ray Dinkel, Harry DePoy, and Ed Stickley looking over a production schedule at Bridgewater Furniture Corporation in 1965.

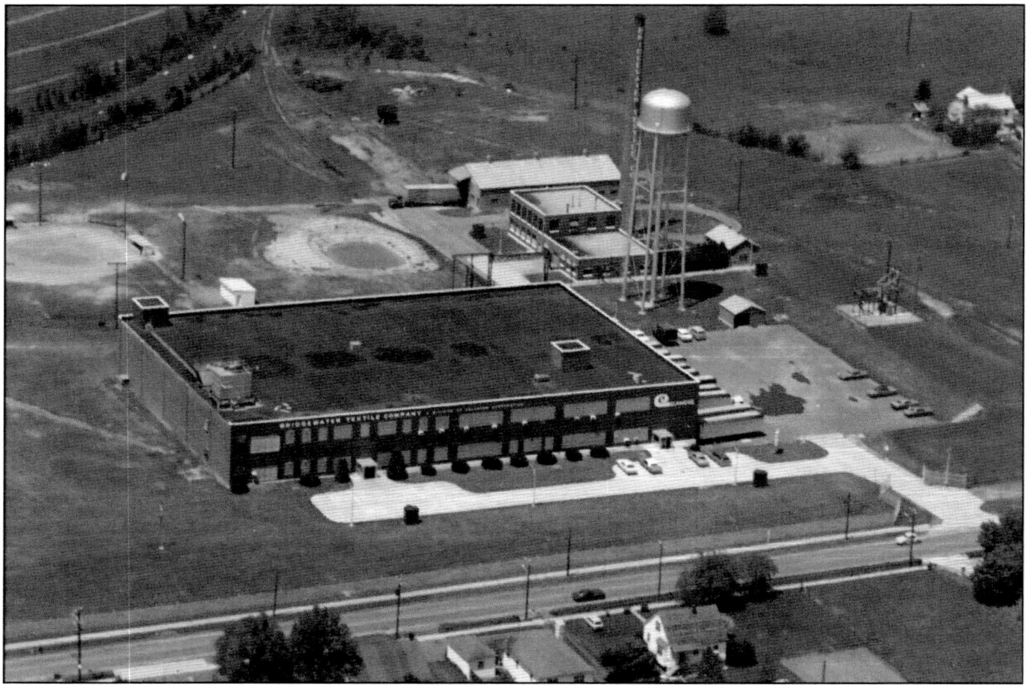

Celanese Fibers Company, located at 701 North Main Street, came to Bridgewater in the mid-1940s. Originally called the Bridgewater Textile Company, it was part of the post-war boom in textiles that took place throughout the south. The citizens of Bridgewater appreciated Celanese but not only for the jobs they provided; in 1949, when the flood decimated the town's water system, they stepped in and provided drinking water for the residents of the town.

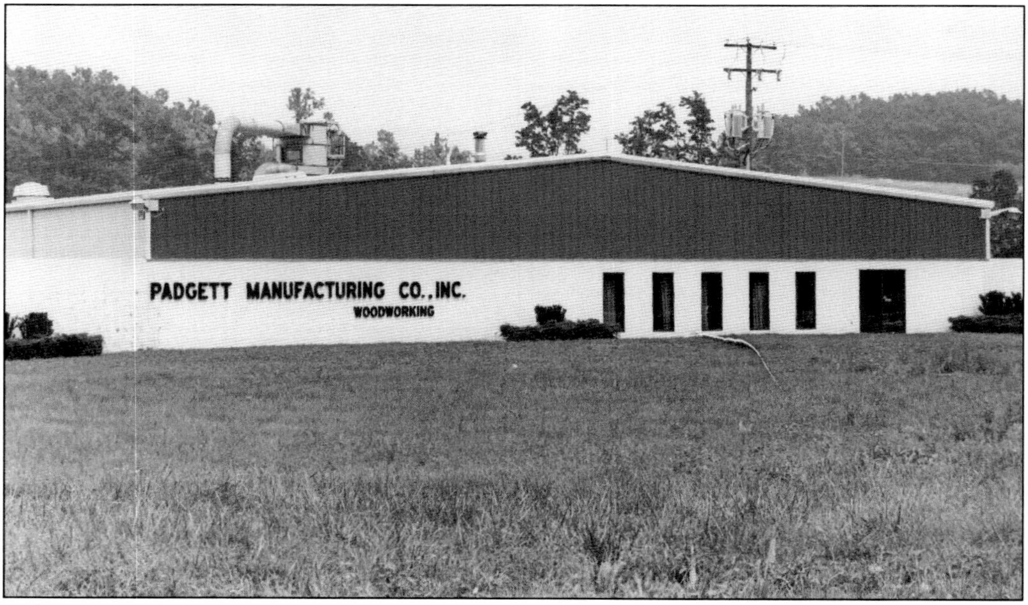


Padgett Manufacturing Company is located on Old River Road and has been in the woodworking business since 1967. While their product line has varied over the years, some of the more notable products include book trucks for the Library of Congress, custom cabinetry, and specialized wooden products for children.

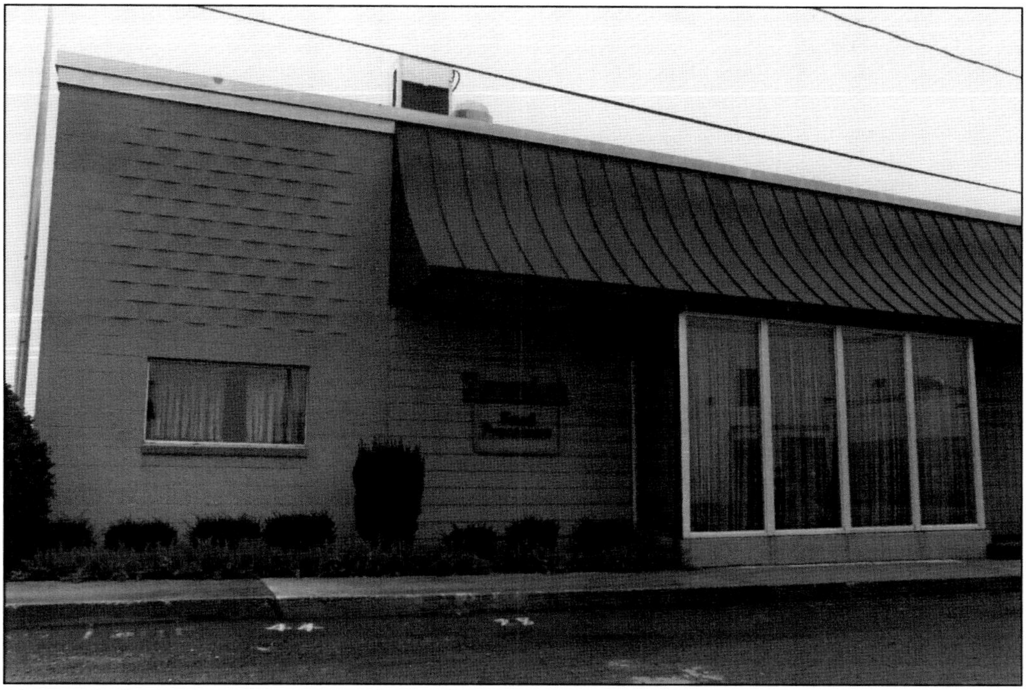

Shenandoah Food Processors was the predecessor to Perdue Farms. This small poultry processor was sold to Perdue in 1984. Over the years, Perdue has expanded their operation in Bridgewater and now employs over 700. Nationwide, Perdue Farms is the third largest poultry producer.

In the midst of the Great Depression, John and Fleta Shickel took a chance that paid off for both their family and the Bridgewater community. They purchased half interest in a small repair business on Dry River Road and began helping the local farm community by sharpening tools, hammering mill saws, and making general repairs for farmers and, eventually, the Chesapeake and Western (C&W) Railway. Since then, the descendants of John Shickel have carried on the business. It has grown from a 900-square-foot wood-frame shop to a modern 50,000-square-foot complex, which continues to serve the agricultural and business community.

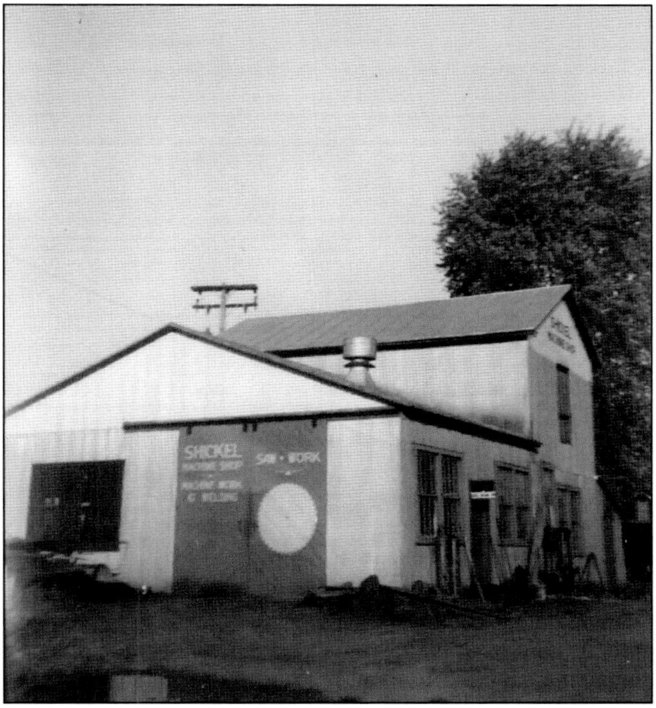

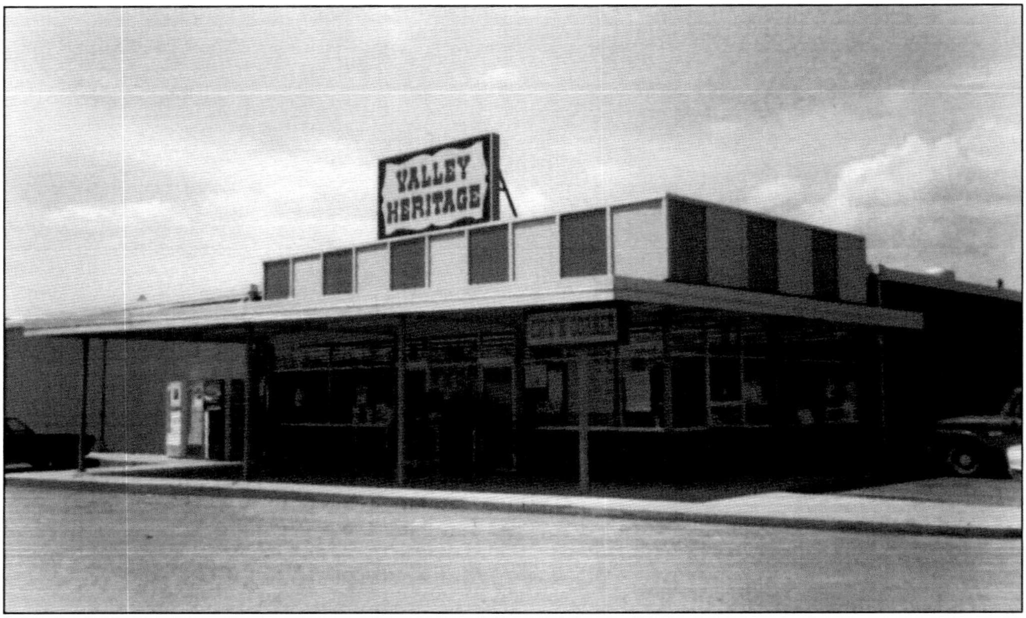


Mick or Mack has closed, as has Bowman's Meat Market and all the other stores from earlier times. Taking their place is the Bridgewater IGA, which started as Valley Heritage nearly 50 years ago. Ralph Eagle, the current owner, opened the Bridgewater IGA at this site in 1973 and probably has the largest business volume of all IGAs in Virginia.

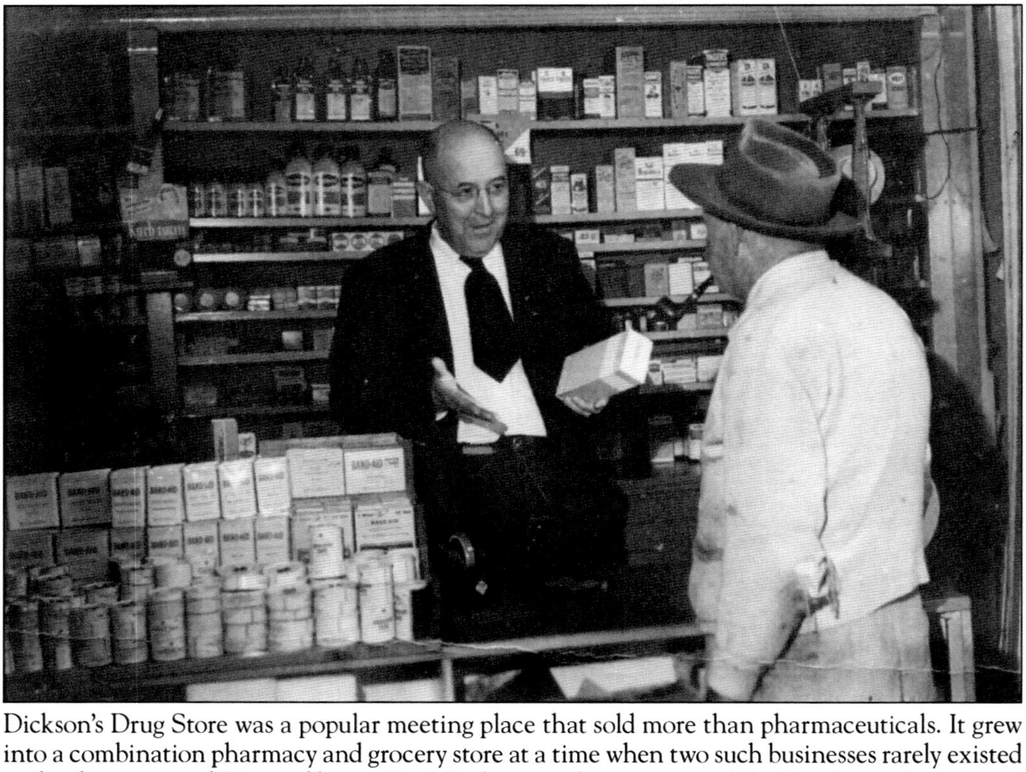

Dickson's Drug Store was a popular meeting place that sold more than pharmaceuticals. It grew into a combination pharmacy and grocery store at a time when two such businesses rarely existed under the same roof. Pictured here, "Doc" Dickson pitches an item to Jake Swecker at the original Dickson's Drug Store.

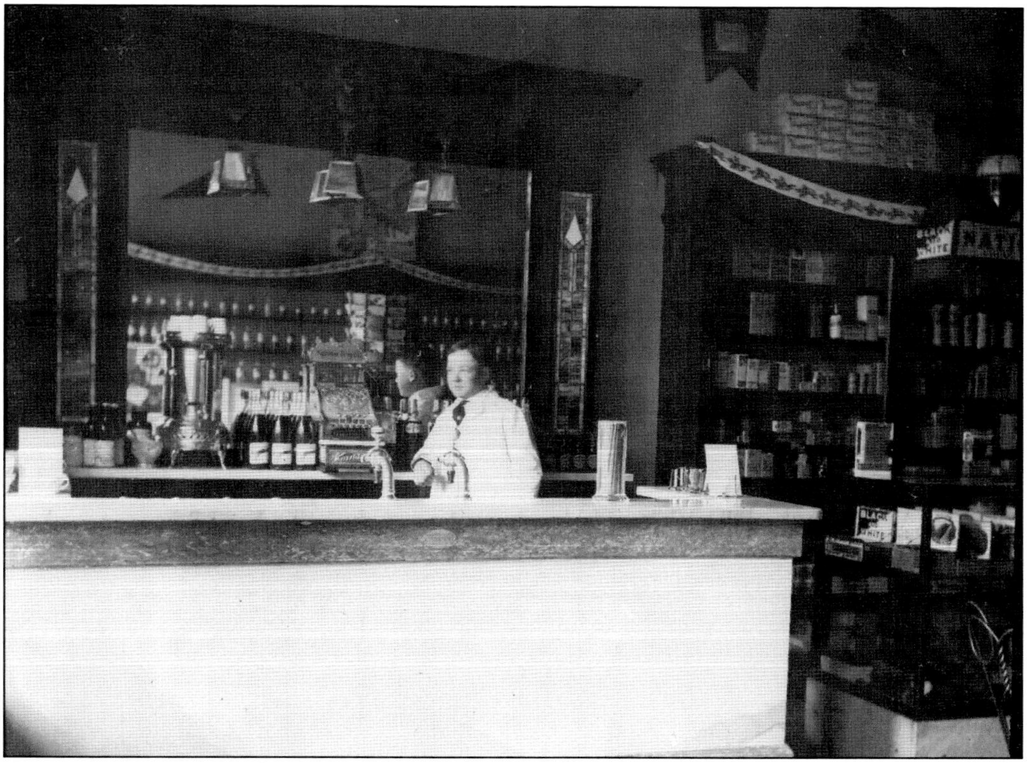

A century ago, most pharmacies contained more than prescriptions and over-the-counter medications. Lunch counters were common, although most were not as elaborate as the one in the original Bridgewater Pharmacy. Ice cream, sodas, sandwiches, and the like were prepared daily by pharmacy employees. At this point in our history, lunch counters were one of the most popular meeting places for citizens to gather.

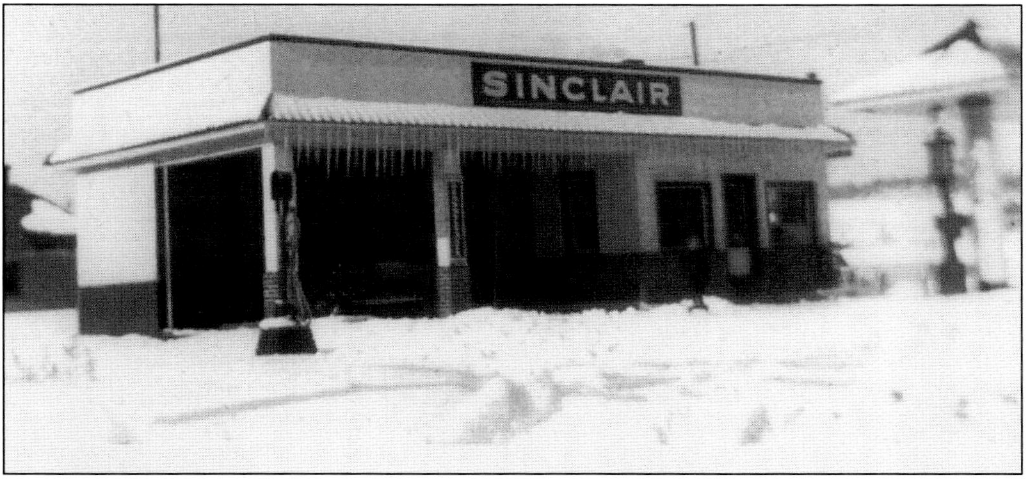


After World War II, the boom of the automobile coincided with an increase in the number of gas stations. During the 1950s and 1960s, the town of Bridgewater had seven such stations. It must be remembered that these were more than typical gas stations. They were truly service establishments where oil, antifreeze, tire pressure, and other important inspections were provided with each fill-up.

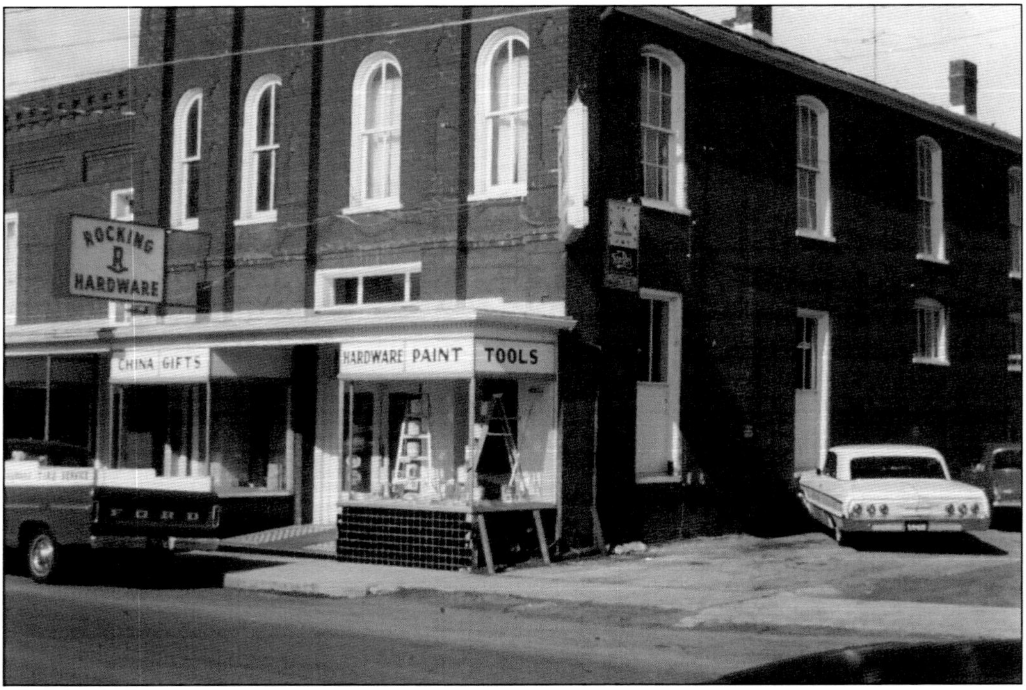


Situated at 205 South Main Street, this was originally Bowman's Hardware Store, but architectural changes make it barely recognizable compared to the former structure. Rocking "R" Hardware occupied this site for many years before moving to a new location. This picture was taken in the mid-1960s.

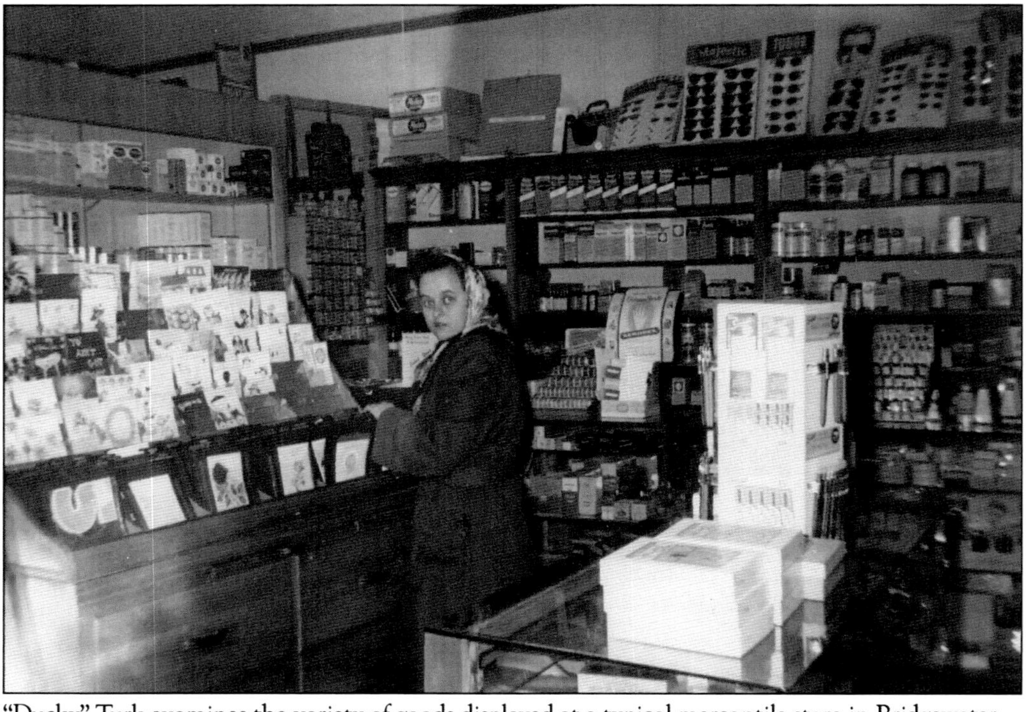

"Ducky" Turk examines the variety of goods displayed at a typical mercantile store in Bridgewater.

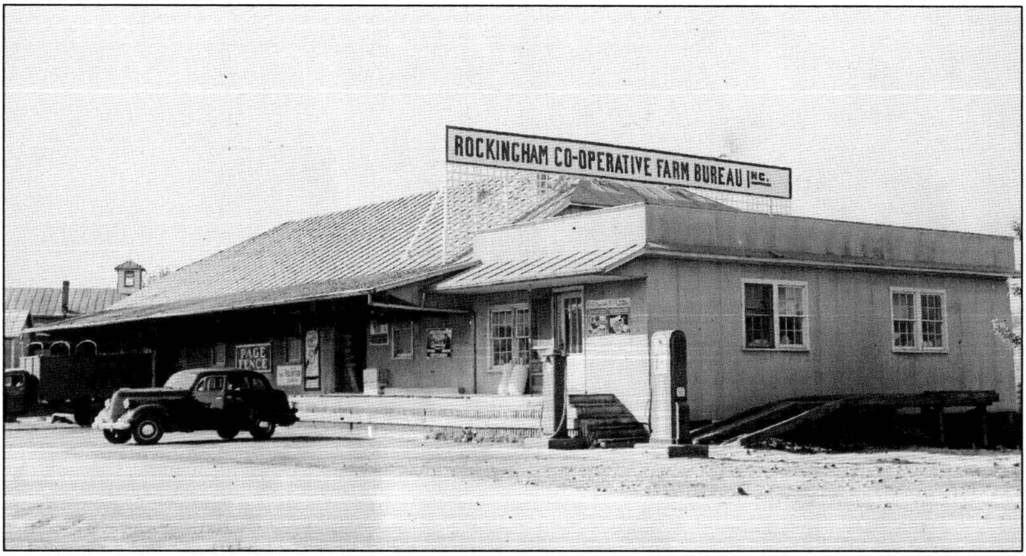


Although a part of Rockingham Cooperative, this company is better known as Valley Heritage to Bridgewater residents. It started more than 50 years ago as a farm cooperative to benefit farmers in purchasing needed items as well as to help with marketing farm goods. It eventually developed into a dry goods store and had a grocery section added. This business is still in Bridgewater and markets mainly farm implements, feed, hardware, plants, and fertilizer.

Bowman's Grocery Store predated the modern supermarket. Of course the selection would be much slimmer than seen today, but the service was unbelievable. It went far beyond bagging groceries. Purchases could be carried to a waiting horse and buggy or even delivered to the customer's home if that was more convenient. If money was tight, the Bowmans would hold the bill until it was more convenient to pay. Like most stores of their time, Bowmans relied more on local farmers than large food distributors. They would buy produce, meat, or other goods from farmers to be resold to the public.

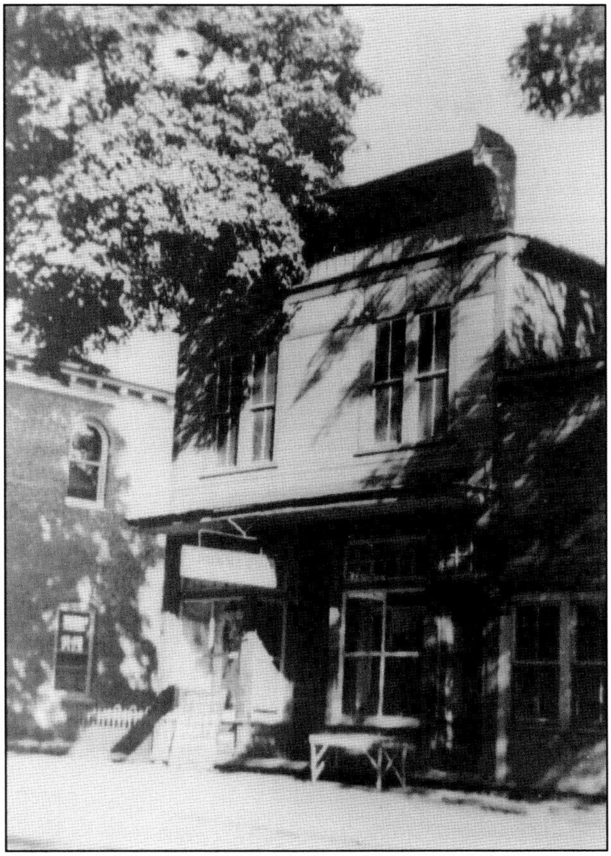

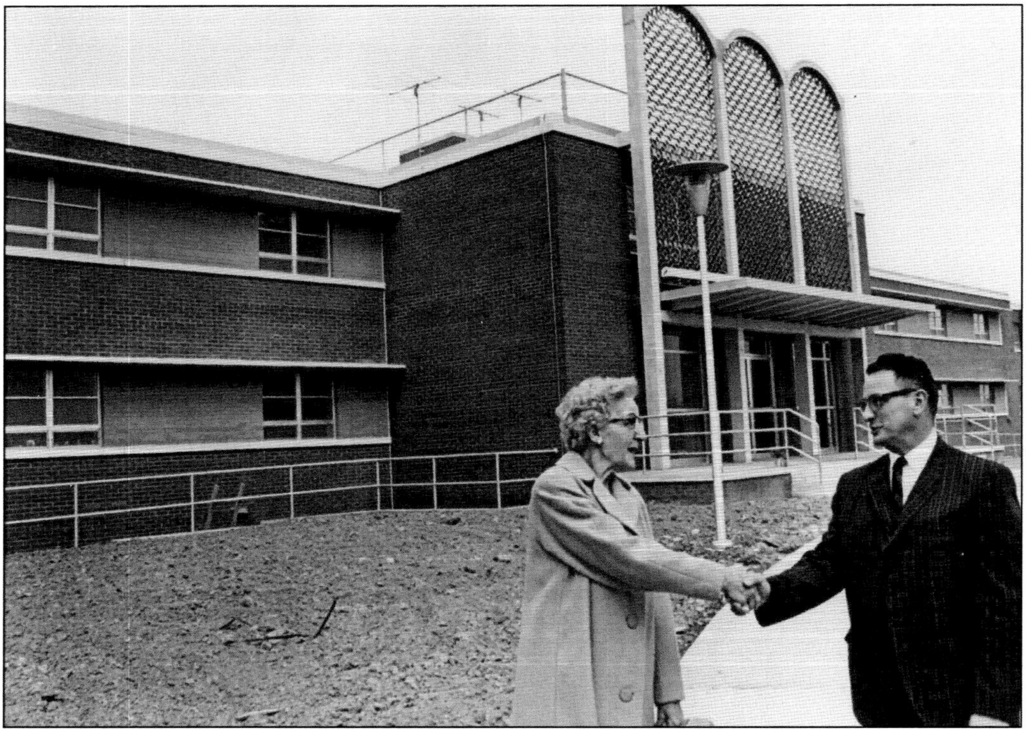

Edith Glick was the first resident of Bridgewater Home. In the picture above, she is welcomed by Dick Stevens, who served as president when the doors of Bridgewater Home (later named Bridgewater Retirement Community) opened in the mid-1960s.

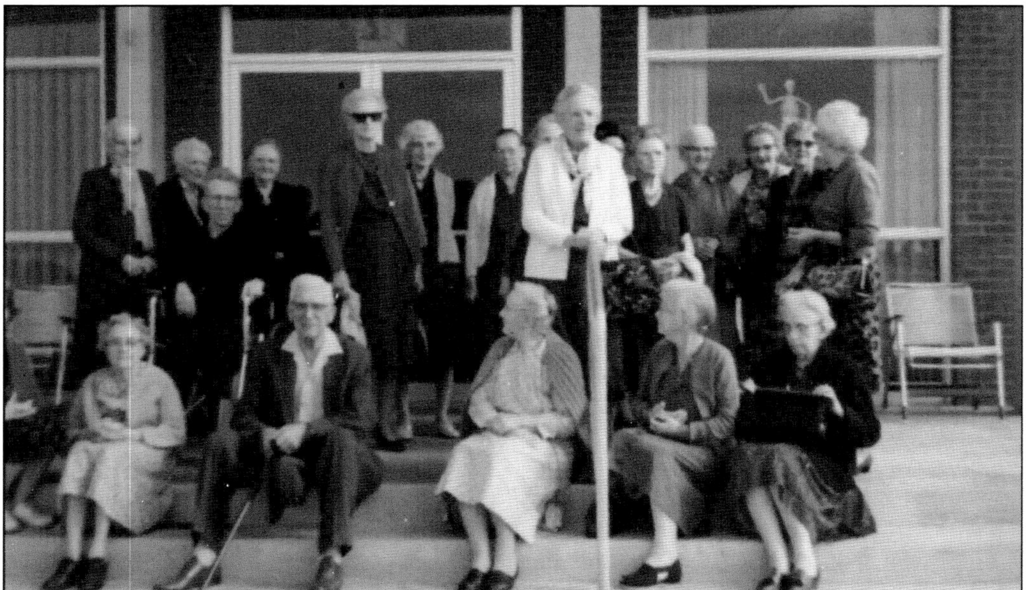

The first residents of Bridgewater Home gather for a group portrait in 1966. Like its neighbor on Dinkel Avenue (Bridgewater College), Bridgewater Home is affiliated with the Church of the Brethren. While the home initially provided only nursing care, they have expanded their operations over the years to include all levels of service for those entering the retirement years.

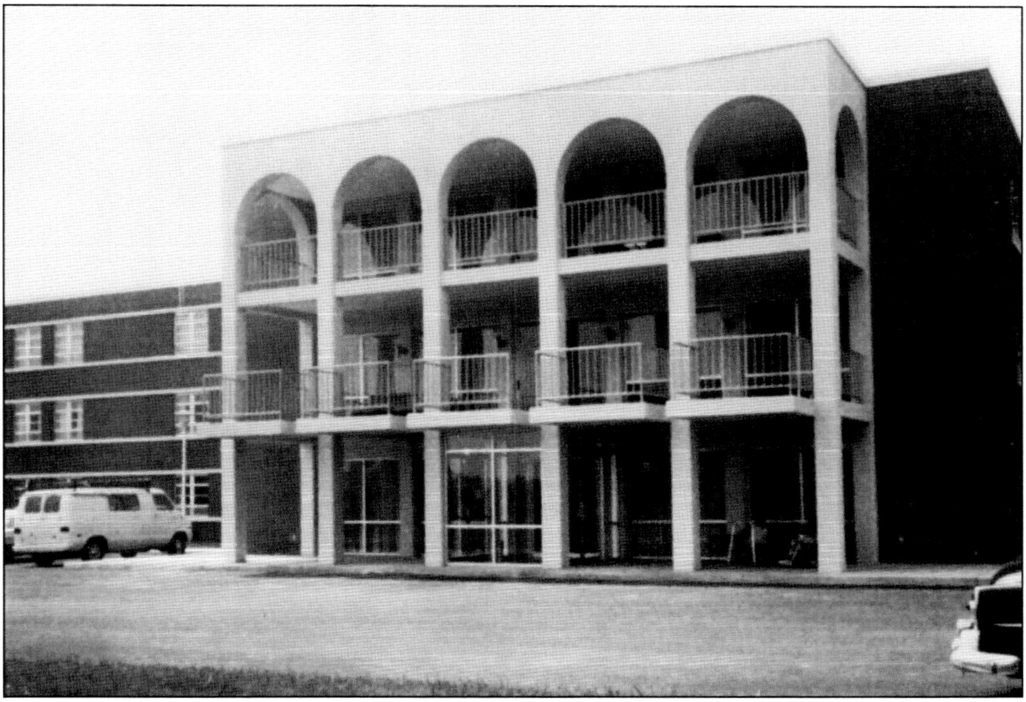

Bridgewater Home today looks very different from this picture taken shortly after the home opened. So much has changed over the last 44 years, but their mission remains the same.

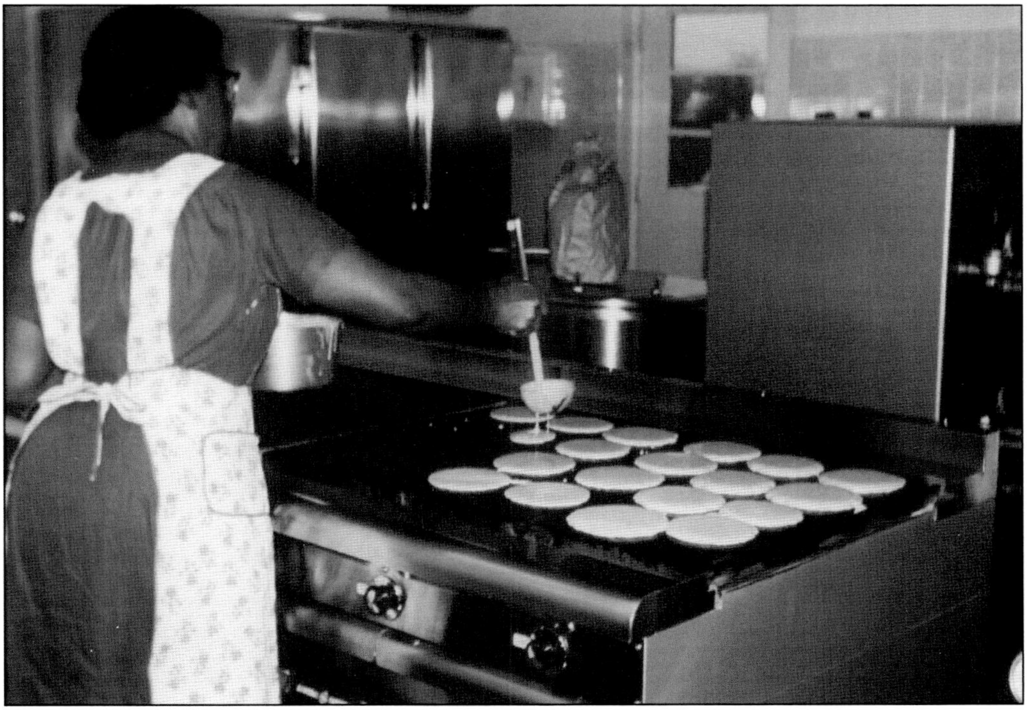

Muriel Whitelow served as a cook at Bridgewater Home for nearly 25 years. She was their first dietary employee and prepared and served the first meal to the new residents on May 1, 1965. She retired in 1986. Her son Carlyle Whitelow still resides in Bridgewater.

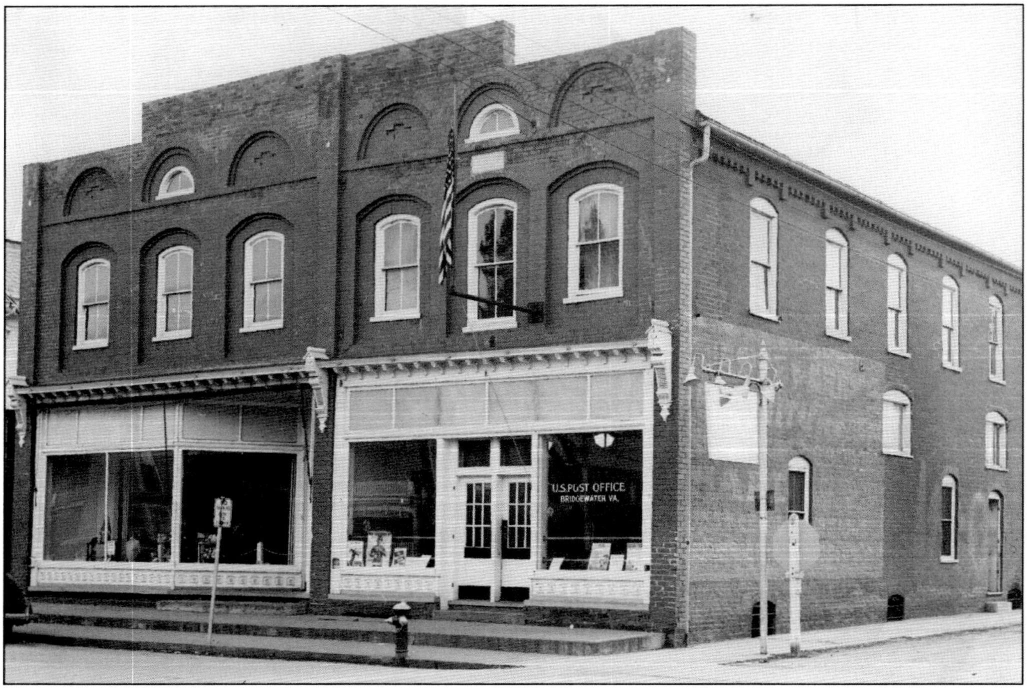


The large building at the corner of Main and East College Streets has been the home for department stores, Bridgewater College, and at one time, the post office. In 1889, when a major fire damaged the only building at the college, this site was rented for classroom space.

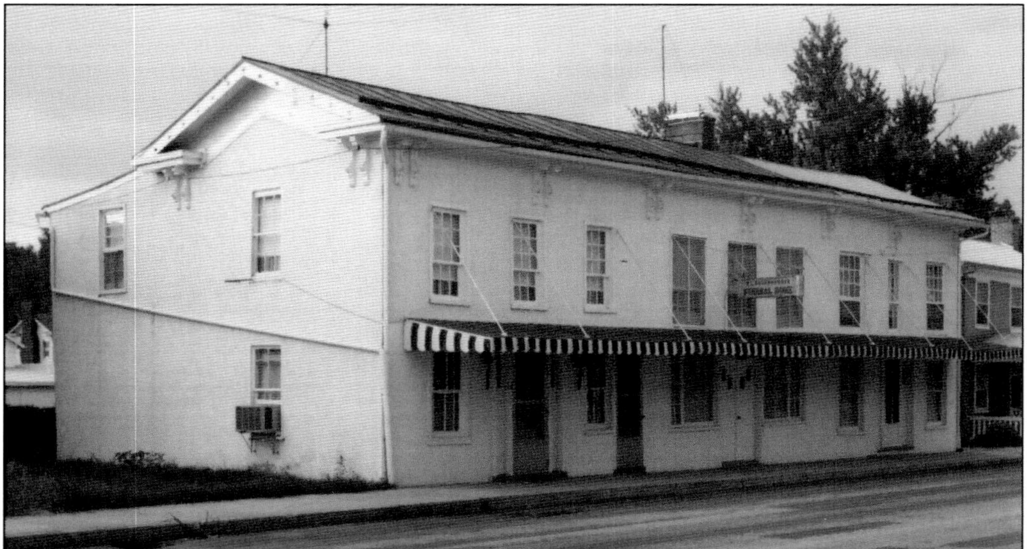

W. L. Rosenberger came to Bridgewater early in the 20th century and opened Rosenberger Funeral Home on South Main Street. After the building was damaged by the 1949 flood, Rosenberger decided to sell his business to Loving Service from Harrisonburg, who conducted services at this site for only a year or two. In 1951, McMullen Funeral Home purchased the business and served the public for the next 39 years. In 1990, it became Johnson Funeral Home and is still in operation. The original building shown here was torn down in 1977, and a newer structure was erected in its place.

# *Five*

# COMMUNITY

From the day the Magills arrived at the banks of North River to the present time, individuals and organizations have stepped forward to lead the Bridgewater community. Some historians think events control history, while others focus on the men or women who make a difference. In most disputes of this nature, both sides are correct. Certainly Bridgewater's history has been shaped by natural disasters, wars, depressions, and fires, but people have been more of a factor than any of these events.

From the Dinkle brothers laying out the town in the 1830s, to their direct descendant Hallie Dinkel leading Bridgewater as mayor in 2010, individuals have made all the difference in the town's evolution. Surely this book will not list every man and woman who has contributed to the progress of Bridgewater. Indeed it would take a massive volume to compile that list. But the people on the following pages will give a snapshot of those who have made a difference.

Leadership is difficult and utterly different from popularity. At key moments in history, those in charge have to make difficult decisions that may not be popular with their citizenry. With the passage of time, it is easy to see whether a decision was good or bad. Unfortunately being a leader requires one to choose a course of action without the advantage of hindsight.

One can only imagine what was it like for Mayor J. A. Riddel in 1920 when he had to tell the voters that taxes would be increased 400 percent to replace a defective water system installed only seven years earlier. Mayor Riddel could have blamed his predecessors or passed his responsibilities on to another generation, but true leadership called for something else. In the end, the public accepted his course of action, because it was the right thing to do.

Like it has been said earlier, everyone's story cannot be told, but please be assured that the men and women seen on the following pages have made Bridgewater a better place to live.

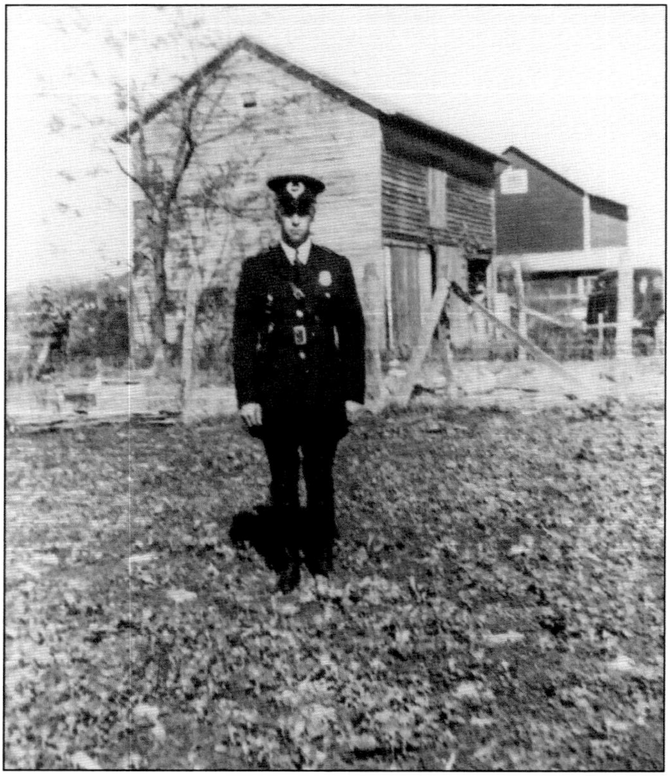

From its inception in 1835 until the 1950s, the police force in Bridgewater generally consisted of one man who held the position of town sergeant. Law enforcement was different in those days. In many cases, the sergeant would be asked to provide his own transportation and have other duties, such as turning on the water pump at the springhouse. Pictured at left is town sergeant Berlin Bodkin, who served Bridgewater in the years following World War II.

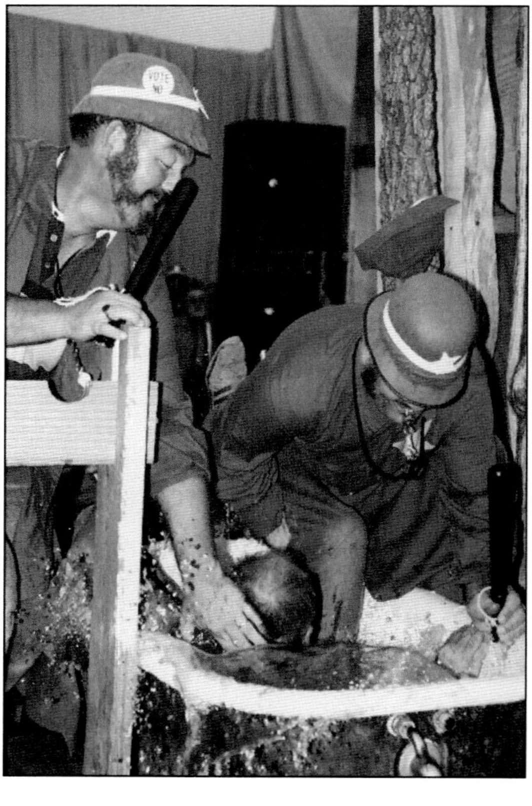

Everyone tried to avoid the Keystone Cops during Bridgewater's anniversary celebrations. For minor infractions such as no facial hair, offenders could find themselves dunked in a bathtub or put in stocks. Here is one unfortunate citizen receiving his punishment from "officers of the law."

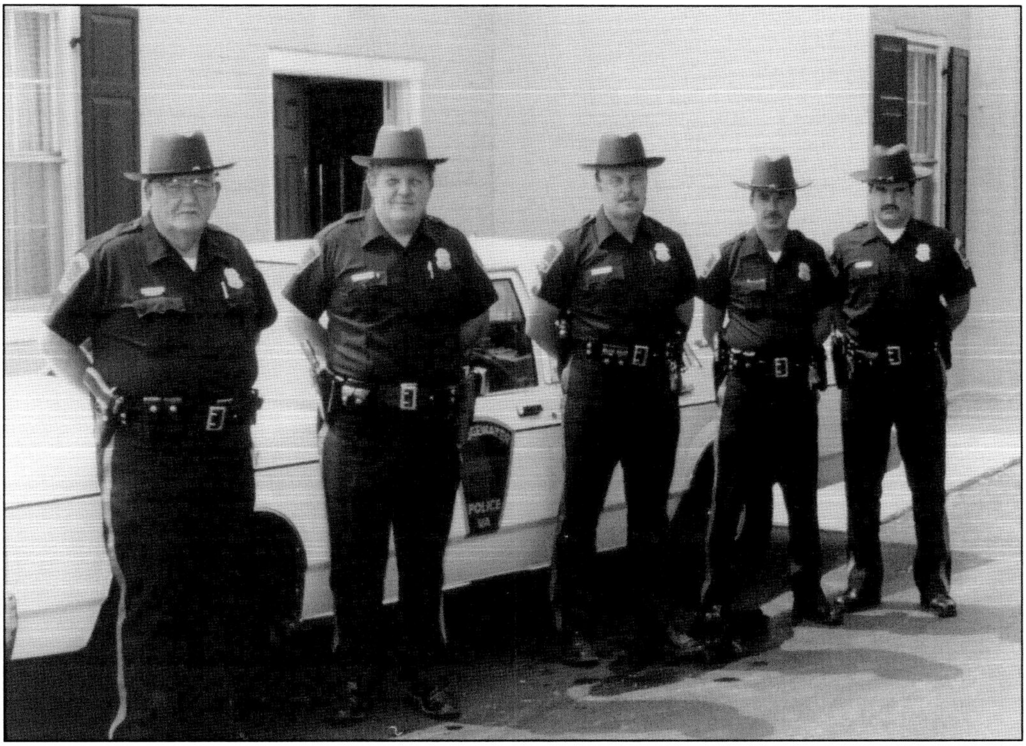

By 1985, the Bridgewater Police Department had grown to five men who provided around-the-clock coverage. Pictured here from left to right are George Harvey, police chief Mark Payne, Sgt. Bob Hill, Ron Dove, and Harry Deavers. In 2010, the department has grown to nine members, including both males and females. Sargeant Hill is now Chief Hill and has served the Bridgewater community for nearly 35 years.

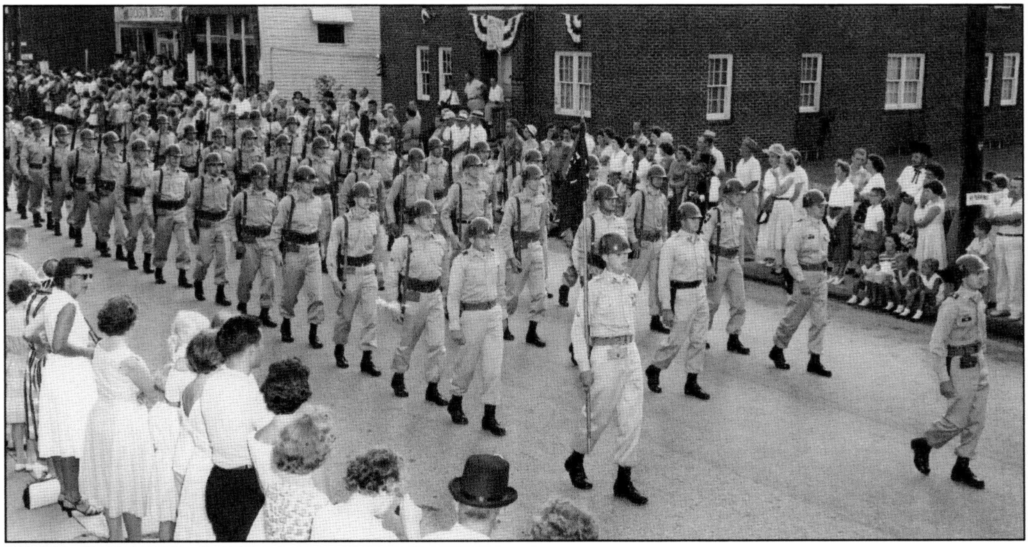

The National Guard assisted Bridgewater during its darkest days in 1949. They provided security, directed traffic, and helped citizens in many ways following the devastating flood of that summer. The National Guard has also celebrated happier moments with the town such as this one in 1960 during the 125th anniversary. (BCAMML.)

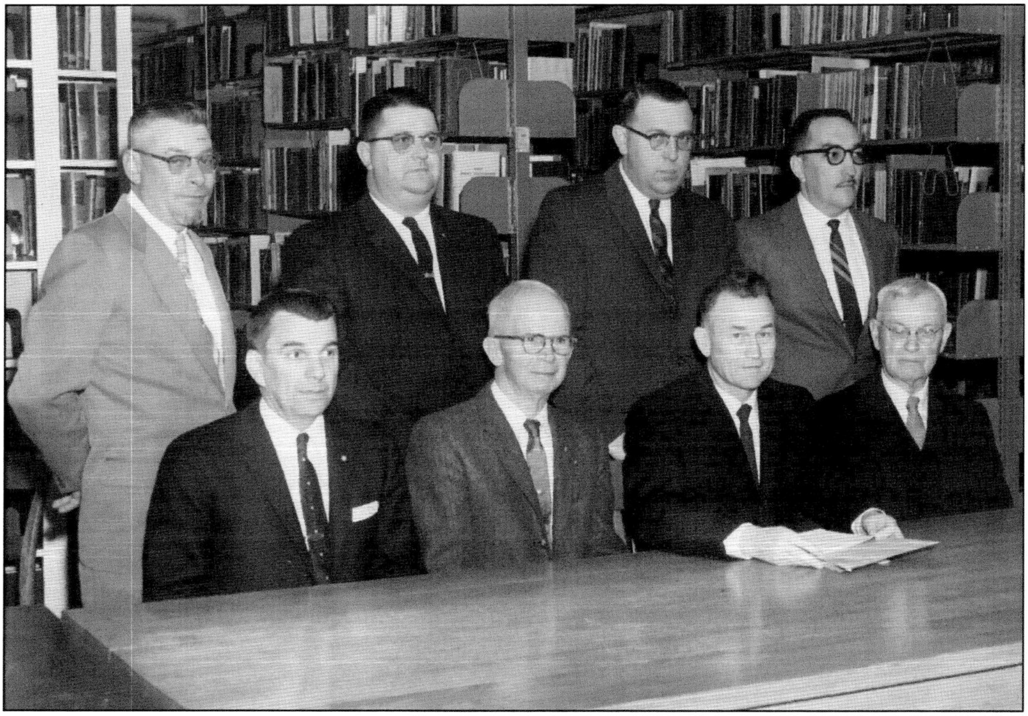

This is the Bridgewater Town Council and other elected officials in 1960 when the town celebrated its 125th anniversary. Pictured from left to right are (first row) M. B. Plecker, assessor C. P. Graham, Mayor C. E. May, and treasurer W. H. Sanger; (second row) Earl Gordon, Roland Arey, William Hisey, and Clyde Pugh. Carlton Shickel and recorder Adam Miller are absent. (BCAMML.)

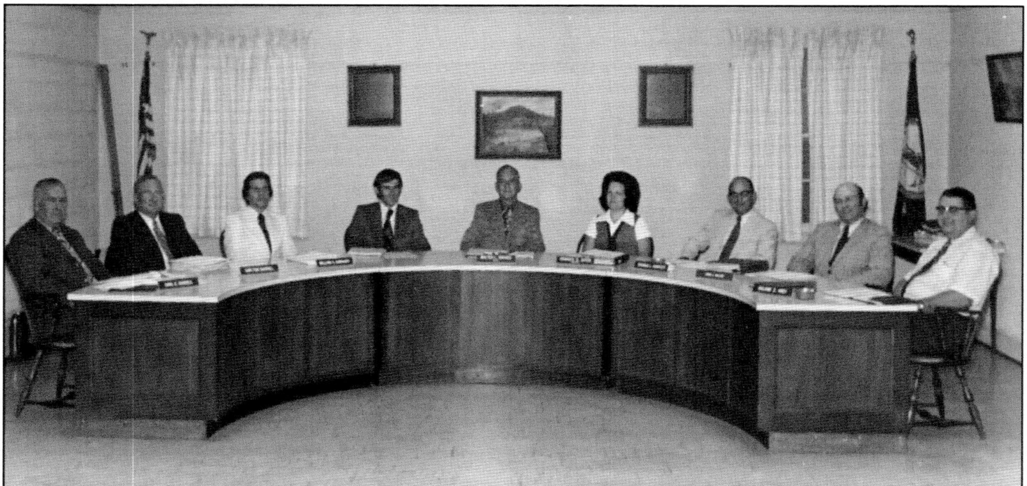

The 1973 town council hired the town's first full-time administrator to handle the day-to-day operations of the town. Pictured from left to right are Carl Rhodes, Carlton Shickel, William Earhart, administrator Bob Holton, Mayor Walter Hodges, clerk Frances Suter, Tom Huntley, John L. Miller, and Roland Z. Arey.

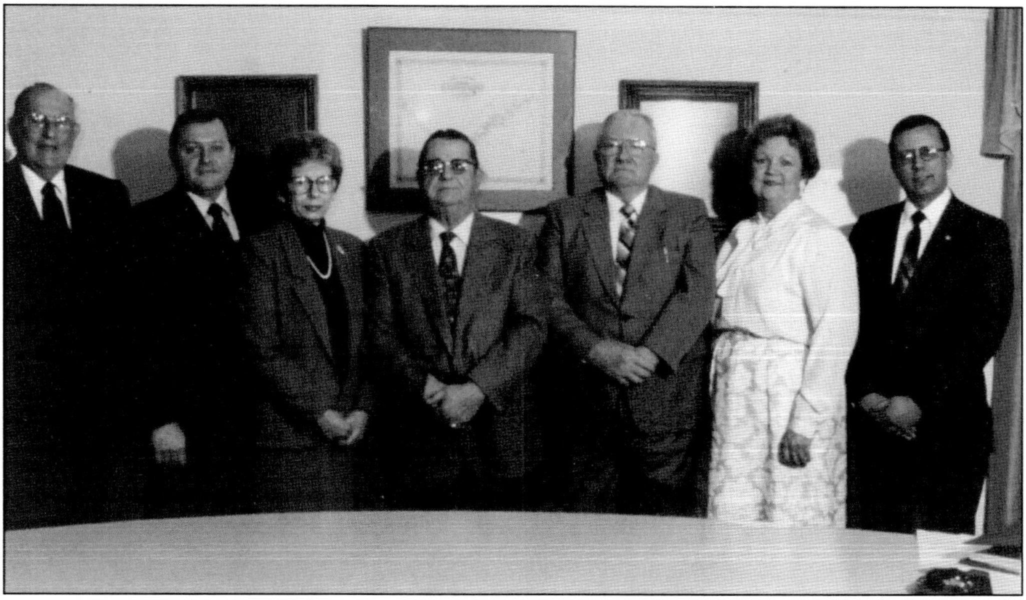

The 1986 election was a significant one for Bridgewater. That year, the first women were elected to town council. Pictured from left to right are Cliff Riddel, Bob Wolfe, Nancy Trout, Mayor Roland Z. Arey, Carlton Shickel, Rosetta Harris, and Melvin Wampler. Rosetta Harris continues on the council to this day as vice mayor and chairs the community relations committee. Nancy Trout's efforts while on council to beautify Bridgewater are seen every day in the trees, shrubs, and flower beds planted throughout town during her term in office.

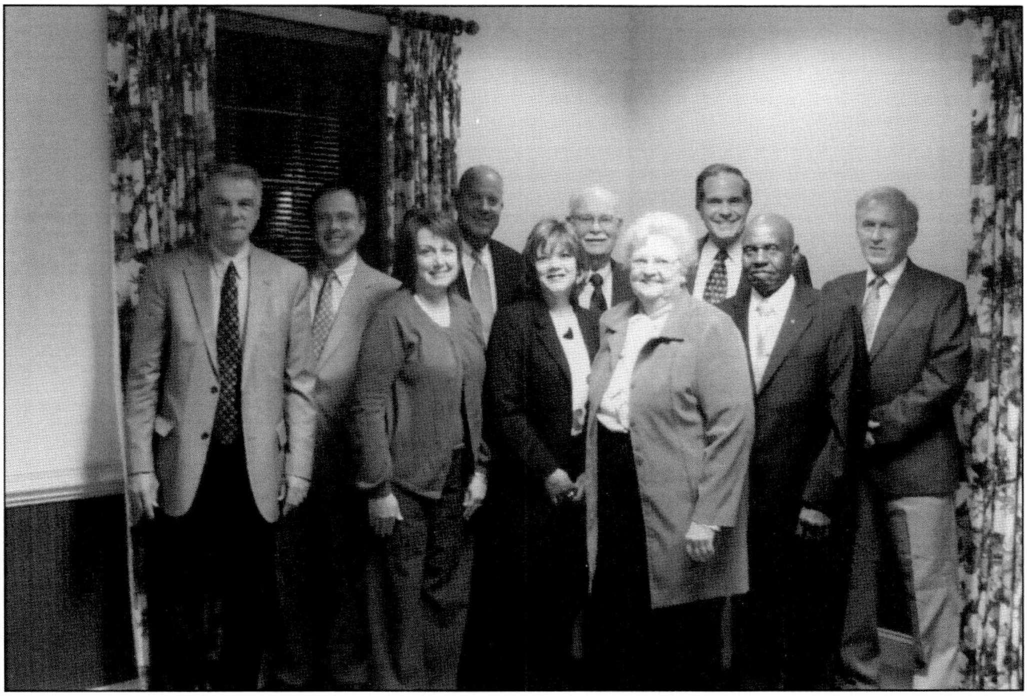

This picture shows the leadership in Bridgewater in 2010. From left to right are Bill Miracle, attorney Jay Litten, treasurer Cherie Bowen, Fontaine Canada, Dillina Stickley, Mayor Hallie Dinkel, vice mayor Rosetta Harris, Ted Flory, Roscoe Burgess, and administrator Bob Holton.

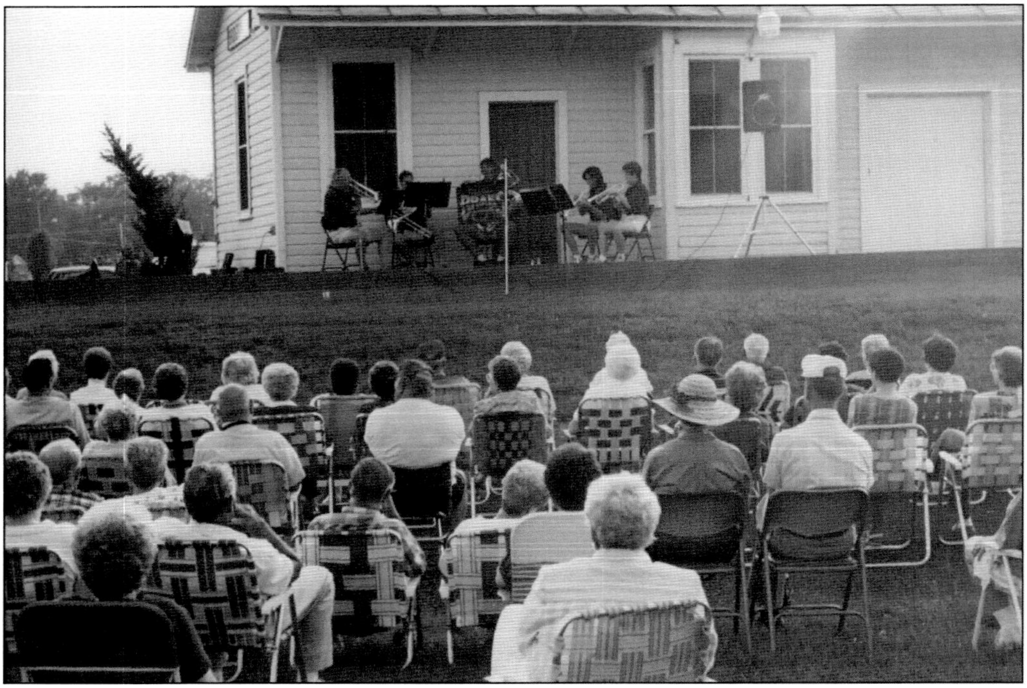

The old depot, which had been left in disrepair a decade earlier, was refurbished and moved to Oakdale Community Park on Mount Crawford Avenue. Here it is used for a variety of events, but the most notable is the summer concert series where area bands provide musical presentations on Sunday evenings throughout the summer. The performances are free to the public and provide a wide assortment of music.

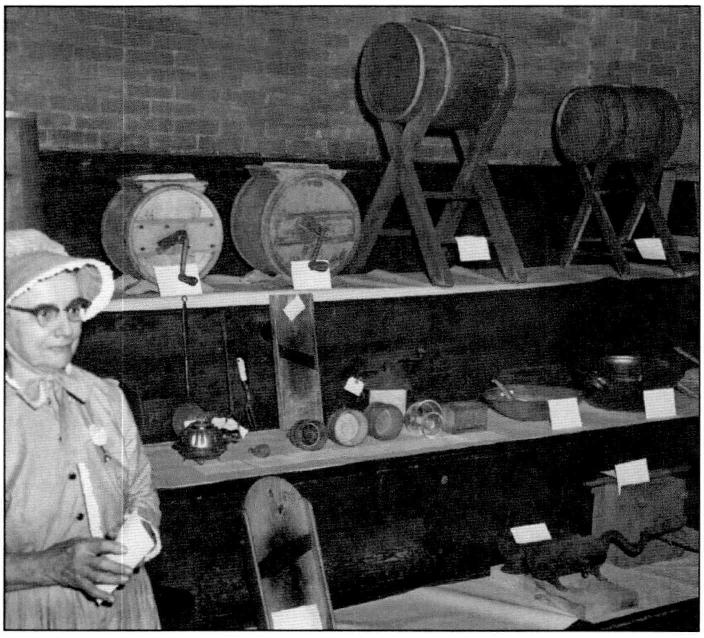

Every 25 years, Bridgewater makes a special effort to remember the past. This is done through a variety of entertainment venues as well as a historical review of how the town came to be. Displayed here are a variety of butter churns that were used in the later 1800s and early 1900s. Butter made in these churns was not only consumed by those that made the commodity but was also exchanged for goods or services from area stores or professionals. (BCAMML.)

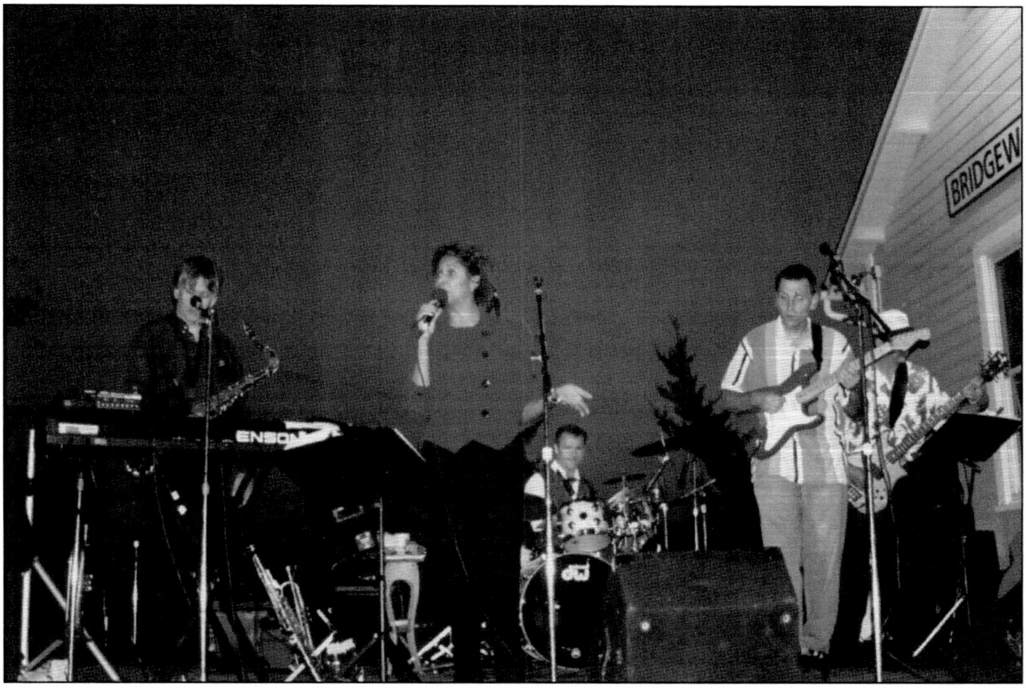


Every small town needs something to celebrate. For most, it is the Fourth of July, while others might devote time and money to a Christmas parade and festive celebration. In Bridgewater's case, the end of summer is a time for music, food, rides, and fireworks. Each Labor Day, 3,000 to 5,000 young and old gather together to listen to a variety of music, enjoy food prepared by local churches and organizations, and close the day with a spectacular fireworks display.

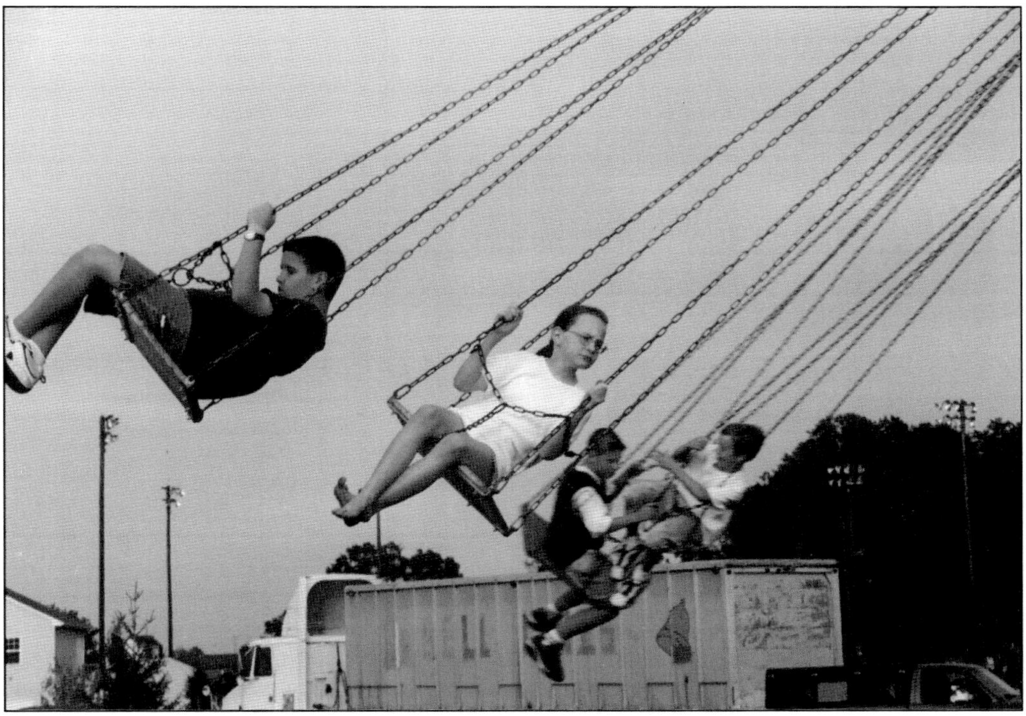

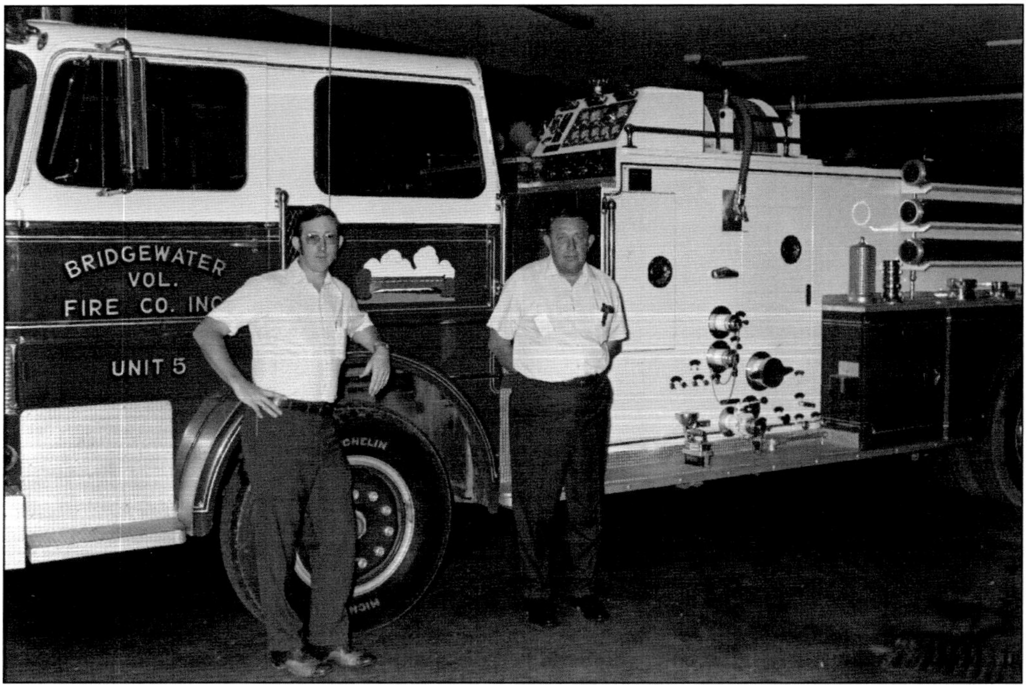


Several disastrous fires in the community started people thinking about the need for volunteer firefighters. In 1938, the Bridgewater Volunteer Fire Company was organized, and by 1940, they ordered their first fire truck. The picture above, taken in the late 1960s, shows Pete Huffman and Bill Hisey, two longtime leaders in this important organization.

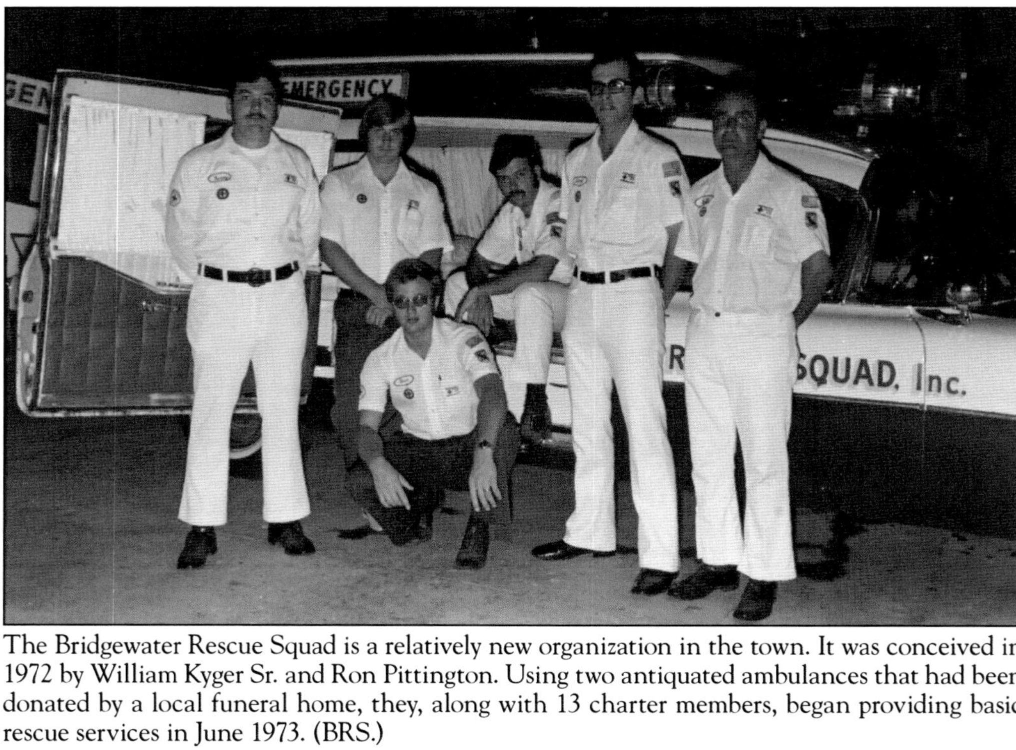


The Bridgewater Rescue Squad is a relatively new organization in the town. It was conceived in 1972 by William Kyger Sr. and Ron Pittington. Using two antiquated ambulances that had been donated by a local funeral home, they, along with 13 charter members, began providing basic rescue services in June 1973. (BRS.)

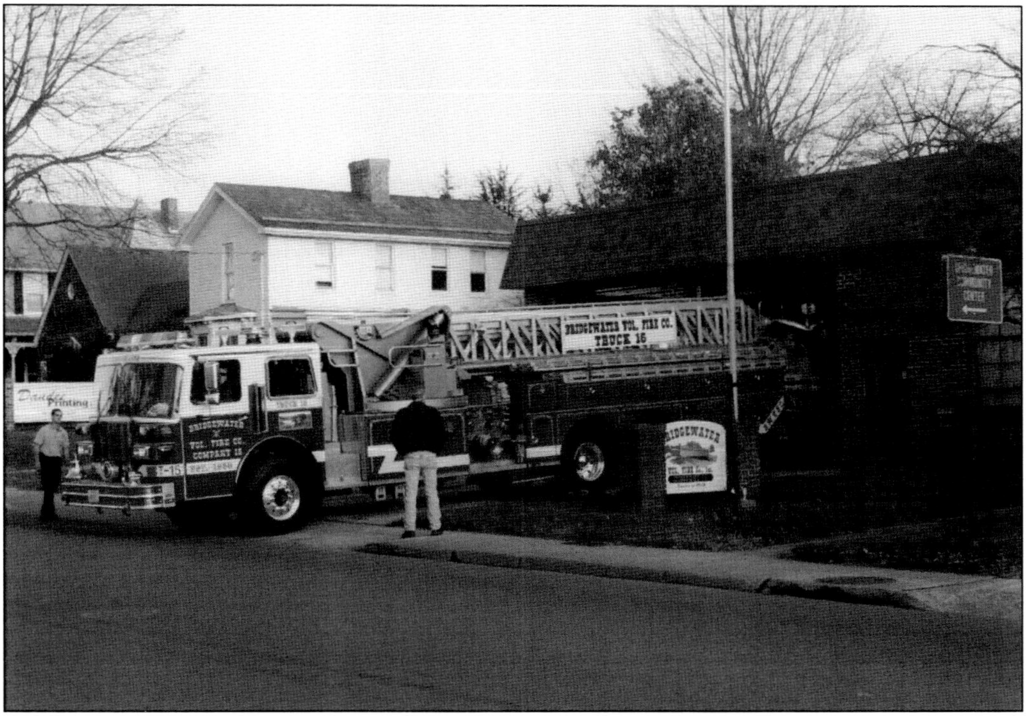


When first organized, the Bridgewater Volunteer Fire Company operated out of an old garage located behind town hall. In 1950, they built a fire station on the east side of Main Street that is still in use. Over the years, the size of the department has grown and today includes not only more fire engines but full-time paid personnel in addition to numerous volunteers. (BRS.)

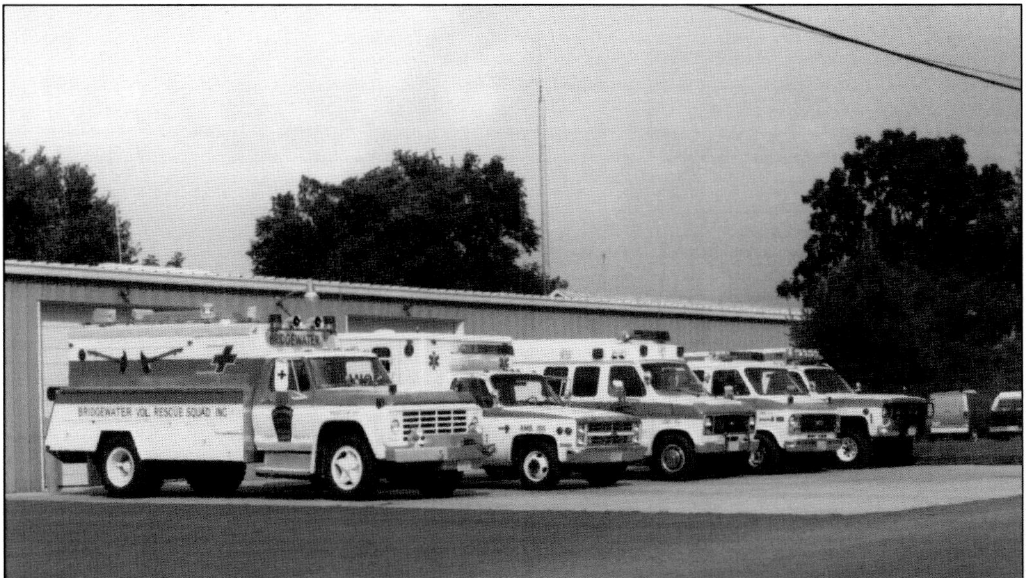

By the time this picture was taken in 1985, the squad had grown to six ambulances plus a crash truck and was serving an area over 600 square miles. Today they have moved to modern facilities on Don Litten Parkway and continue to serve the community and surrounding area with the same drive and determination that existed when they were founded in 1972.

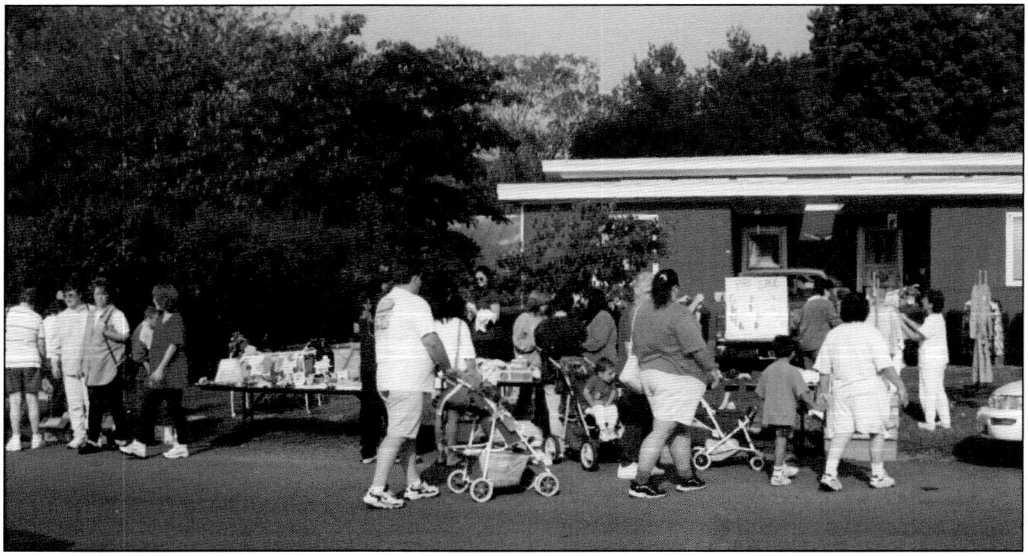

Every spring and fall, the town council sponsors a community-wide yard sale that draws such a large crowd that many residential streets are blocked. Guests come from as far away as Ohio and other states bordering Virginia. Many of these people are former residents of Bridgewater who use this special occasion to revisit their hometown and rekindle memories and friendships from days gone by.

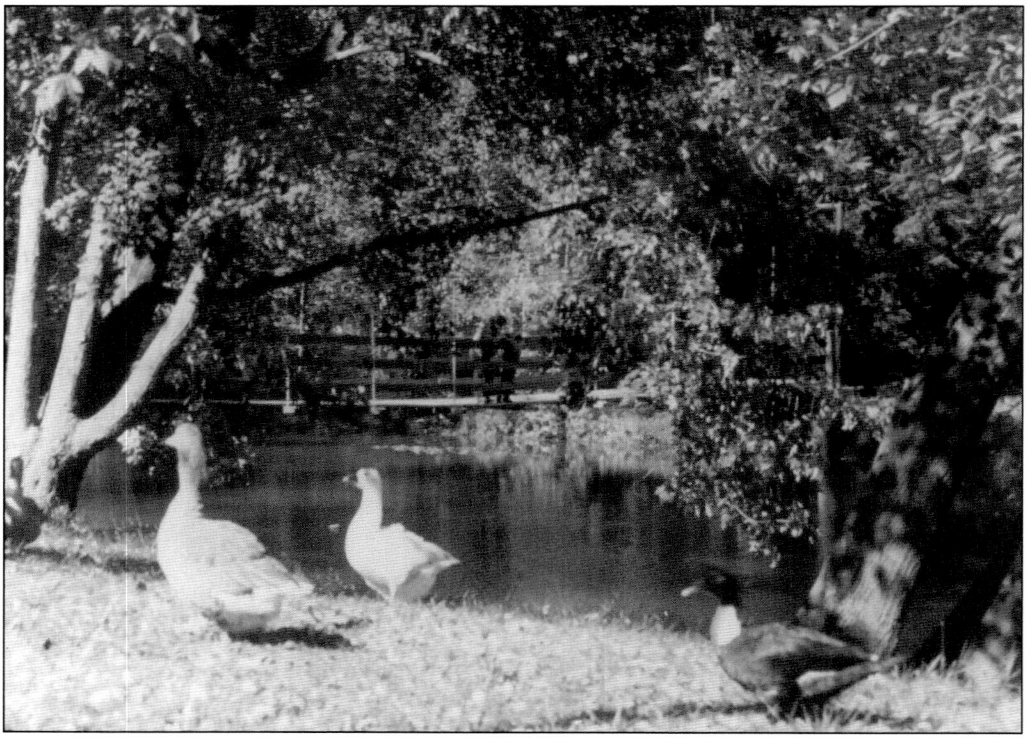

Wildwood Park began as a private club but was purchased by Bridgewater in the mid-1960s. It is perhaps the most beautiful natural setting in town and is filled with young and old every day during the warmer months.

# *Six*

# Crossing North River

Jacob Dinkle is credited with building the first bridge across North River at Magills' Ford, near where the present bridge stands. It was described as a low bridge set on posts and lying near the water. Presumably this structure was damaged or destroyed by floodwaters, because historical documents state that another bridge was built by Abram S. Williams in 1853.

This bridge only lasted nine years, or until 1862, when Thomas "Stonewall" Jackson ordered the bridge to be burned to slow a possible advance of Union soldiers. Often during the Civil War, bridges were burned to impede the progress of opposing forces or to prevent fresh troops from reinforcing weary armies. Some battles were fought and lost while idle troops watched from the other side of the river, unable to help their comrades.

Near as can be found in historic records, this bridge was not replaced until after the Civil War. Interestingly Jackson made a temporary bridge near this location by placing six-horse wagons in the stream alongside one another with their tongues upstream and then planking them over. He used this makeshift bridge on May 19, 1862, to advance his entire army across North River on its way to Harrisonburg.

The third bridge was completed in October 1866 by John W. Woods, who is also credited with constructing four other bridges in Rockingham County between 1866 and 1870. This bridge was noted for its support in the middle. Unfortunately the northern half of this bridge was swept away by a flood on September 29, 1870. Three months later, Col. William F. Pifer completed a fourth bridge that also had a middle support. It, too, met its demise in floodwaters on November 24, 1877.

By April 1878, the fifth bridge had been completed by William H. Grove and is the one commonly seen in town letterhead and publications. It crossed at a length of 240 feet or more and is said to be the longest single-span wooden bridge in the world.

In their May 1916 meeting, the Rockingham County Board of Supervisors awarded the contract for the construction of Bridgewater's sixth bridge to the Bridge and Iron Company of Roanoke. Their low bid of $8,766 included removal of the wooden structure, completion of all the mason work, and construction of the iron bridge. It was to be completed in six months. The seventh and final bridge is still in use today and was constructed in 1955.

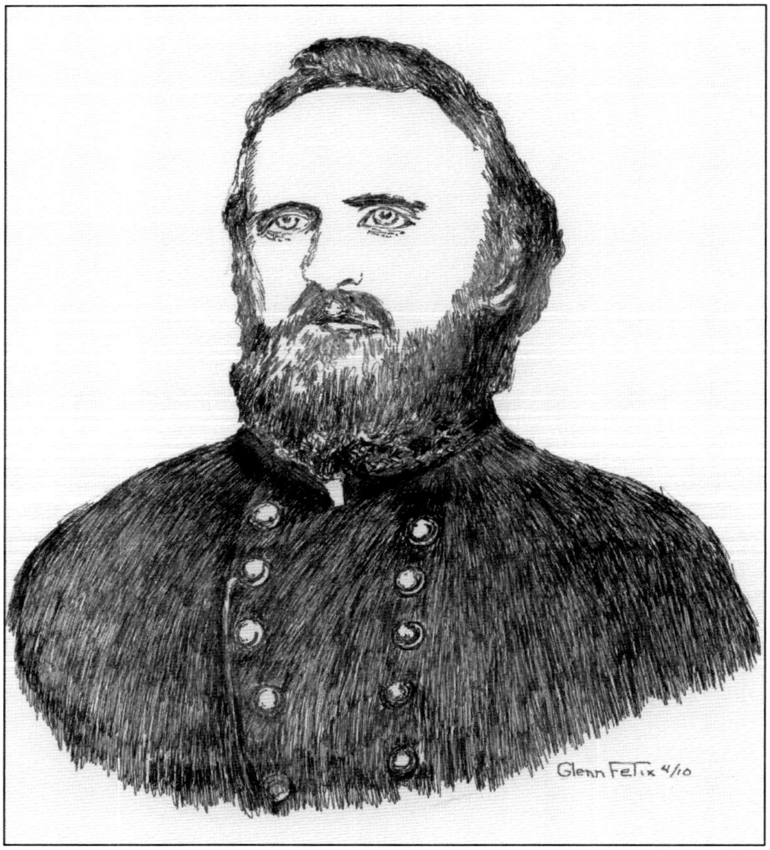


In 1862, Gen. Thomas "Stonewall" Jackson ordered the bridge across North River to be burned to slow the advance of Union soldiers. Later that year, Jackson constructed a temporary bridge made of wagons placed in the stream and covered with wooden planks to allow his entire army to cross North River on their way to Harrisonburg. (Sketched by Glenn Felix.)

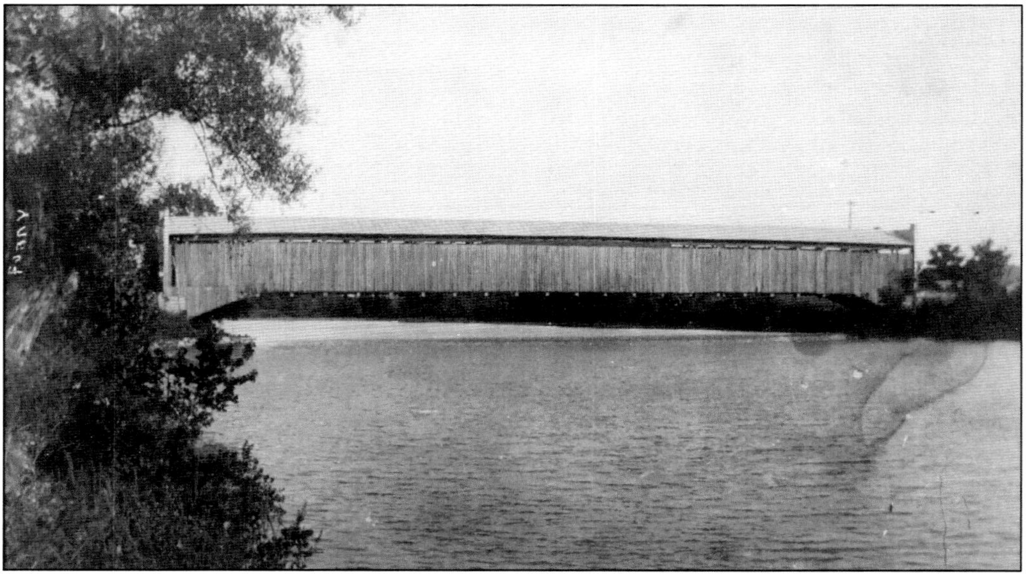

The most famous bridge crossing North River is this one constructed by William H. Grove in 1878. At a length of 240 feet, it was said to be the longest single-span wooden bridge in the world.

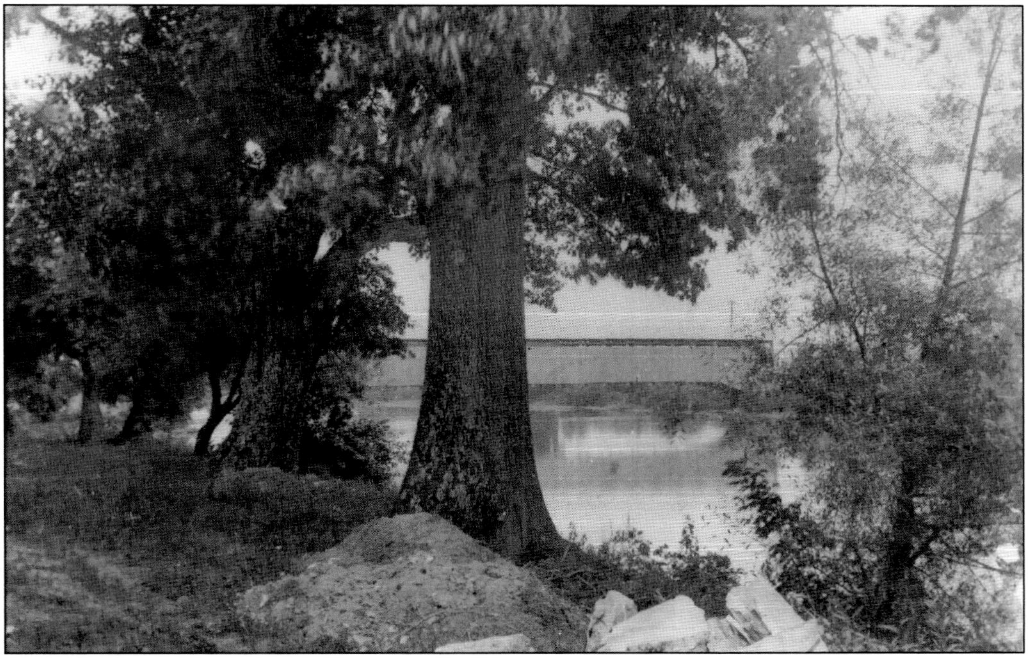

The wooden bridge lasted 38 years and survived several floods. Even though the covered bridge has been gone for nearly a century, it is still used as the symbol of the community and can be found on brochures, letterheads, advertisements, and local publications when referring to Bridgewater.

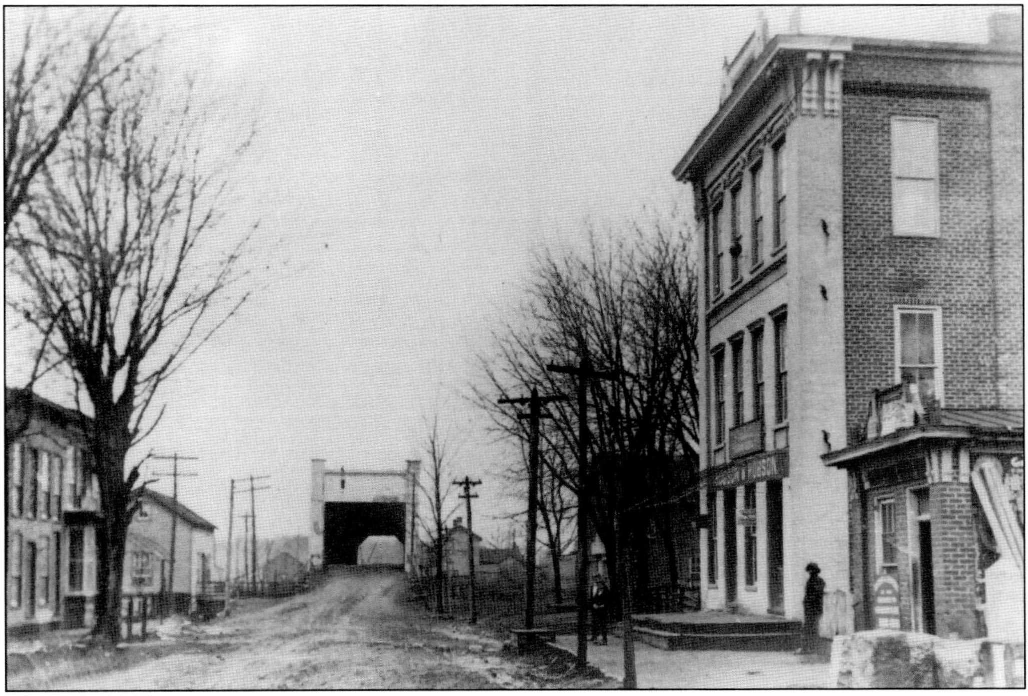

This is how Bridgewater looked to the traveler as he or she passed through town heading south. To the right is Rinker's Marble Yard and next to it is Allemong's store, later known as Robson and Robson. By this time, electrical service had arrived in Bridgewater as evidenced by the numerous utility poles along Main Street.

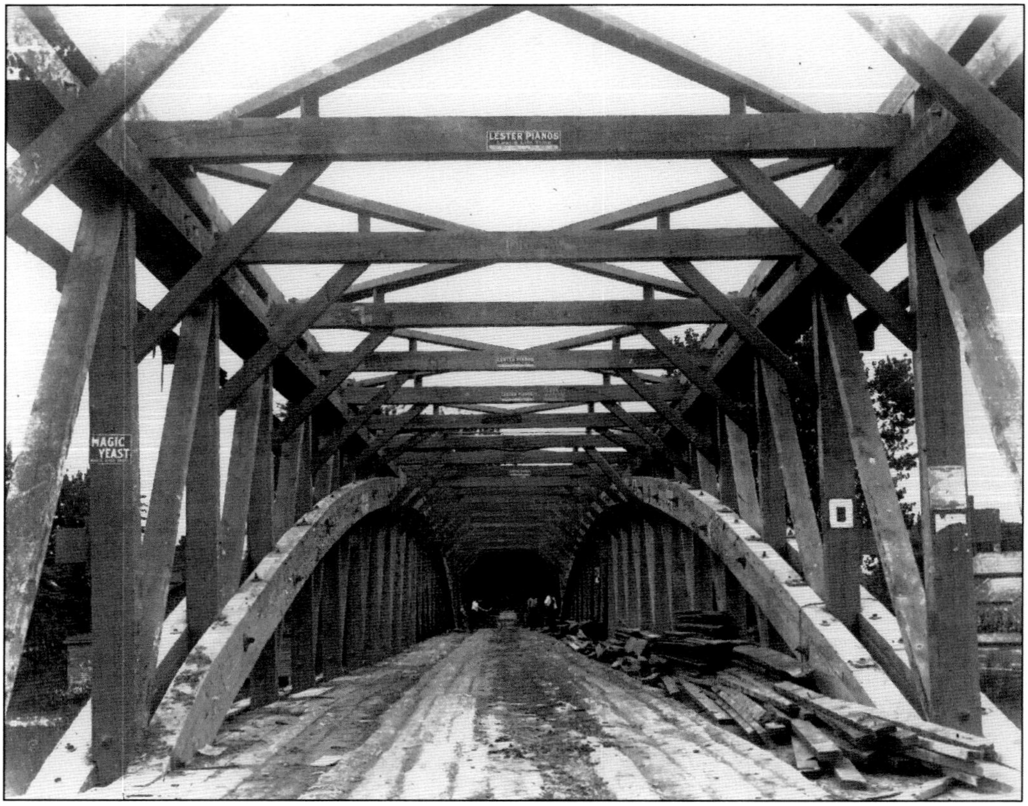


In 1916, it was decided that the wooden bridge would be replaced by a more modern iron structure. The contractor took down the wooden bridge piece by piece prior to constructing the new one.

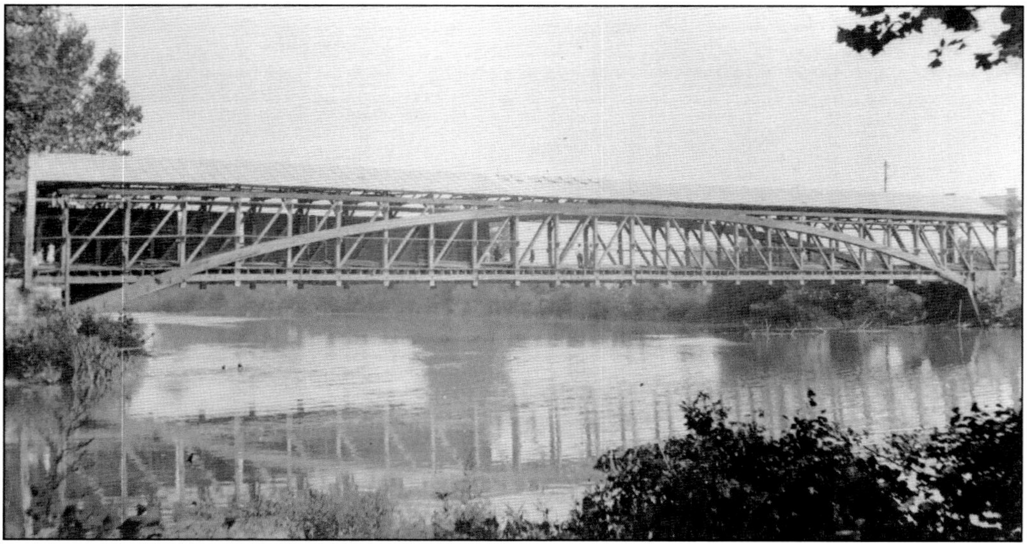

Seeing the "skeleton" of the wooden bridge gives one a better appreciation for the engineering and construction skills shown by William Grove. It was built before the days of cranes, backhoes, and power equipment, let alone technical design methods available today, and was truly an engineering marvel of its time.

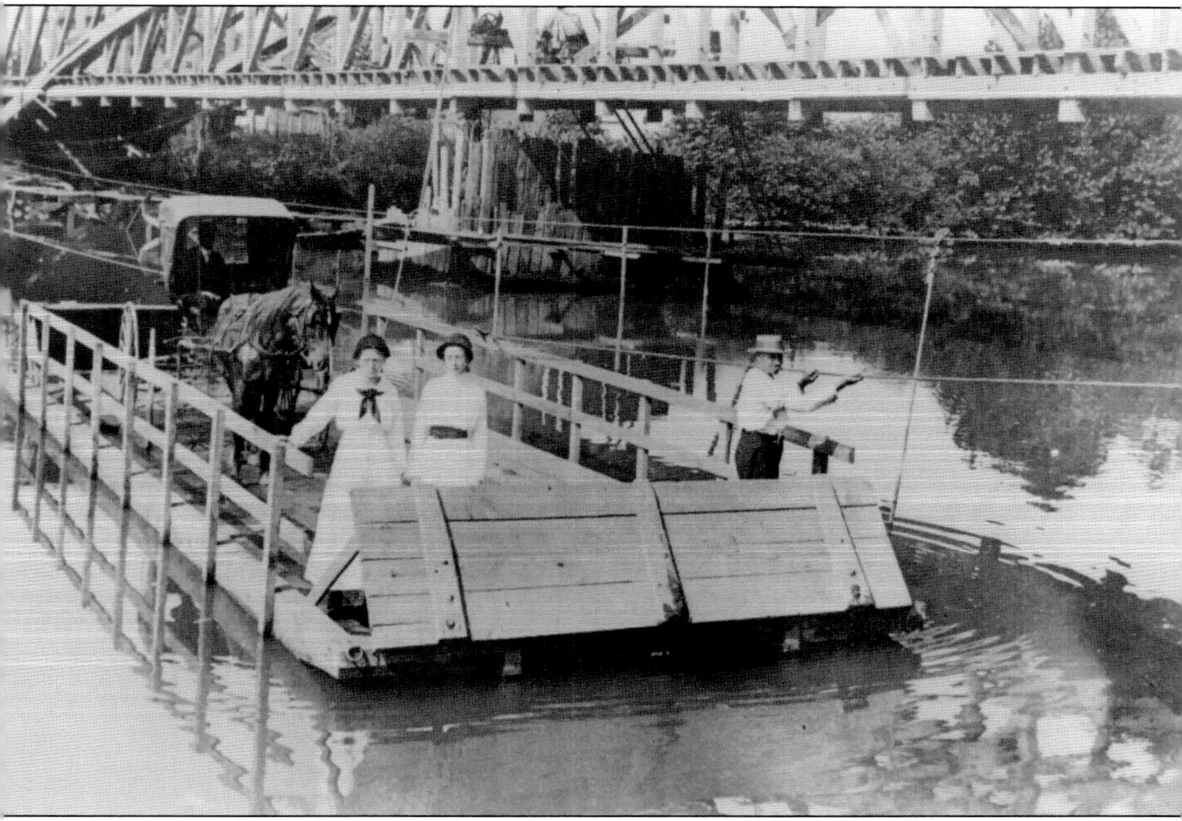

As soon as the wooden bridge was taken out of service, ferries were put into operation to haul travelers from one side of the river to the other. The *Daily News Record* dated August 22, 1916, reports of the first accident occurring on the ferryboat. A young farmer, Wade Huffman, was returning home in a one-horse buggy and used the ferry service to cross the river. "As the boat neared the middle of the river a boy dived (sic) from the side-rail into the water. The flying leap and splash frightened the horse and it backed the vehicle against the gang plank and when it gave way the buggy and driver dropped out of sight, but the young man came to the surface just about as quickly as he went under." The ferrymen pulled the drenched passenger on board and later towed the buggy ashore. All ended happily. The horse was re-hitched to the buggy, and the young man continued his journey home.

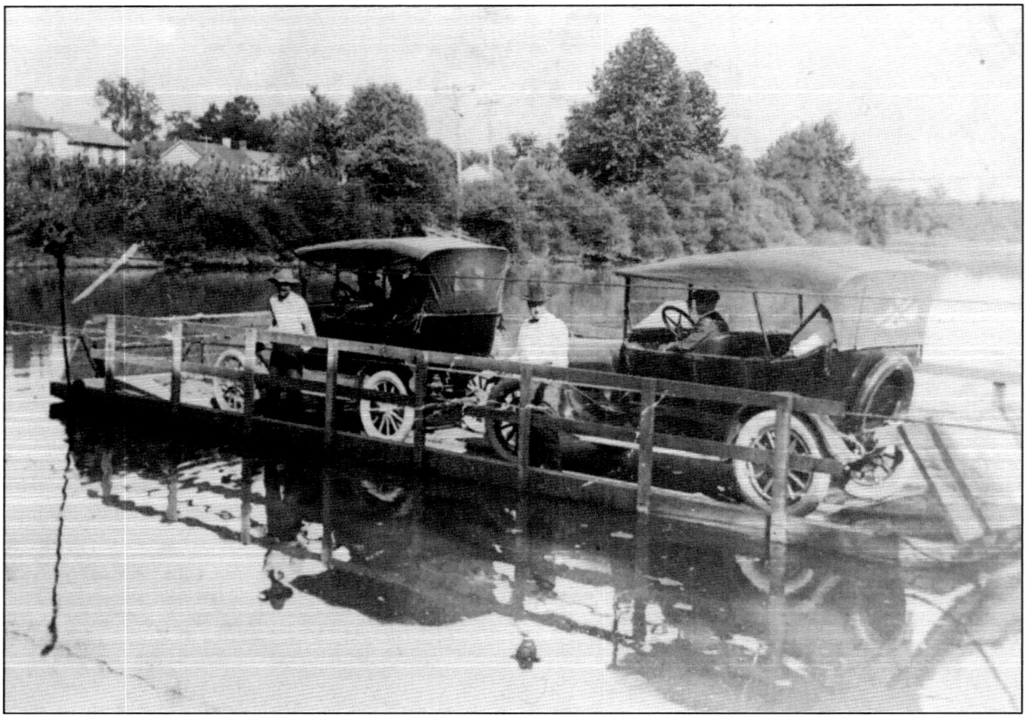

Although the automobile was becoming increasingly popular, most people in rural communities such as Bridgewater still traveled by horse and buggy. Due to the popularity of Warm Springs and other resort areas south of Bridgewater, it was not uncommon to see cars such as these passing through town.

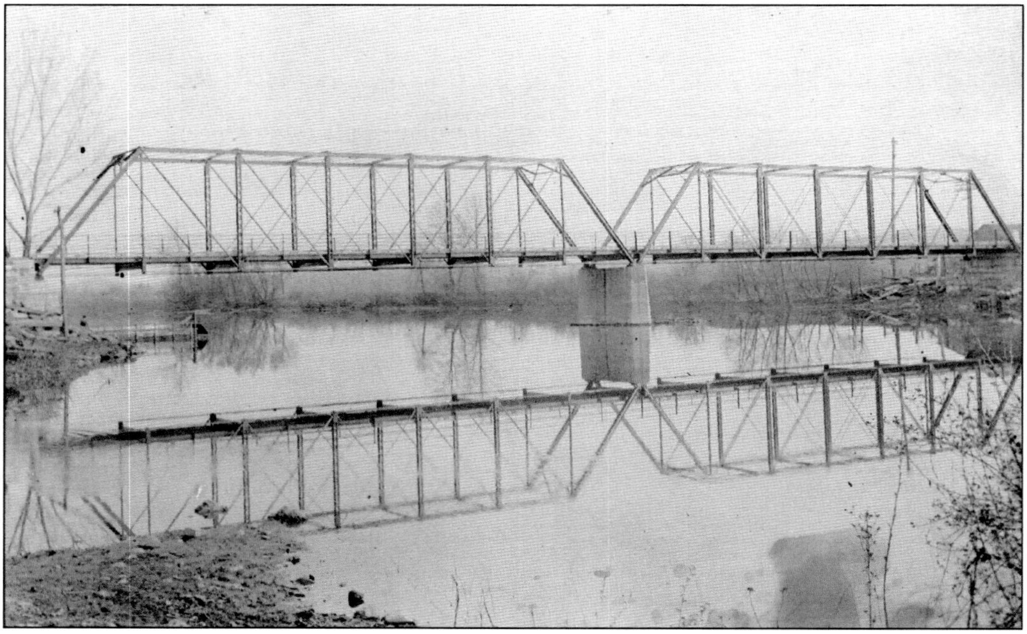

After three years, the new bridge was open to the public. While no one really knows why it took six times longer to construct than was estimated, it is believed that the diversion of men and materials to the World War I effort was a major factor.

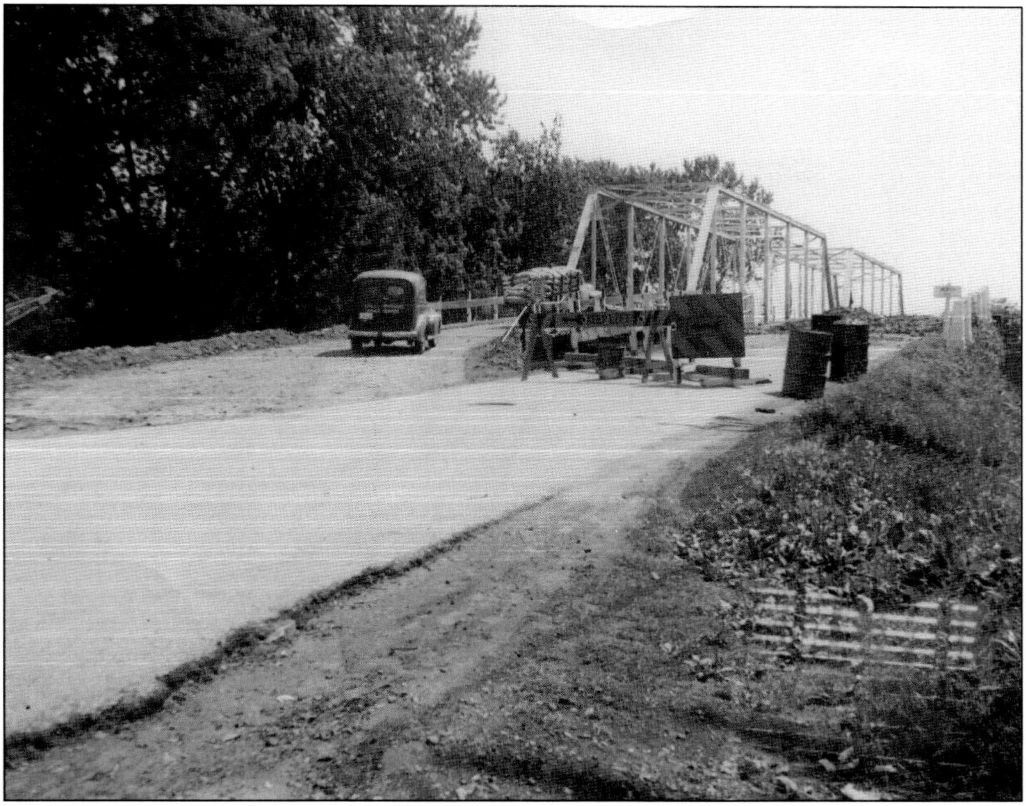

Finally open to traffic after the end of World War I, the iron bridge provided safe passage across North River until it was replaced in 1955.

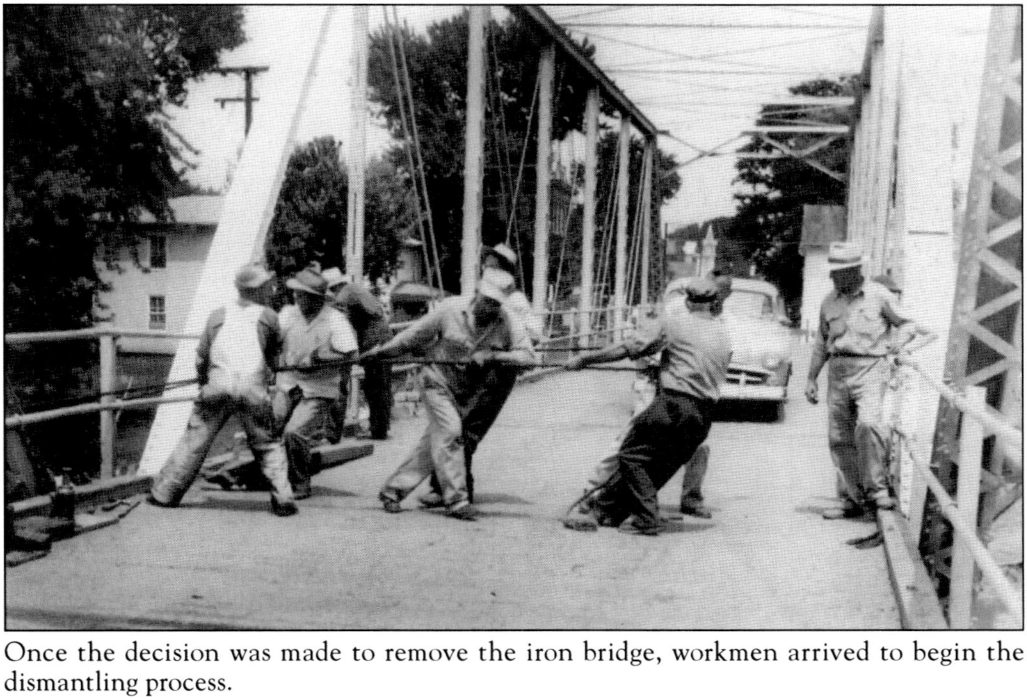

Once the decision was made to remove the iron bridge, workmen arrived to begin the dismantling process.

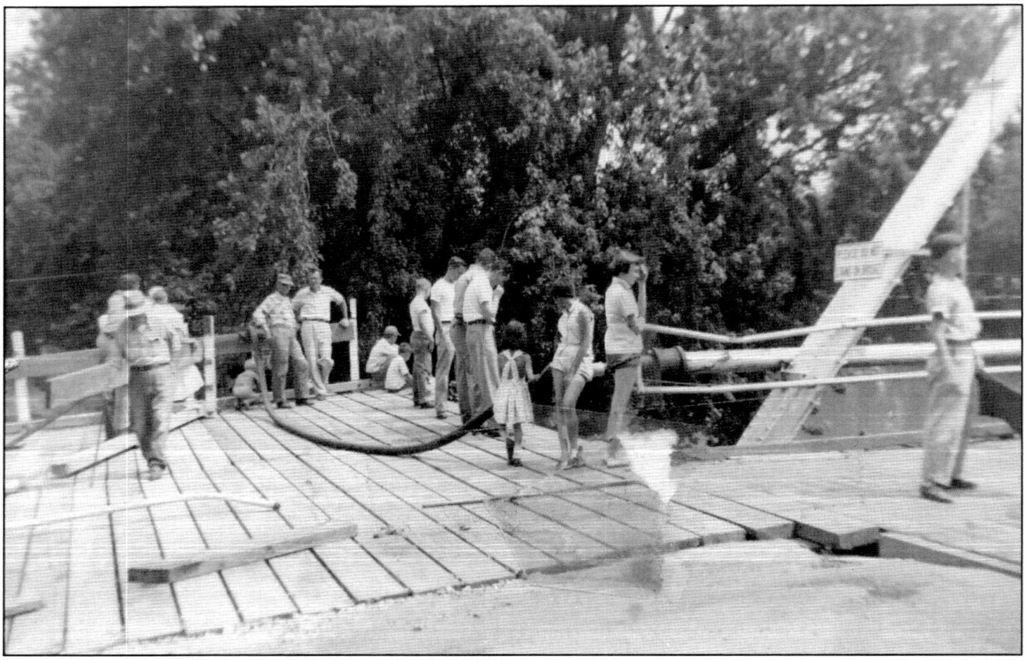

As one bridge went up and another came down, crowds gathered to watch the activity. It was not unusual in past times for construction sites to have a social element about them as "sidewalk superintendents" offered advice and criticism to the workers.

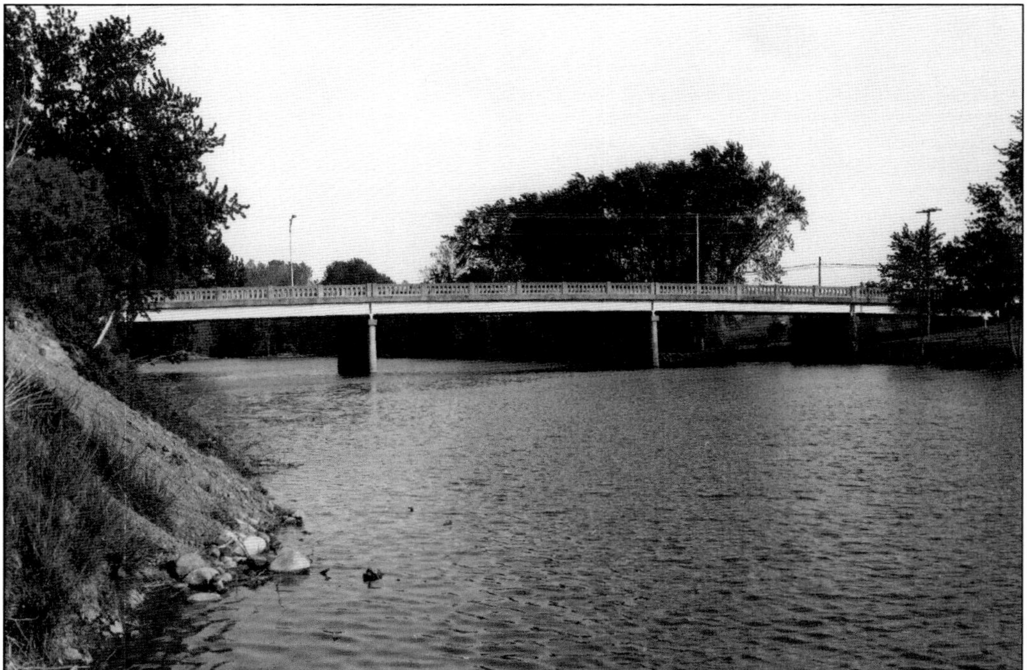

In the mid-1950s, the new concrete-and-steel bridge opened to the public and remains in service today. It was constructed at a cost of $162,000 by the Virginia State Highway Department, which is now known as the Virginia Department of Transportation.

# *Seven*

# Transportation

Prior to turnpikes, bridges, and the railroad, transportation in Bridgewater centered on the river. Flatboats hauled goods downstream to the Shenandoah River, which allowed them entry to the Potomac and major markets such as Front Royal and other points north, including the nation's capital. Roads were an impractical means of travel, because many of them were primitive paths suitable only for horse and rider or occasionally a small carriage.

The story of transportation in Bridgewater really starts with the construction of the Warm Springs Turnpike. In 1830, the Virginia General Assembly passed an act incorporating the Warm Springs and Harrisonburg Turnpike Company. The road that they built provided a modern route for transporting farm products, furs, herbs, and cast iron articles from the Mossy Creek Ironworks located just south of town to market. Eventually the turnpike connected with other roads and became the means of travel between Washington, D.C., and destinations in Tennessee, Kentucky, and points in present-day West Virginia.

Transportation in Bridgewater did not change until 1895, when more than 10,000 showed up for the long-awaited arrival of the railroad. For the first time, Bridgewater found easier access to the outside world.

One generation later, the automobile took the nation by storm, and transportation once again changed. Paved roads became the norm. The railroad waned and finally disappeared as it became commonplace for families to own at least one car.

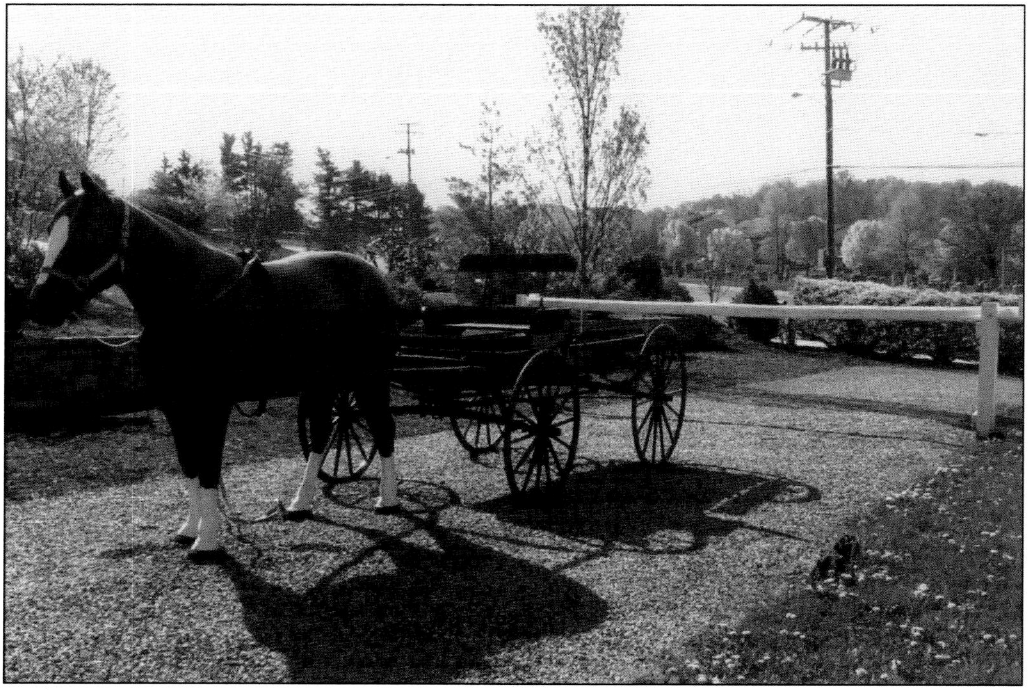

Bridgewater has a plan for keeping its history alive for new generations. Pocket parks along Main Street bring to life different parts of history. Warm Springs Turnpike Park, located at the north end of town, tells the story of the first road and the travelers who used it. In the park is a horse and buggy as well as a recreated tollgate much as it appeared 150 years ago. The wall adjacent to the road is made up of foundation stones from the original Church of the Brethren that had been located at this site.

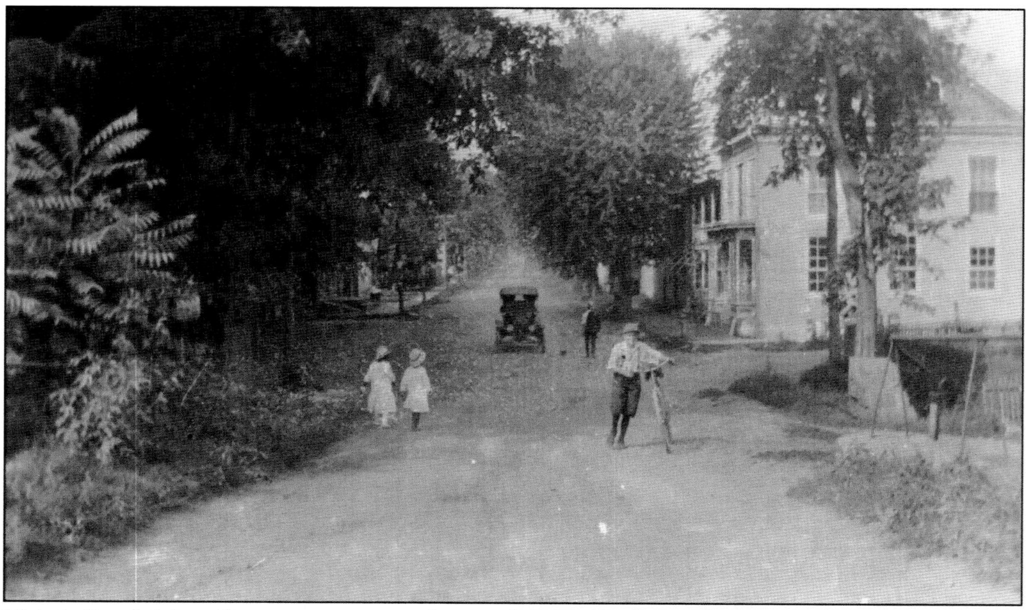

This is South Main Street as it appeared around 1900. Traffic at that time consisted of bicycles, horse-and-buggies, and the rare appearance of an automobile. Many of the buildings on South Main Street are still in place 100 years later.

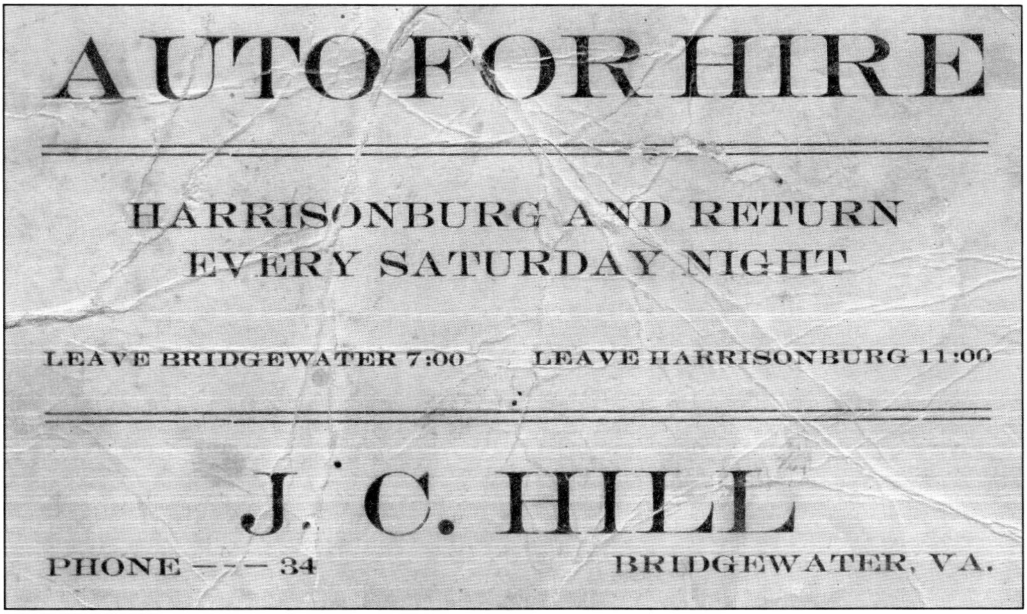
AUTO FOR HIRE

HARRISONBURG AND RETURN
EVERY SATURDAY NIGHT

LEAVE BRIDGEWATER 7:00 LEAVE HARRISONBURG 11:00

J. C. HILL

PHONE — — — 34 BRIDGEWATER, VA.

Whenever a need arises, an entrepreneur will appear with a way to meet it. One such person was J. C. Hill, who used his car to drive locals to Harrisonburg for a night on the town every Saturday. He left Bridgewater at 7:00 p.m. and returned from Harrisonburg at 11:00 p.m. To show how long ago this was, note that his telephone number was "34."

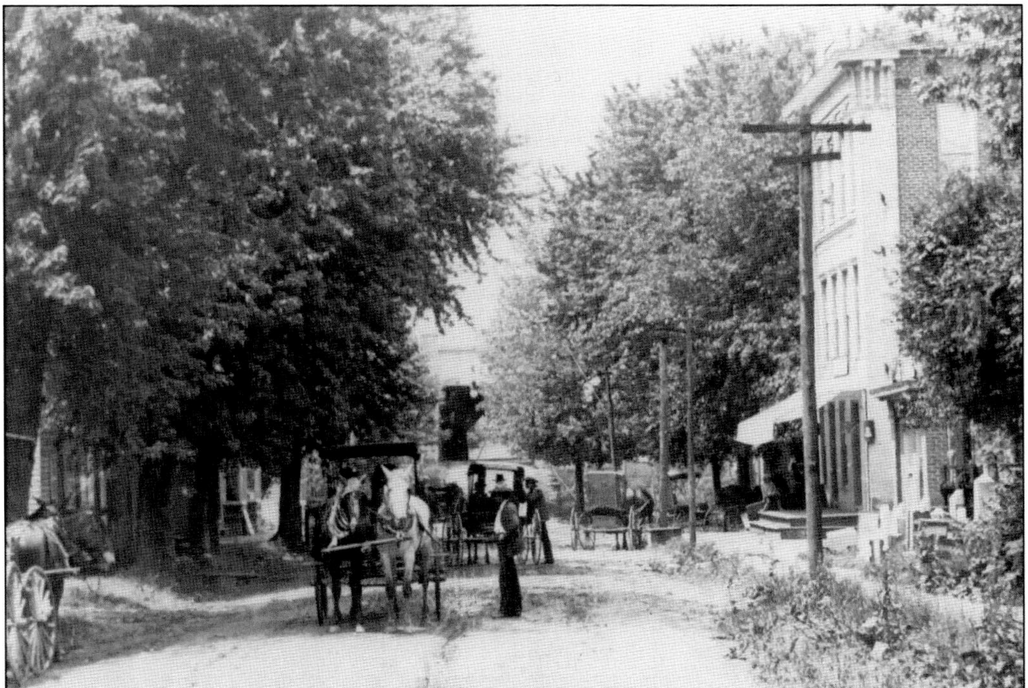

This is how South Main Street looked at the dawn of the 20th century. Notice the covered bridge in the background. While it is nostalgic to look back on the good old days, not all was good. The street was made of dirt and cinders, which became a muddy mess after each rain. Weeds grew waist high along the side of the road, and the drainage ditches were used to dump garbage.

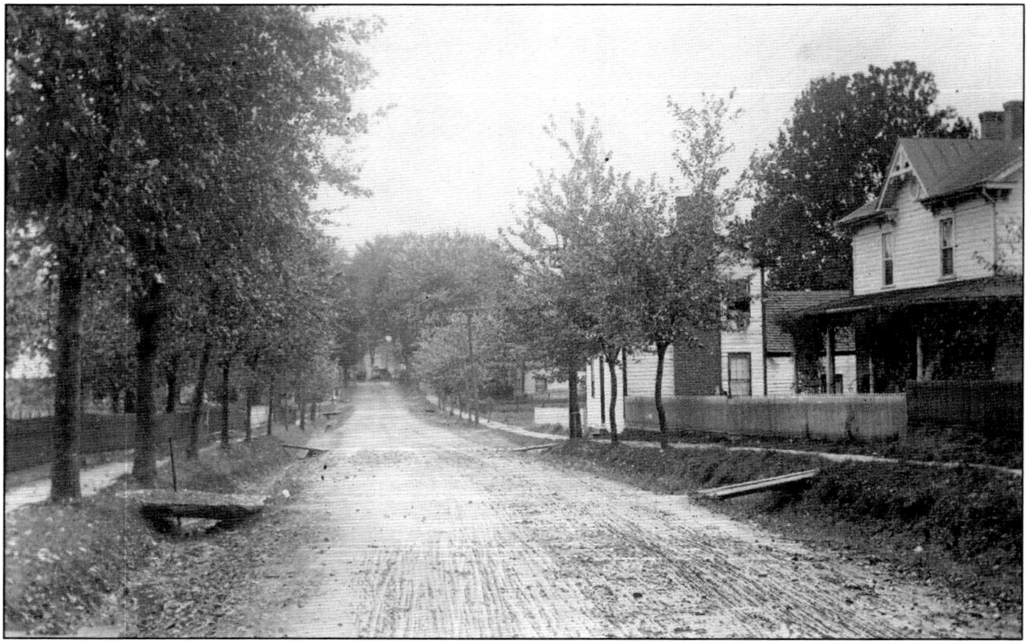

Prior to the arrival of electricity to Bridgewater, all streets were tree lined. Trees provided shade during hot summer days and added natural beauty throughout the year. Even though most citizens regretted the removal of hardwoods such as maple, oak, and chestnut, Bridgewater was ready to move into the 20th century and welcomed the electric light.

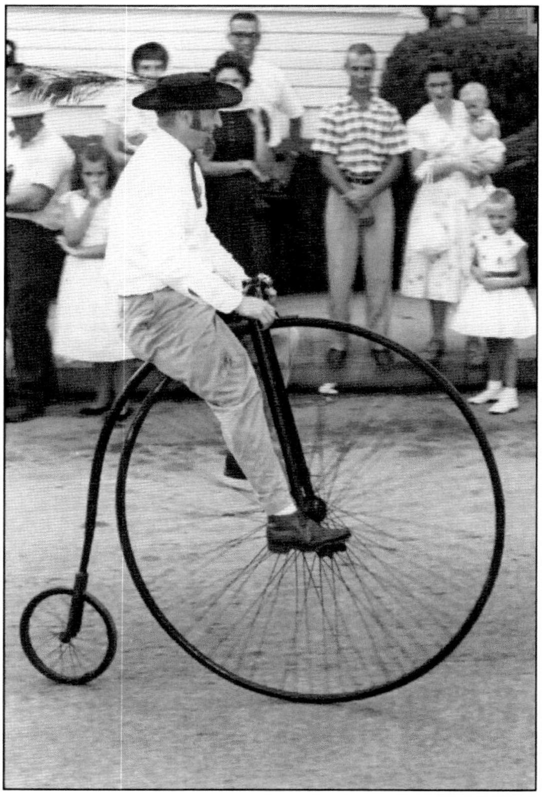

Here Dr. Dwight Shull shows off his antique bicycle during a summer parade. Bicycles have evolved much like automobiles. Early days of transportation might have included self-propelled equipment such as seen here.

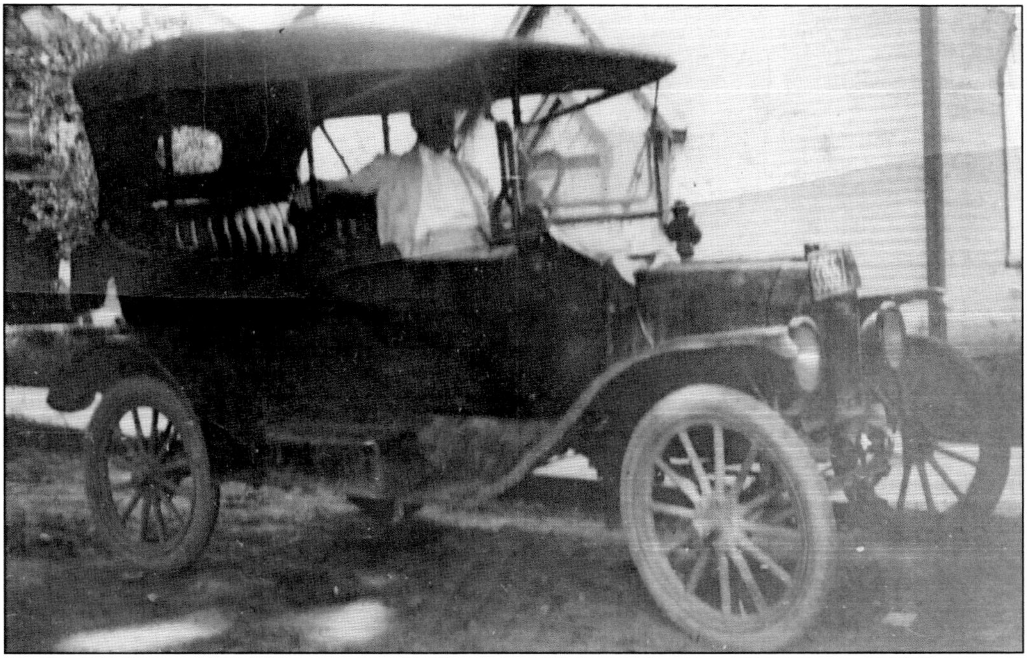

This picture taken around 1915 shows one of the first Model-T Fords in Bridgewater. The arrival of the car changed life in many ways. For example, it was no longer safe for chickens to wander up and down Main Street, and suddenly there was a need to fence in cattle and other livestock. Ordinances were passed requiring people to keep their cows at home and chickens out of the road.

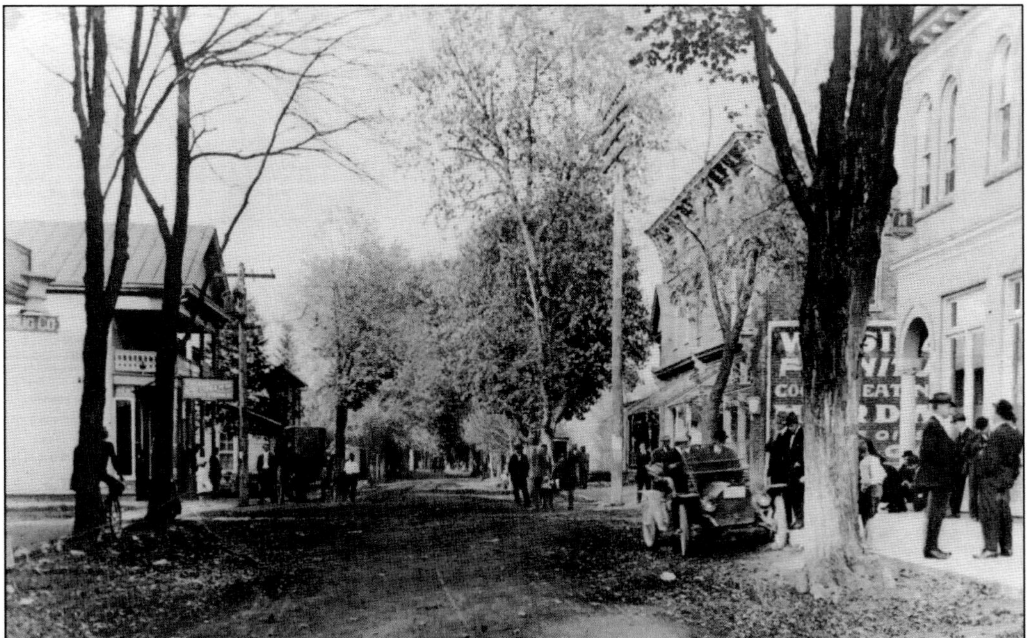

Some of the more popular pictures of Bridgewater are those involving Main Street scenes from years ago. With the arrival of the automobile, citizens felt the need to provide a hard surface on Main Street. This was done by applying layers of hot tar and gravel to the existing dirt road. Along with electricity and telephones, this helped move Bridgewater into the 20th century.

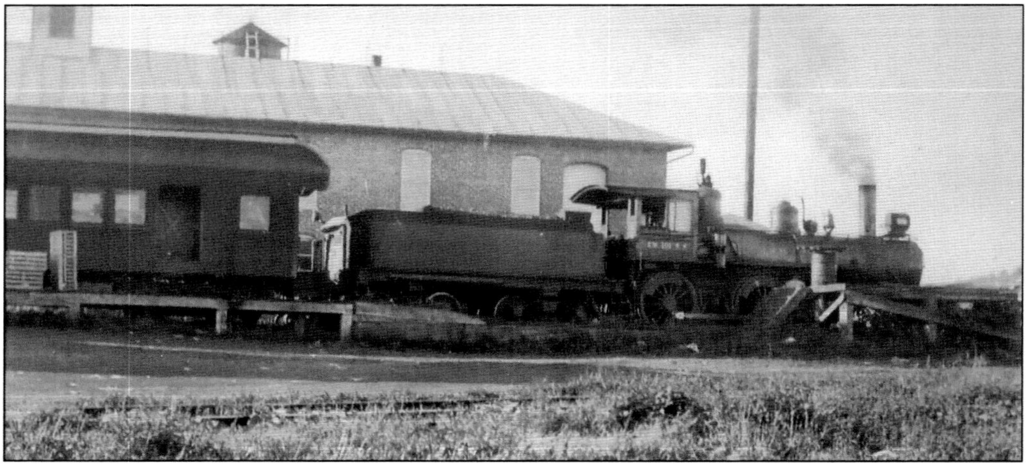

The C&W (Chesapeake and Western) Railway opened up the outside world, not only for travel, but to also provide a way to ship and receive goods from Washington, Baltimore, and other metropolitan areas.

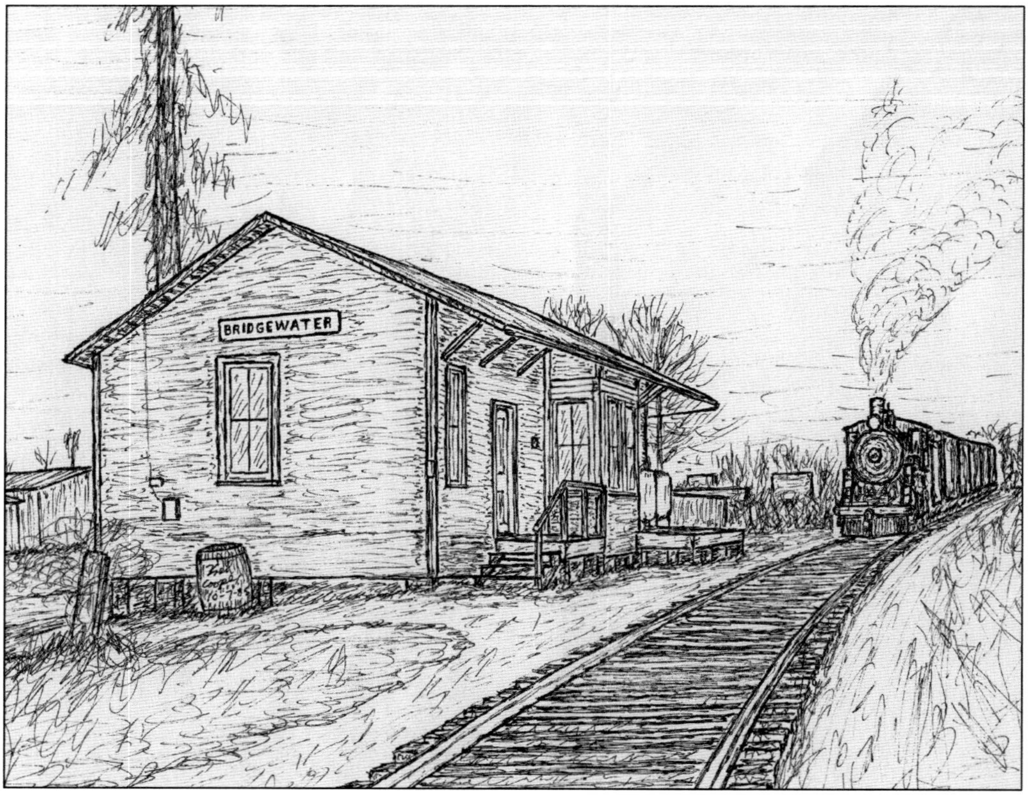


After nearly a quarter of a century of starts and stops, Bridgewater citizens were skeptical of whether rail service would ever arrive. Once the commitment was received from Chesapeake and Western in 1895, excitement began to build as everyone anticipated the completion of the Bridgewater line by the end of the summer. In July, dynamite blasting used to level the ground for the railroad bed could be heard in the nearby town of Dayton. By August, the activity had reached Bridgewater. As the day grew near for the arrival of the first train, a committee was organized to form a grand welcoming jubilee.

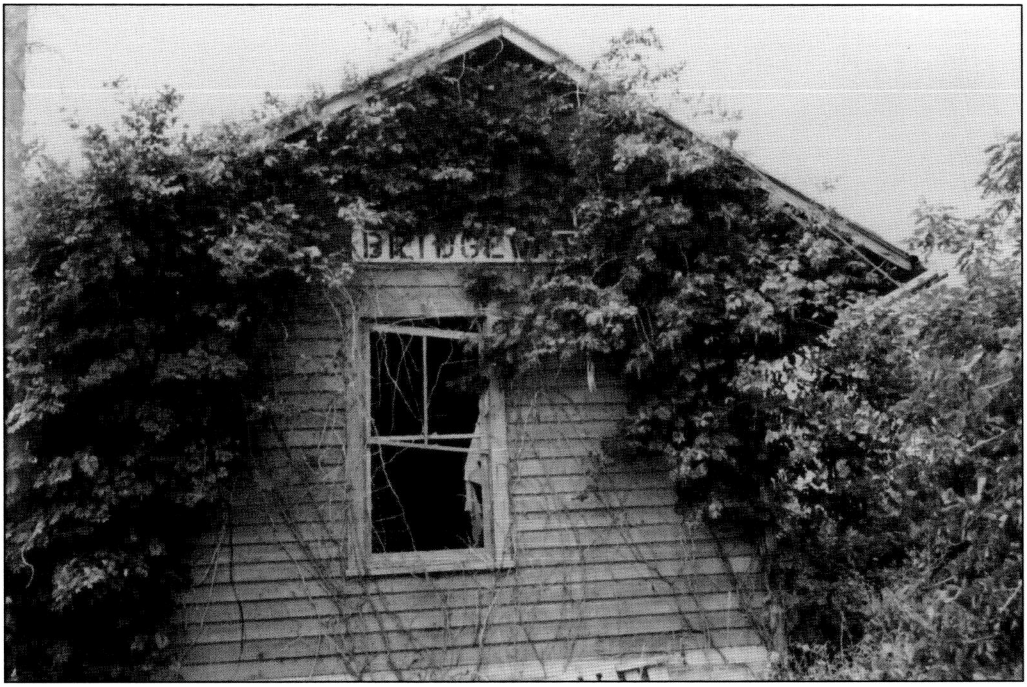

Looking at the abandoned railroad depot shown above, it is hard to believe that on the day the first train came to Bridgewater as many as 10,000 people were there to greet it. Suddenly a much bigger world opened up to area residents. Trips to Niagara Falls and other "exotic" locales could be purchased if one could afford the round-trip ticket, which might cost as much as $10. The first freight hauled to Bridgewater was a carload of cans purchased by the Bridgewater Cannery, but other consignments soon followed.

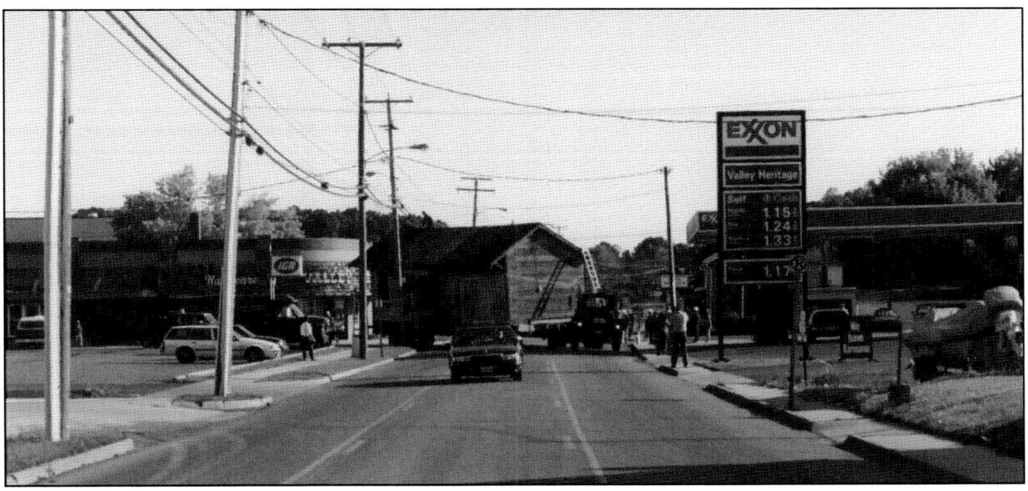


Rail service no longer comes to Bridgewater, but the depot that was such a part of the town's history has survived. Here it is traveling down Main Street on a flatbed truck moving to its new location at Oakdale Community Park. It has been restored to the appearance it had a century ago.

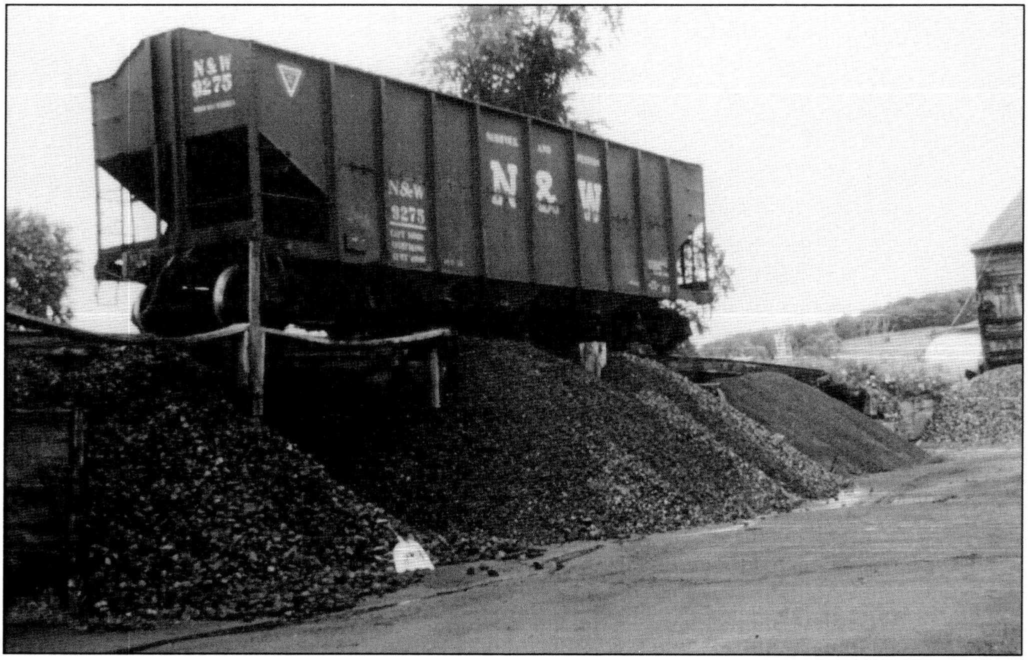


Prior to the days of heat pumps and gas furnaces, homes were heated by coal or wood. All towns had a coal yard where residents could purchase coal for personal use. In addition to the home owner, most factories and businesses were customers at the coal yard as well.

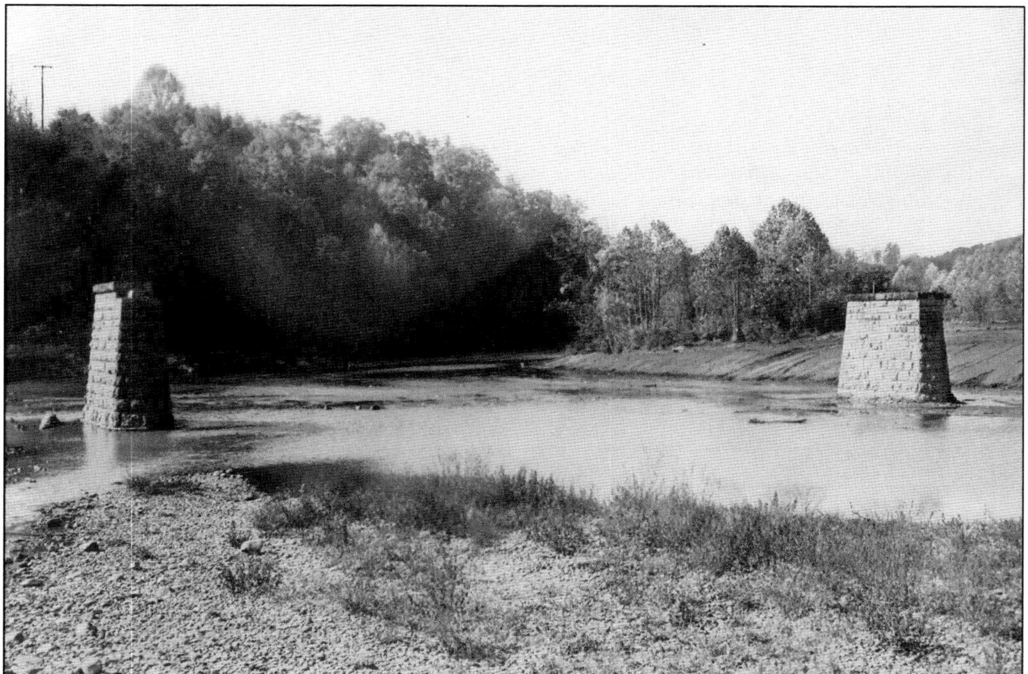

During World War II, the steel rails were removed and used for scrap metal. Two stone trestles are all that remain of the train tracks crossing North River. Prior to this, trains traveled from Stokesville to Bridgewater and on to Harrisonburg and Elkton on a regular basis. After that, passenger service ended and never returned.

*Eight*

# TAMING NORTH RIVER

It is unknown whether Noah ever sailed his ark through Bridgewater, but it certainly is possible with the number of floods in the area. Many local amateur historians could be confused when referring to the flood of '85—it could be the flood of 1885 or 1985. Likewise, the flood of '96 could apply to 1896 or 1996. Records show that Bridgewater has experienced at least seven major floods since 1870.

Of all these, perhaps the 1949 flood is the one people remember the most. Other floods resulted in the loss of property, but the 1949 one took the lives of three women who were unexpectedly in the path of quickly rising waters. Mary Riddleberger Bowman, Margaret Bricker, and Margaret's daughter Frances all drowned in the swirling torrent of the North River one rainy June night.

Out of the disaster of the 1949 flood came the combined effort of the U.S. Army Corps of Engineers and the Bridgewater Town Council to build a flood-control levee near the intersection of the North and Dry Rivers to prevent a repeat of this catastrophe. In this chapter are not only pictures of the flood but of the workers who spent many months constructing a barrier between the men, women, and children who live in Bridgewater and the rivers that, on occasion, leave their banks with a vengeance.

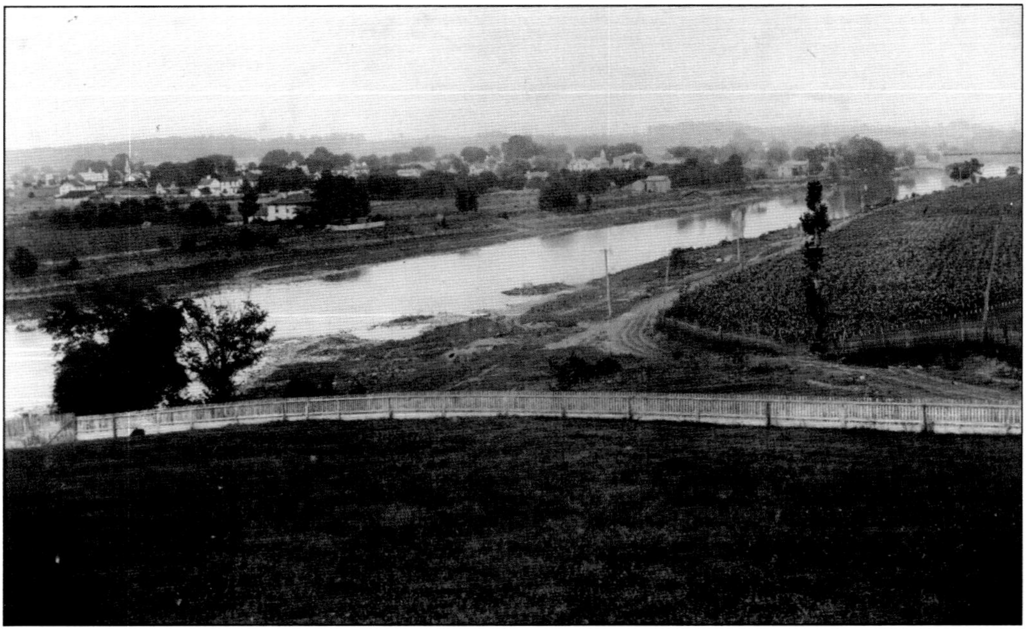

This is the only known picture of the town after the 1885 flood. Erosion of the riverbank as well as the silting-in of the river bed is seen in the picture.

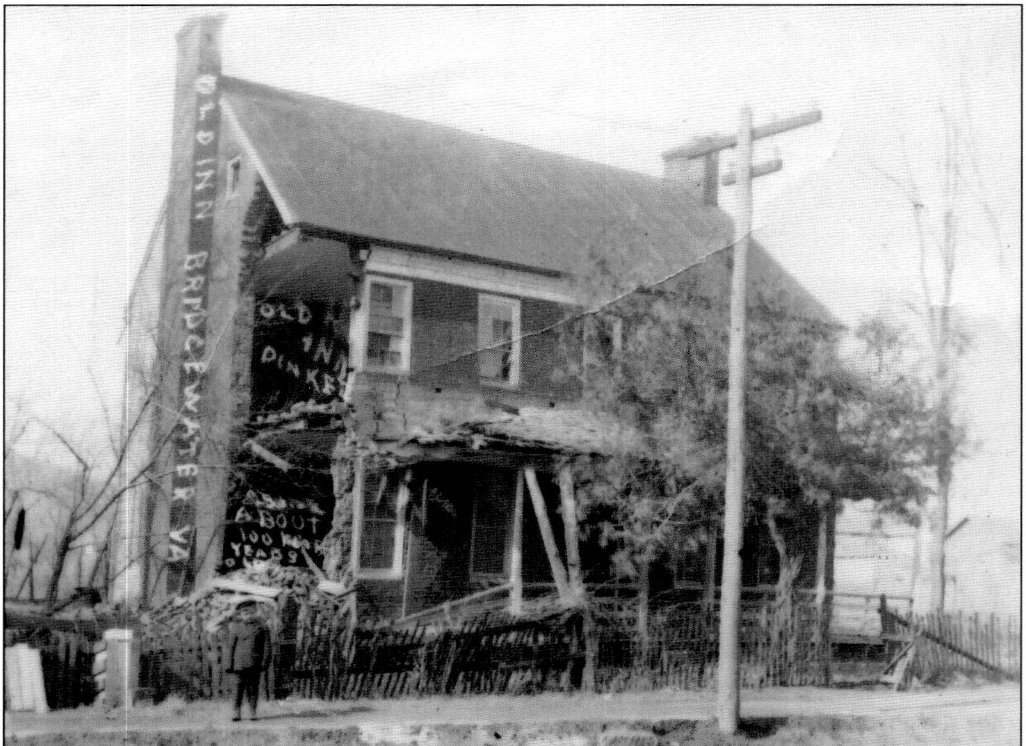


This is Dinkle Tavern after one of the floods in the late 1800s. This picture must be later than 1873, since telegraph poles came to Bridgewater that year. Floods occurred in 1877, 1885, and 1896. Whatever year it was, the tavern received considerable damage, particularly on the south wall.

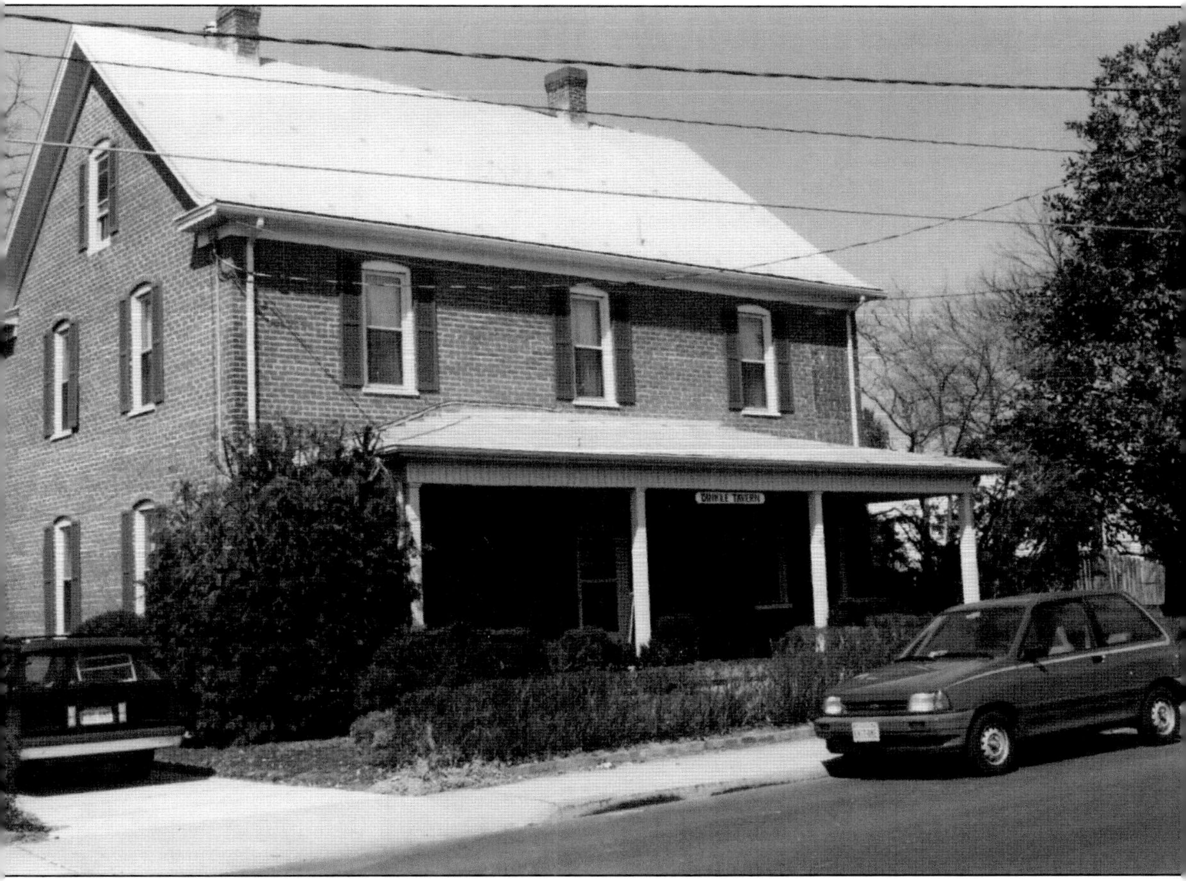


Dinkle Tavern had several more floods to endure in 1949, 1985, and 1996 but has survived them all and looks like this today. Evelyn Row described the 1949 flood this way: "During the early June of 1949 gentle rains had saturated the slopes of the Allegheny Mountains when on June 17, within a few hours, seven inches of rain fell on the headwater area of North River 25 miles west of Bridgewater. Walls of water rushed headlong to the valley carrying boulders, trees, as well as other plant and animal life." By 1950, Dr. Row had repaired the damage caused by the flood of 1949 and restored his home to its original condition. It is a little-known fact that Dr. and Mrs. Row were experts at developing hybrid irises. Their yard became an attraction not only for locals but for those traveling through town during the summer months.

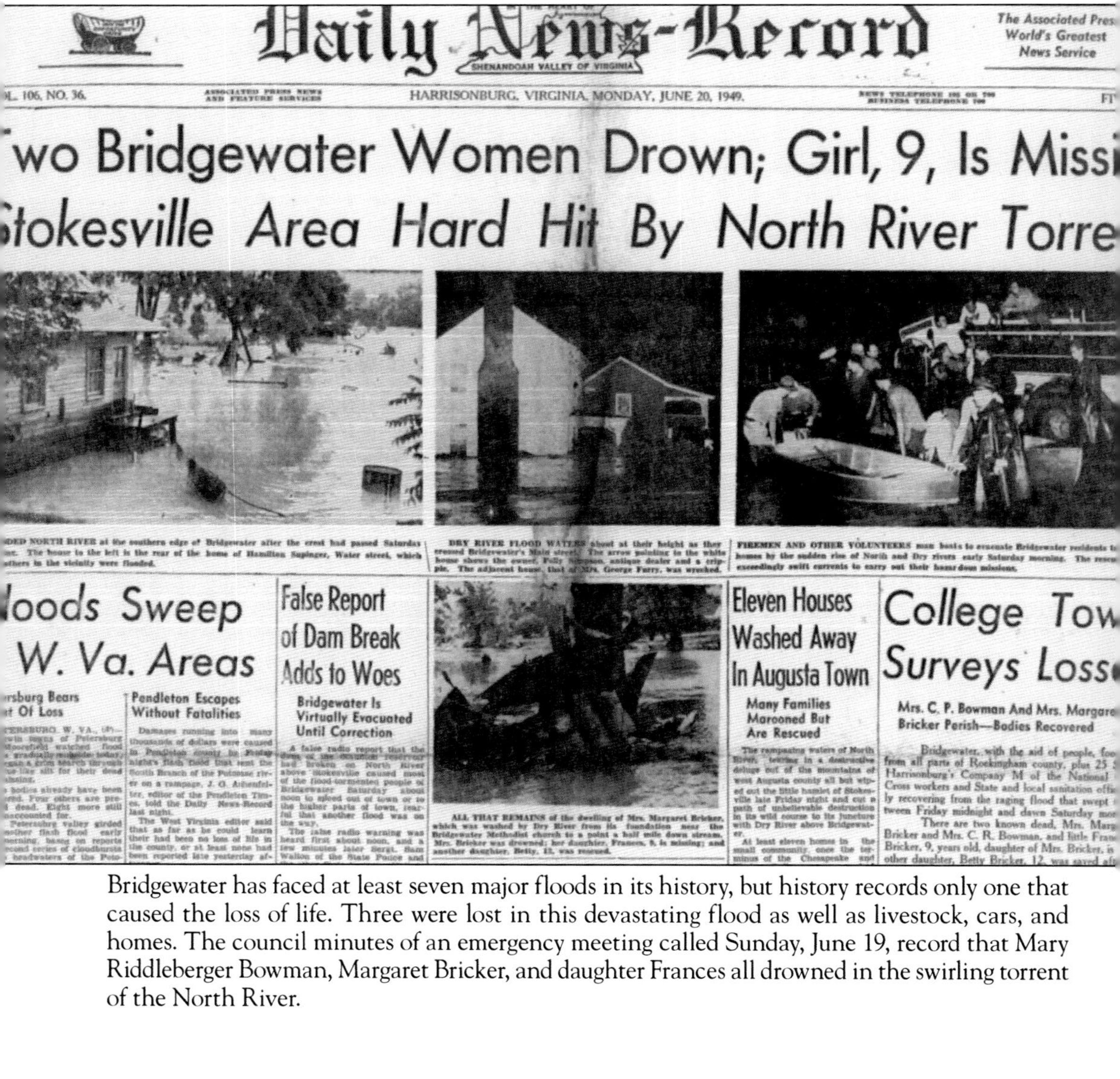

Daily News-Record

SHENANDOAH VALLEY OF VIRGINIA

The Associated Press World's Greatest News Service

…L. 106, NO. 36. HARRISONBURG, VIRGINIA, MONDAY, JUNE 20, 1949.

# …wo Bridgewater Women Drown; Girl, 9, Is Missi…

# …tokesville Area Hard Hit By North River Torre…

…DED NORTH RIVER at the southern edge of Bridgewater after the crest had passed Saturday …. The house to the left is the rear of the home of Hamilton Sapinger, Water street, which …others in the vicinity were flooded.

DRY RIVER FLOOD WATERS about at their height as they crossed Bridgewater's Main street. The arrow pointing to the white house shows the owner, Folly Simpson, antique dealer and a cripple. The adjacent house, that of Mrs. George Furry, was wrecked.

FIREMEN AND OTHER VOLUNTEERS man boats to evacuate Bridgewater residents … homes by the sudden rise of North and Dry rivers early Saturday morning. The rescu… exceedingly swift currents to carry out their hazardous missions.

## …loods Sweep W. Va. Areas

…rsburg Bears …t Of Loss

Pendleton Escapes Without Fatalities

Damages running into many thousands of dollars were caused in Pendleton county by Friday night's flash flood that sent the South Branch of the Potomac river on a rampage, J. O. Ashenfelter, editor of the Pendleton Times, told the Daily News-Record last night.

The West Virginia editor said that as far as he could learn their had been no loss of life in the county, or at least none had been reported late yesterday af-…

## False Report of Dam Break Adds to Woes

Bridgewater Is Virtually Evacuated Until Correction

A false radio report that the … had broken on North River above Stokesville caused most of the flood-tormented people of Bridgewater Saturday about noon to speed out of town or to the higher parts of town, fearful that another flood was on the way.

The false radio warning was heard first about noon, and a few minutes later Sergt. Sam Walton of the State Police and …

ALL THAT REMAINS of the dwelling of Mrs. Margaret Bricker, which was washed by Dry River from its foundation near the Bridgewater Methodist church to a point a half mile down stream. Mrs. Bricker was drowned; her daughter, Frances, 9, is missing; and another daughter, Betty, 12, was rescued.

## Eleven Houses Washed Away In Augusta Town

Many Families Marooned But Are Rescued

The rampaging waters of North River, tearing in a destructive deluge out of the mountains of west Augusta county all but wiped out the little hamlet of Stokesville late Friday night and cut a path of unbelievable destruction in its wild course to its juncture with Dry River above Bridgewater.

At least eleven homes in the small community, once the terminus of the Chesapeake and …

## College Tow… Surveys Loss…

Mrs. C. P. Bowman And Mrs. Margare… Bricker Perish—Bodies Recovered

Bridgewater, with the aid of people, foo… from all parts of Rockingham county, plus 25 … Harrisonburg's Company M of the National … Cross workers and State and local sanitation offic… ly recovering from the raging flood that swept … tween Friday midnight and dawn Saturday mor…

There are two known dead, Mrs. Marg… Bricker and Mrs. C. R. Bowman, and little Fran… Bricker, 9, years old, daughter of Mrs. Bricker, is … other daughter, Betty Bricker, 12, was saved af…

Bridgewater has faced at least seven major floods in its history, but history records only one that caused the loss of life. Three were lost in this devastating flood as well as livestock, cars, and homes. The council minutes of an emergency meeting called Sunday, June 19, record that Mary Riddleberger Bowman, Margaret Bricker, and daughter Frances all drowned in the swirling torrent of the North River.

In the days after the 1949 flood, citizens surveyed the damage, looked for the missing, and made plans to rebuild lives and replace what was lost. Such is the case in this picture.

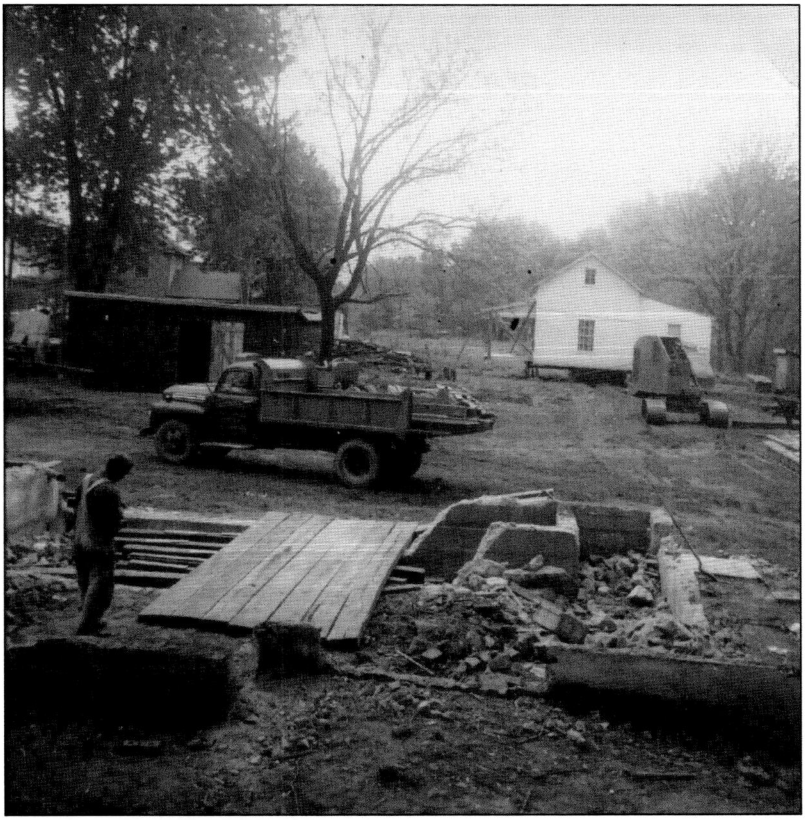

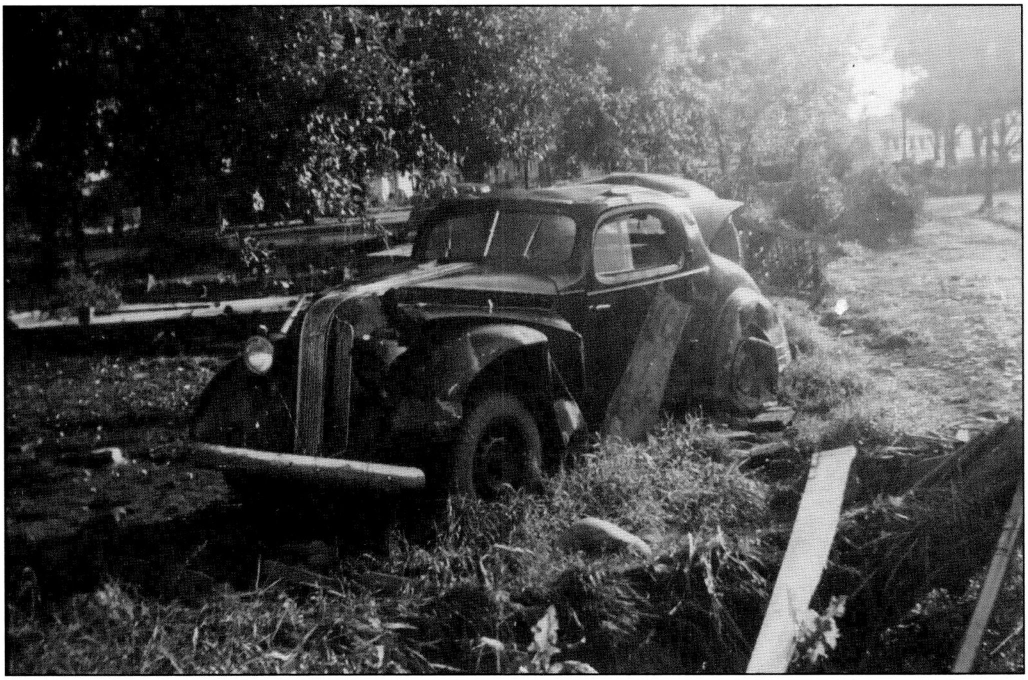

The flood of 1949 destroyed property as well as lives. Many automobiles were damaged beyond repair by the deep floodwaters running through town.

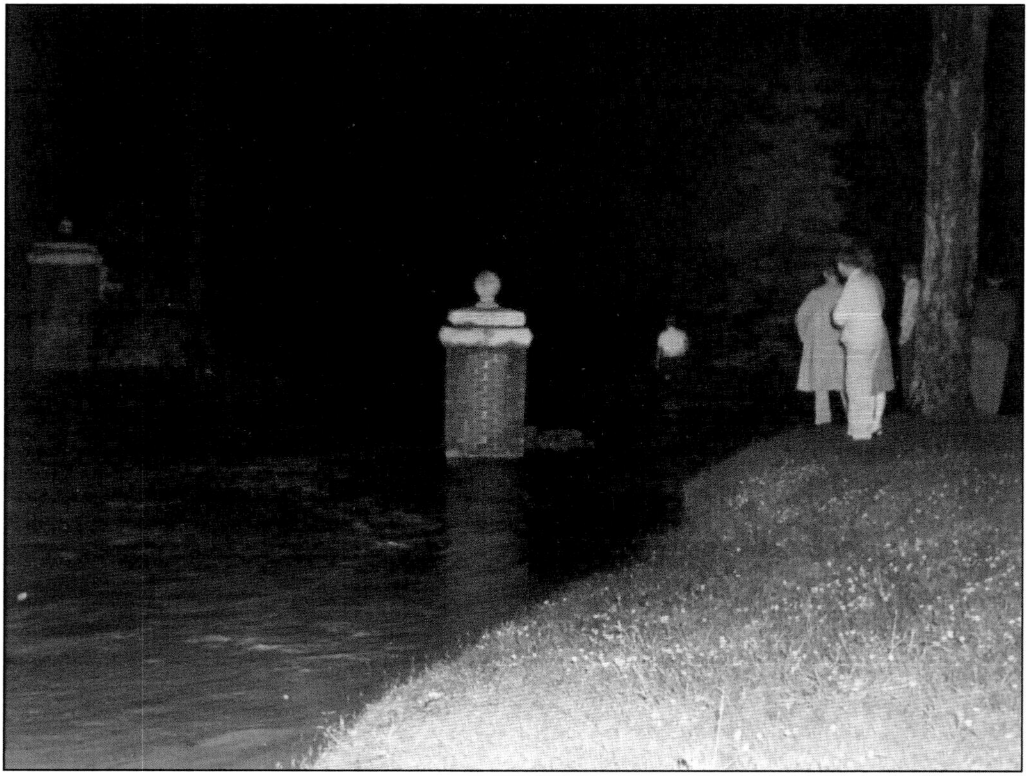

Students and citizens watched in amazement as floodwaters rose through the night of June 17, 1949. It had been an unusually wet month when more heavy rain began falling on June 17. The saturated ground could hold no more. Witnesses say that rain fell in sustained torrents from mid-afternoon to past midnight. Car headlights could not penetrate the rain more than 5 feet. The excess water poured into the North River and Dry River, causing both to rise at unprecedented rates.

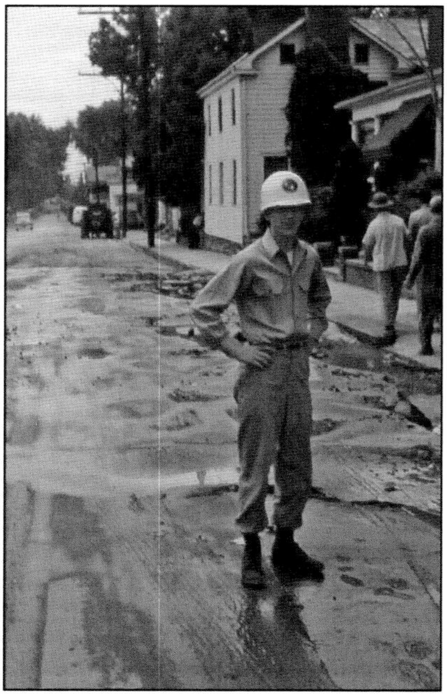

During disasters, human behavior can go to extremes. Some people are at their best, while others can stoop to deeds they would not consider in better times. The National Guard came to Bridgewater during June 1949 to help provide security for the businesses and homes damaged by the flood as well as to keep the overly curious away while owners and friends attempted to clean up the damage. (HRHS.)

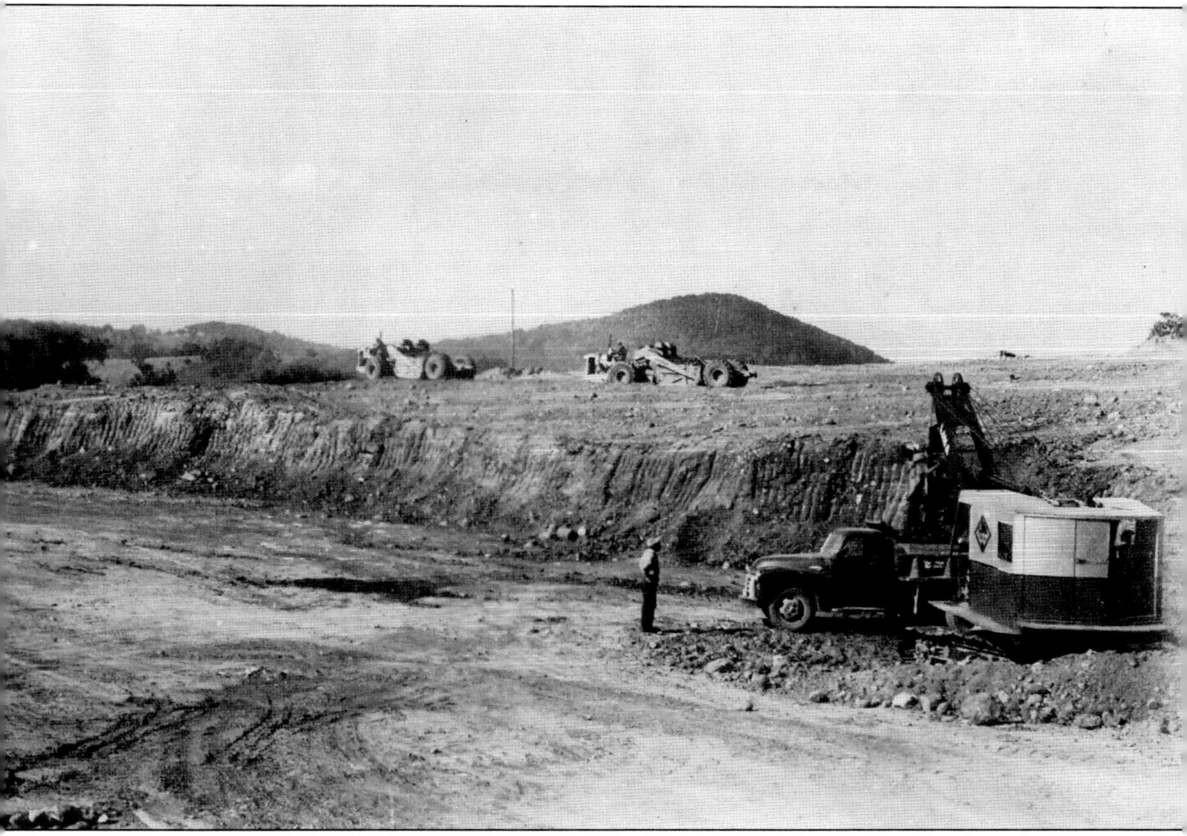

After the 1949 flood, the U.S. Army Corps of Engineers partnered with Bridgewater to build a flood-control levee. Thousands of cubic yards of clay and topsoil were hauled to complete this project. Fortunately a deep vein of clay was found a short distance away. Here workers are loading it for transport to the levee site. Once completed, this structure stood fast through two major floods in 1985 and 1996. In both cases, the levee held its ground without suffering damage and protected Bridgewater from harm.

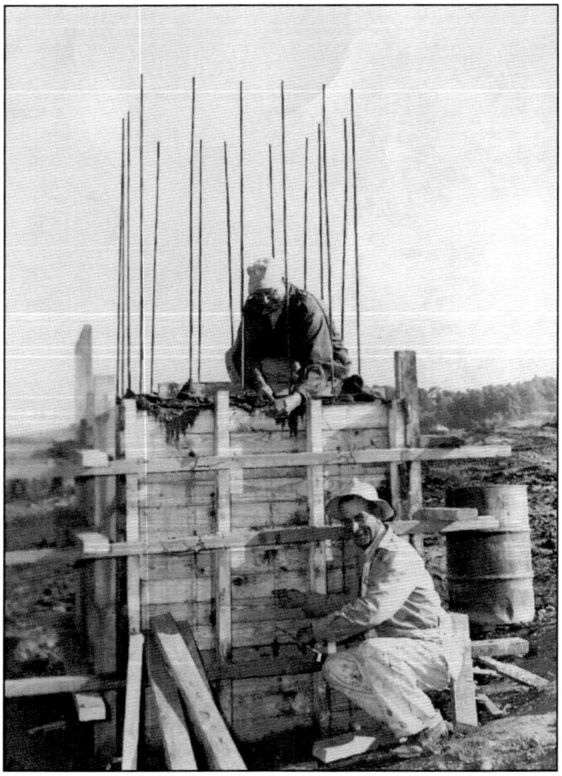

Here workers are building floodgates at strategic locations along the levee to help control the flow of storm water from one side to the other.

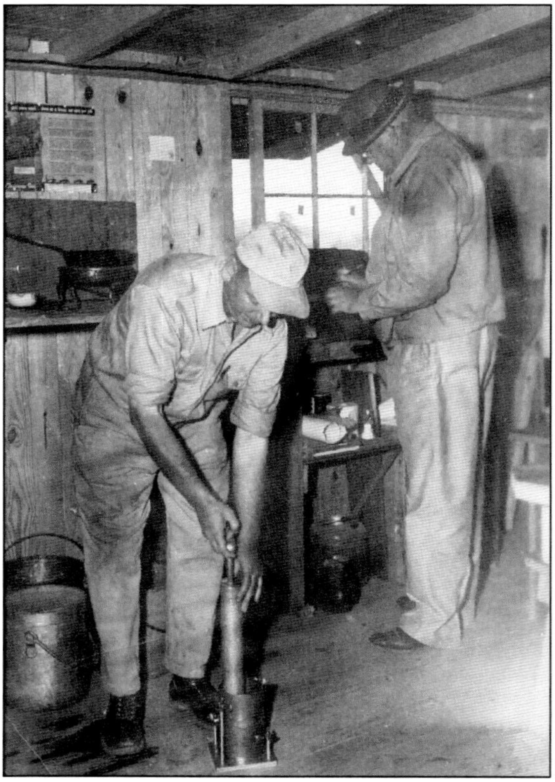

Workers check core samples during levee construction in 1950. The care they took in construction and the dedication taken since that time in maintaining it has protected Bridgewater in both the 1985 and 1996 floods. In a day and time when levees are known to fail, it is important to remember that this one never has.

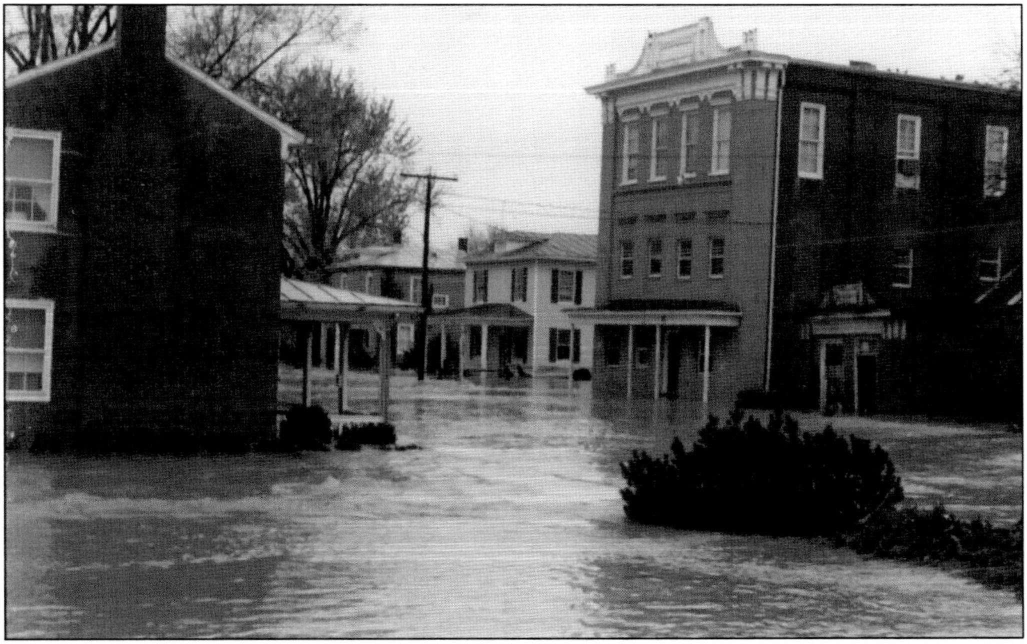

Floodwaters crested around 3:00 a.m. on November 5, 1985. The following morning, South Main Street was still underwater and would be so for most of the day.

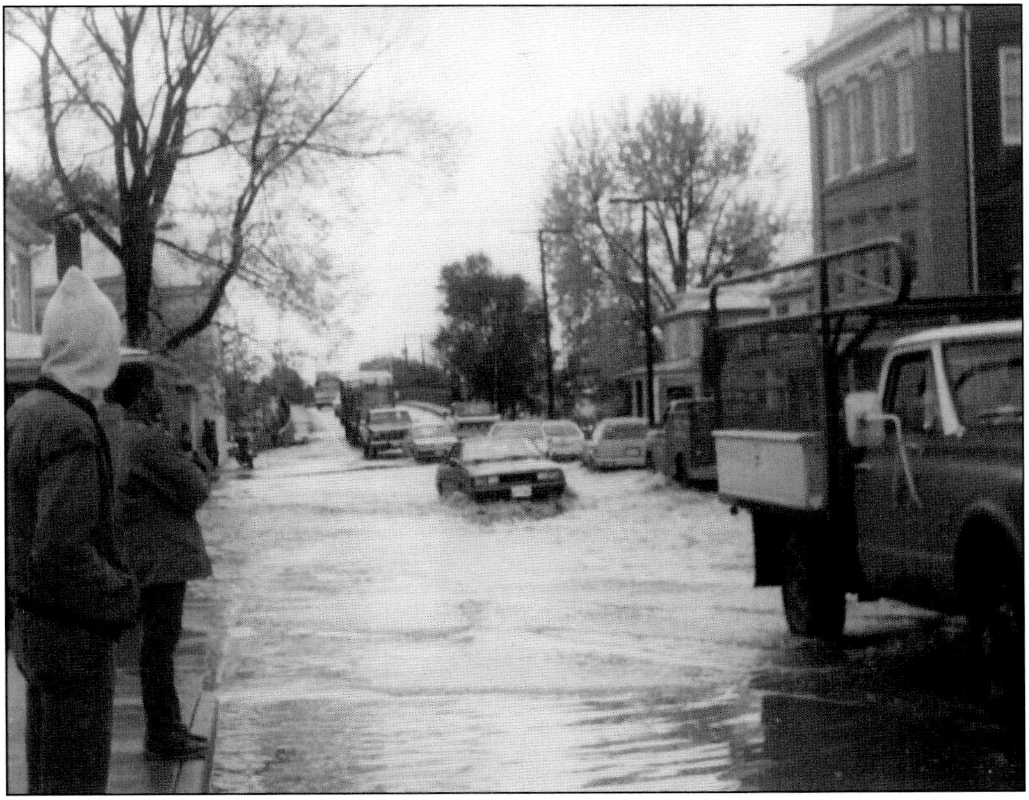

As the day wore on and the flood level dropped even further, traffic began to return to Bridgewater. Home owners surveyed the damage to their property and that of their neighbors.

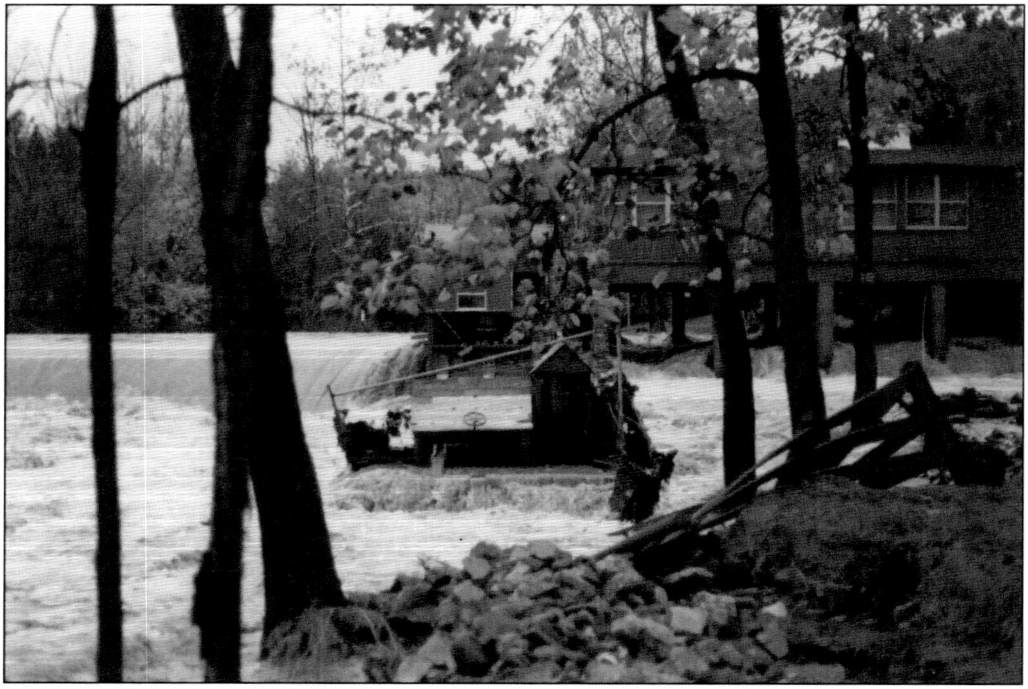

Theoretically 100-year floods should only come once every century. Bridgewater experienced three such catastrophes in 37 years. What are the odds? Pictured here is the 1985 flood as it appeared at Wildwood Park. The clubhouse structure seen at the right of the picture survived this flood but the not the following one.

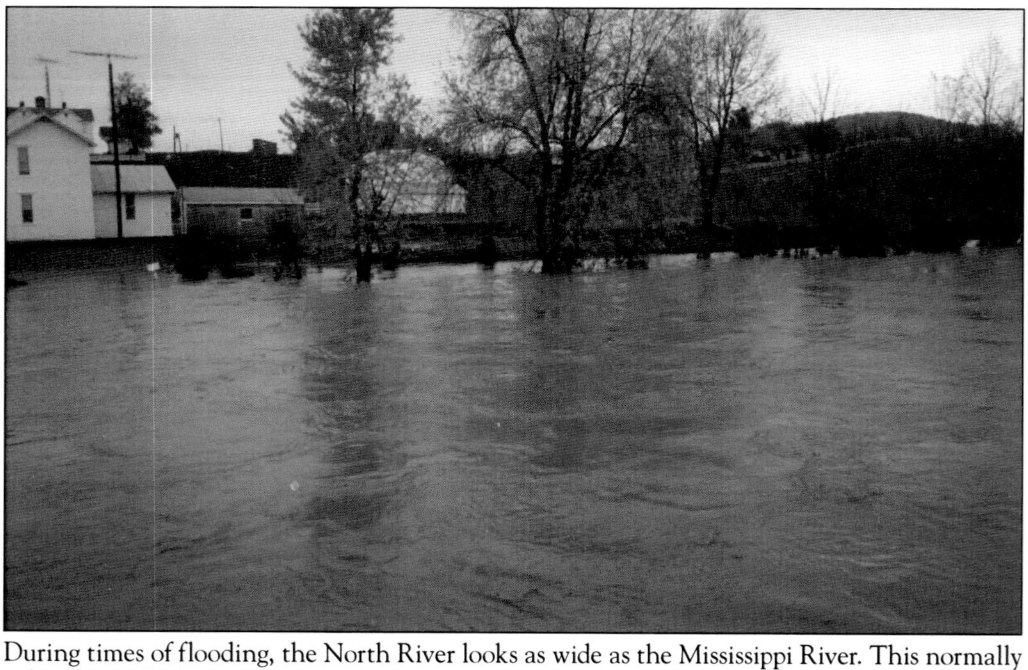

During times of flooding, the North River looks as wide as the Mississippi River. This normally calm channel of water is a site for fishermen, canoeing, and picnics. When destructive floods occur, the full power that nature can generate is readily understood.

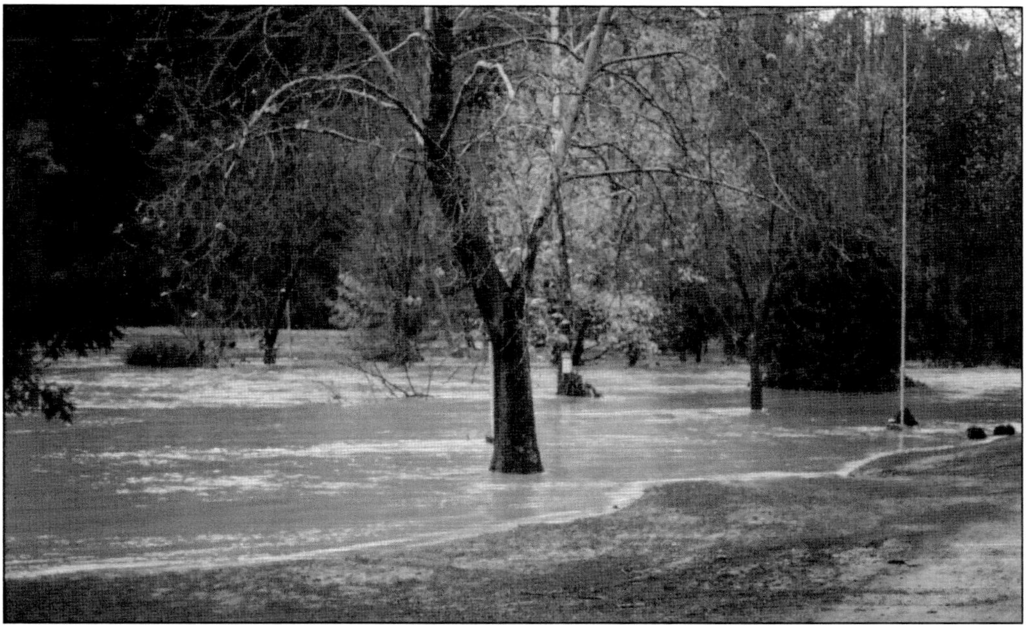

The 1996 flood may have shown less damage than previous ones, but some buildings that survived in 1949 and 1985 did not make it this time. The clubhouse at Wildwood Park was permanently damaged as was a town maintenance shop situated along the river. About half a dozen houses were purchased by FEMA and the Town of Bridgewater after this flood to remove them from flood-prone areas. All of the land acquired in this manner has been deeded to Bridgewater's park system and will be able to survive future floods with relatively little harm.

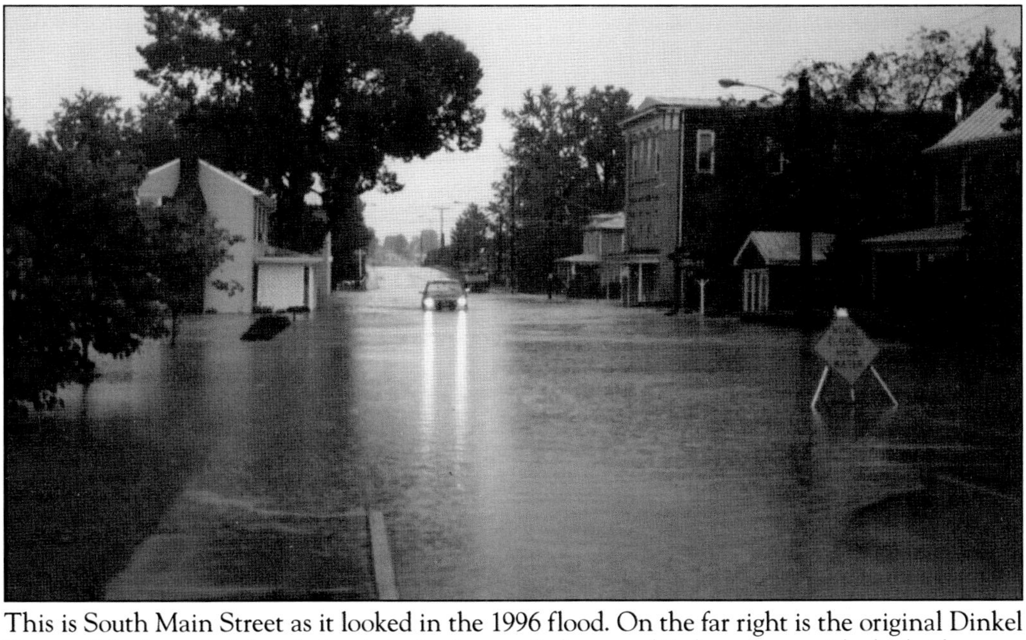

This is South Main Street as it looked in the 1996 flood. On the far right is the original Dinkel Tavern. The large building below it is the former Robson and Robson store with the bridge over the North River at the center of the picture. The house beyond Robson and Robson has been removed with the assistance of FEMA. In its place is Seven Bridges Park, which commemorates the history of bridges spanning North River.

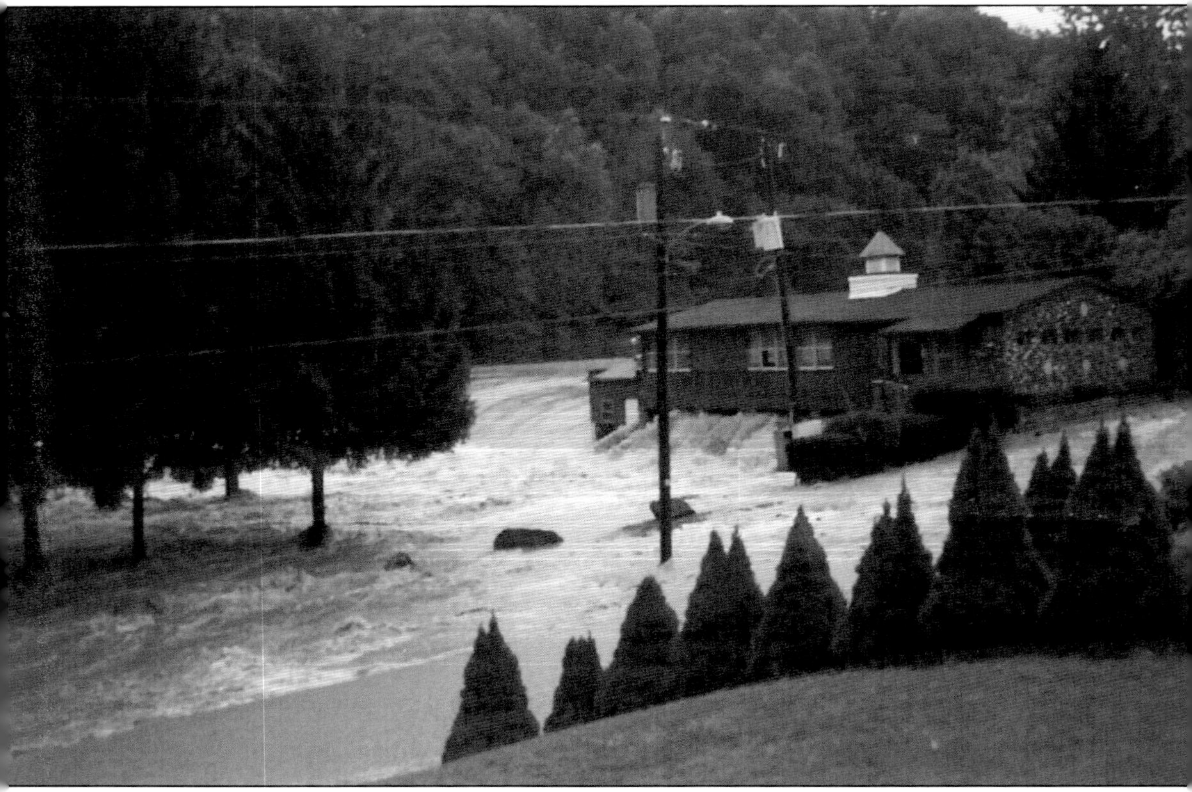

This picture shows the last days of the clubhouse at Wildwood Park. Perhaps some damage had occurred before and gone unnoticed, or maybe this flood (1996) was strong enough to do all the harm. Whichever is correct, the clubhouse was severely damaged and torn down a short while later. Wildwood Clubhouse in good times was operated as a private club that sponsored dances, dinners, and boating in the North River. When purchased by the Town of Bridgewater in the mid-1960s, it was opened to all as a public park.

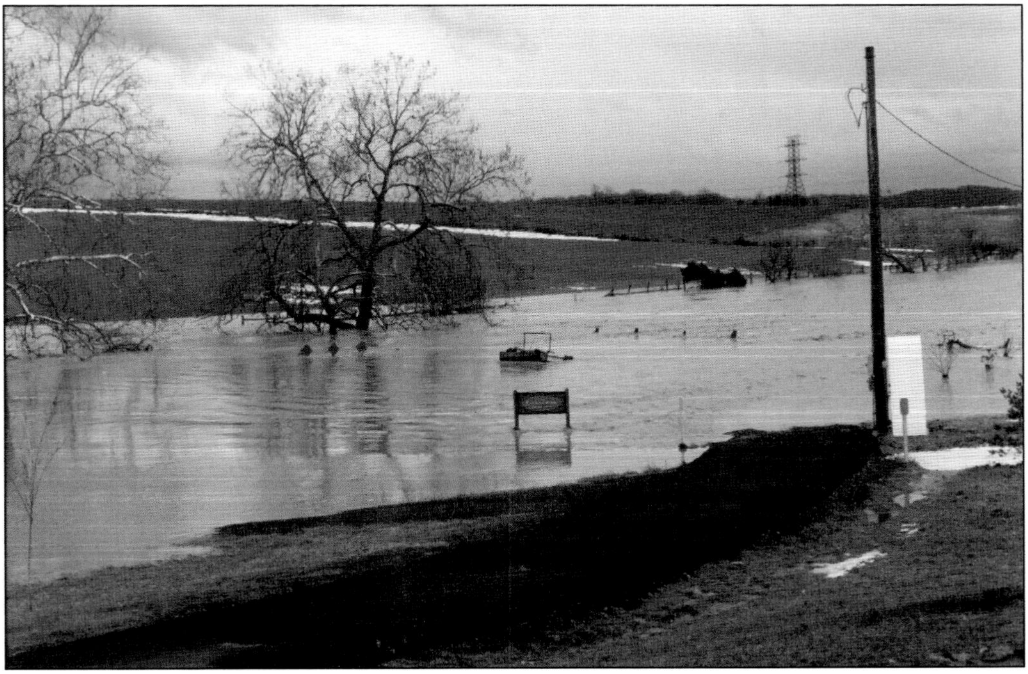

Cooks Creek Arboretum is a model for the development of floodplain land. One would expect a major flood such as this one from 1996 to leave destruction in its path. However, the arboretum is made up of native trees and plants that can withstand floodwaters occurring in low-lying areas.

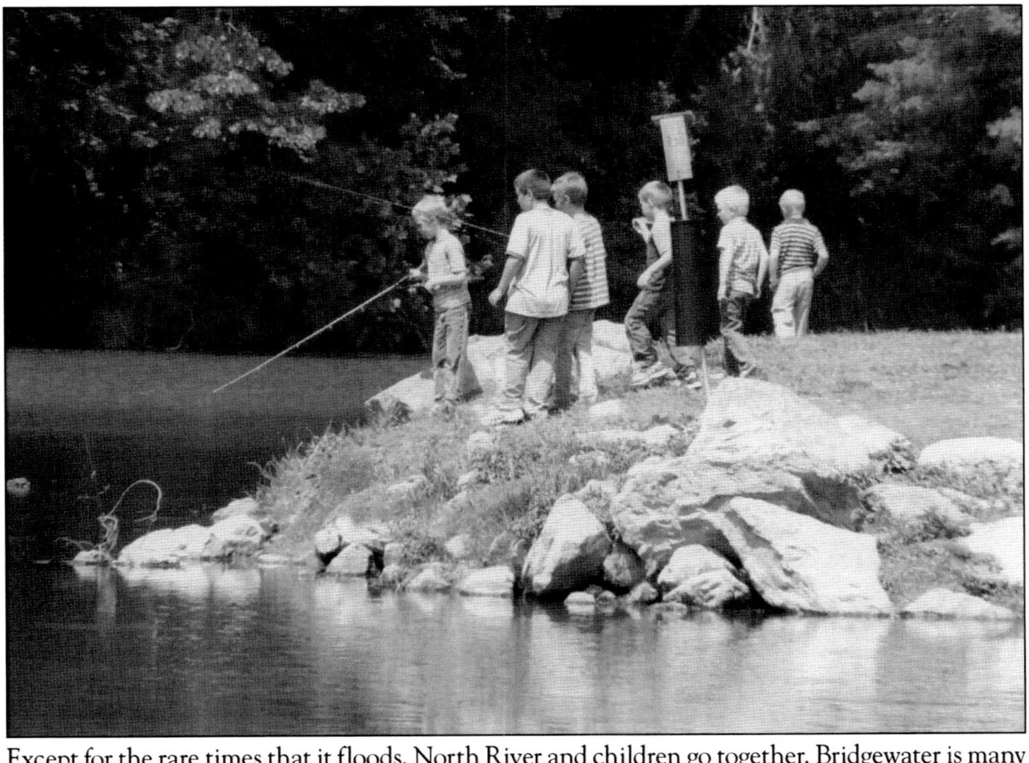

Except for the rare times that it floods, North River and children go together. Bridgewater is many things, but one of its greatest attributes is the fact that it is a great place to be a kid.